D0929858

The Early Film Music
of Dmitry Shostakovich

The Oxford Music/Media Series
Daniel Goldmark, Series Editor

oxford
music/media series

The Early Film Music
of Dmitry Shostakovich

Joan Titus

OXFORD
UNIVERSITY PRESS

OXFORD
UNIVERSITY PRESS

Oxford University Press is a department of the University of Oxford. It furthers
the University's objective of excellence in research, scholarship, and education
by publishing worldwide.Oxford is a registered trade mark of Oxford University
Press in the UK and certain other countries.

Published in the United States of America by Oxford University Press
198 Madison Avenue, New York, NY 10016, United States of America.

Library of Congress Cataloging-in-Publication Data
Titus, Joan, 1975– author.
The early film music of Dmitry Shostakovich / Joan Titus.
pages cm
Includes bibliographical references and index.
ISBN 978-0-19-931514-7 — ISBN 978-0-19-931515-4 —
ISBN 978-0-19-931516-1 — ISBN 978-0-19-045683-2
1. Shostakovich, Dmitrii Dmitrievich, 1906–1975. Motion picture music.
2. Motion picture music—Soviet Union—History and criticism. I. Title.
ML410.S53T58 2016
781.5'42092dc23
2015028106

3 5 7 9 8 6 4 2
Printed by Sheridan, USA

This volume is published with the generous support of the AMS 75 PAYS Endowment
of the American Musicological Society, funded in part by the National Endowment
for the Humanities and the Andrew W. Mellon Foundation.

To Kiko, for showing me the importance of a break

To Margarita, for kindness and faith

And to Christian, for patience and love

CONTENTS

ACKNOWLEDGMENTS

There is no doubt that this book was created with the help of countless kind individuals and institutions across the world. This particular research began over fifteen years ago as a spark that was ignited by my mentor, Margarita Mazo, to whom I am eternally grateful. I am thankful for the helpful encounters from many others since then, particularly my friends and colleagues abroad. I express my heartfelt thanks to Irina Shostakovich, Ol'ga Digonskaya, and Ol'ga Dombrovskaya at the Shostakovich Apartment Archive in Moscow for their graciousness, and helping in countless ways; among them, allowing me access to manuscripts, videos, and permission to work with the Shostakovich *fond* in the Russian State Archive of Literature and Art (RGALI) and the archives at the All-Russian Museum Association of Musical Culture named after M. I. Glinka (VMOMK) in Moscow. Many thanks also go to the late Manashir Yakubov, Naum Kleiman, and Lyudmila Kovnatskaya for their insights and advice, especially early in my research. I was also supported in terms of access and permissions by director Vladimir Lisenko, Elena Fetisova, and Irina Medvedeva (formerly) of the Glinka Museum (VMOMK); Vladimir Dmitriev and Irina Popova at the State Film Archive (Gosfil'mofond) in Belye Stolbye; and Galina Kopïtova at the Russian Institute of Art History in St. Petersburg (RIII). Special thanks also go to the Russian State Archive of Literature and Art (RGALI) and their wonderful staff, director Larisa Sergeevna Georgievskaya and the Central State Archive of Literature and Art (TSGALI), the All-Russian State Institute of Cinematography named after S. A. Gerasimov in Moscow (VGIK), the Russian Institute of Art History in St. Petersburg (RIII), and the library staff at Lenfil'm Studios in St. Petersburg for kind assistance and access to their libraries, and manuscript and bibliography rooms. I am incredibly grateful for the generous support of those who hosted me while in Russia—my thanks to Pavel Shulgin and Aleksandr Eremeev at the Heritage Institute in Moscow, to Levon Akopian (Hakobian) for his extraordinary hospitality and sharp wit, and to Lena and Andrey Tsurinov/a for their kindness in St. Petersburg.

This and other related research has been kindly supported by the US Department of Education, University of North Carolina at Greensboro and the Ohio State University, particularly the Foreign Language Area Studies (FLAS) fellowships; UNCG Office of Sponsored Programs, the International Programs Center (especially Associate Provost Penelope Pynes); School of Music, Theater and Dance; and the Ohio State Graduate School and Slavic Center. I also thank the American Musicological Society for the AMS 75 PAYS Endowment publication subvention that was awarded to this book. I am grateful to all of these institutions and centers that have been incredibly supportive of my and other research in Russian studies.

Years ago, I was approached by the amazing Norm Hirschy about transforming some of my work into a book; since then, Norm and Daniel Goldmark have been remarkable in their help through this process and their invaluable support. My deepest thanks go to them. I am also thankful and fortunate to have had various friends and colleagues who have been critical readers, supporters, and have engaged in useful and interesting conversations, among them Danielle Fosler-Lussier, J. Ronald Green, Angela Brintlinger, Alexander Burry, David Haas, Pauline Fairclough, Arved Ashby, and the blind reviewers of the book. I am bolstered by the wonderful help of such friends and students as Vladimir Orlov, Ol'ga Digonskaya, Christian Anderson, and Wei Dai, who helped with archival work when I was unable to travel and who assisted with transcriptions and setting the examples. My thanks also go to my wonderful UNCG students in advanced graduate seminars of past years who were eagerly engaged with many ideas in this book.

I feel fortunate to have so many wonderful friends and family who have been immeasurably supportive. Among them are Alejandro Madrid, Olga Haldey, Arved Ashby, Anna Ochs, Terry Klefstad, Pauline Fairclough, Vladimir Orlov, Ol'ga Digonskaya, Julie Brown, Robert and Lucille Fleischmann, Roberta Titus, and many others who I may have neglected to mention here. Christian Anderson has been wonderful in his patience and enthusiasm for this project; his love means the world to me.

ABBREVIATIONS OF ARCHIVES
AND LIBRARIES CONSULTED

GOSFIL'MOFOND	Gosudarstvennïy Fond Kinofil'mov Rossiyskoy Federatsii (Gosfil'mofond Rossii)/State Fund of Cinema of the Russian Federation (Gosfil'mofond of Russia), Belye Stolby
VMOMK	Vserossiyskoye Museynoye Ob'edineniye Muzïkal'noi Kul'turï imeni M. I. Glinki/All-Russian Museum Association of Musical Culture named after M. I. Glinka, Moscow
LENFIL'M	Kinostudiya Lenfil'ma (Lenfil'm Film Studios), St. Petersburg
RGALI	Rossiyskiy Gosudarstvennïy Arkhiv Literaturï i Iskusstva/Russian State Archive for Literature and Art, Moscow
RGB	Rossiyskaya Gosudarstvennaya Biblioteka/Russian State Library, Moscow
RIII	Rossiyskiy Institut Istorii Iskusstv/Russian Institute of Art History, St. Petersburg
RNB	Rossiyskaya Natsional'naya Biblioteka/Russian National Library, St. Petersburg
SA	Arkhiv Shostakovicha/Shostakovich Family Archive, Moscow
TSGALI SPB	Tsentral'nïy Gosudarstvennïy Arkhiv Literaturï i Iskusstva SPB/Central State Archive for Literature and Art, St. Petersburg
VGIK	Vserossiyskiy Gosudarstvennïy Institut Kinematografii imeni S. A. Gerasimova/All-Russian State Institute of Cinematography named after S. A. Gerasimov, Moscow

NOTE ON TRANSLITERATION
AND TRANSLATION

The transliteration system used in this book follows the US Board on Geographic Names and the system used in the current *Grove Music Online*. These systems are similar to the Library of Congress system (without diacritics), with the exception of the use of "ya," "yu," "ye," and "y" instead of "ia," "iu," "e," and "i." As recommended by the Chicago Manual of Style, I do not follow this system for names of well-known figures that have a commonly used equivalent in English, such as Tchaikovsky or Eisenstein. For quotations, I retain the original spelling of the source. Unless otherwise noted, all translations are my own.

ABOUT THE COMPANION WEBSITE

www.oup.com/us/earlyfilmmusicofshostakovich

Oxford has created a Web site to accompany *The Early Film Music of Dmitry Shostakovich*. Material that cannot be made available in the book, namely video examples, is provided on this site. The reader is encouraged to consult this resource in conjunction with the chapters. Examples available online are indicated in the text with Oxford's symbol ⓟ.

The Early Film Music
of Dmitry Shostakovich

CHAPTER 1

༄

Introduction

In 1954, Dmitry Shostakovich wrote:

> There should be a complete mutual understanding between composers and
> [film] directors. For this, both [fields] should be studied, for a composer without
> knowledge of the laws of cinema cannot fulfill his work so that it may have an
> organic blending with the film's dramaturgy.[1]

Shostakovich was one of the first musicians to formulate and articulate the
role of the film composer in Soviet Russia. As his statement indicates, it was
a collaborative process, and he had the opportunity to develop his understanding of the cinema through working with multiple directors over the
course of his film music career. He began work as a film composer in 1928,
after several years of experience in the cinema as a *pianist-illustrator*, and
after having written the opera *Nose* (1928). Shostakovich had an almost
fifty-year working relationship with Soviet cinema; his last score was for
Korol' Lir (*King Lear*, dir. Grigory Kozintsev, 1971).

Shostakovich's early scores, which date from the late 1920s to the
mid-1930s, reveal his first negotiations with cinema. The opportunity to
compose his first film score coincided with the twilight years of silent cinema, and his following scores with the beginnings of sound-on-film in the
Soviet Union. He was necessarily a witness to the impact of the Cultural
Revolution on the film industry and on music communities. Intelligibility
to the masses, the desire to make Soviet film popular, and the intent to create a specific and original role for the film composer were undeniably the
issues with which Shostakovich, directors, and sound designers worked.

Working for the film industry was a form of schooling for Shostakovich; he learned about the language of cinema, and how to create sound for image in decades when cinema and its politics were undergoing significant change. With directors and other film partners, Shostakovich experimented with new techniques as dictated by the evolving technology, and borrowed from the musical past in terms of form, style, technique, and tropes. These borrowings and experimentation demonstrated the necessity of transgressing genres in order to find a film music language—a form of musical narration—that would suit film. Even by the late 1930s, finding a common musical parlance was challenging:

> If actors, directors, and cameramen have weapons of theory and an arsenal of special cinematographic means, then we musicians, thus far, are gropingly working [with] little to no knowledge of the features and technology of film. And yet, writing music for film without [the required] theoretical and technical knowledge is the same thing as orchestrating a piece of music without knowing the nature of the sound of the orchestra, [or] for which instruments to write.[2]

Connecting with the musical past was a way that directors and composers coped with the struggle to find a film music language that would satisfy the demands of Soviet cinema. Even in 1939, after almost a decade of film scoring experience, Shostakovich was still seeing a trend of composers having difficulty navigating film culture and finding within it a musical subculture. Musical tropes, or codes, were part of the musical past, and helped in navigating the current cinema practices; connecting to those codes allowed for continuity with film and other musical cultures. Participants within those cultures, including composers, film directors, and audiences, responded to codes and heard across genres at the time; and Shostakovich, in his work for cinema, utilized codes and other music tools with which he was familiar in order to contribute to a common ground for film scoring.

Music codes, among other elements, are an aspect of musical narration; and an interest in narration in Shostakovich's music is familiar to listeners. Richard Taruskin's comment on reading the composer's Fifth Symphony has responded to a kind of narration: "Definitive reading, especially biographical reading, locks music in the past. Better let it remain supple, adaptable, ready to serve the future's needs."[3] Such a plea illustrates how hearing narratives in Shostakovich's music became a common trend, and has led me to ask how and why audiences construct narratives to Shostakovich's music; and why film music has failed to become part of that discussion.

In Shostakovich studies in the West, and certainly in past studies of many composers and their repertories, the concert music component of the composer's oeuvre generally has been favored over other types of media, such as film and theater music. Although some writers of complementary backgrounds have written about Shostakovich's Other music, particularly in Europe,[4] such music has failed to inspire significant scholarly attention elsewhere, and has not been ranked in importance alongside his well-known symphonies and string quartets.[5] There are several explanations for this phenomenon. Only recently, since the 1980s, has any film music been regarded as serious enough for study in the United States.[6] Meanwhile, it was Shostakovich's concert music that had initially received attention in the West and in Soviet Russia. Studying his film music was out of the question—he wrote such music for the money, as it is often related[7]—and according to some post-Soviet perspectives, such music cannot be "good."[8] The concept of "Soviet" at one time engendered a negative response: no Soviet art could possibly be good art.

Such perceptions have been and are continuing to be reevaluated. Katerina Clark's seminal text on the Soviet novel indicated a sea-change in the Western study of Soviet literature.[9] Responding to the idea that all Soviet products are necessarily terrible, Clark has argued for the study of Soviet literature as it functioned, instead of how it may be valued. Parallel to this discussion, historians such as Boris Groys have evaluated the implicit dichotomy of modernism and socialist realism, and have challenged the idea that one experimental trend died as another more conservative and therefore inartistic trend developed in its place.[10] My past work has built on that reevaluation and has sought to show how Shostakovich's film music resists categorical description. Instead, I have discussed how he situated himself as a composer for film and negotiated the politics of a newly redefined film industry.

This book continues that work of reconceptualizing Shostakovich as a film composer who negotiated the politics of a state and its industry, and poses questions about the relationship between musical narration, audience and composer, Soviet Russian cinema, and concert and/or stage music. Six case studies selected from Shostakovich's early film scores, from 1928 through 1936, are the primary focus, and each engages the construct of Soviet intelligibility, the filmmaking and -scoring processes, and the cultural politics in creating Soviet film music and the role of the film composer. These examinations involve multiple components, including an investigation of how film teams conceived of music for film, and how elements were drawn from facets of musical culture. Reception, defined as the earliest contexts for the creation of his film music together with the current context for audiences that read his music, and the scores as musical texts and as part of the collaborative process of filmmaking are part of this discussion. Music manuscripts, many of which are extant fragments, and film and music archival materials enrich these studies by illuminating the process of the work teams, studios, and composer. The epilogue provides a reflection on earlier chapters, and muses on issues related to musical narration. In addition to examining Shostakovich the composer or Shostakovich's music, Shostakovich is also evaluated as a concept in itself—not just a person defined in such a way, or who created such popular music. The iconicity of Shostakovich and his music's intelligibility, particularly after his death, are an implicit part of these examinations of his music for early Soviet cinema, and are explicitly but briefly discussed in the epilogue.

Narrative, specifically musical-cinematic narration, is one of several lenses through which I focus my discussion. The study of narrative, or narratology, has been a significant endeavor in the humanities, including musicology, and has attempted to make sense of how various forms of media draw together a series of events. Narratology is no stranger to film studies; the crux of most structuralist film analysis lies in detecting the way in which something is told in images, that is, how a story may be told in discourse.[11] For Western music, narrative has been an enduring issue, especially in regard to debates from the nineteenth-century forward over the concept of *topoi*, the idea of program music, opera, and film. Within these contexts, it is no surprise that many listeners fabricate their own stories to Shostakovich's concert music, with or without knowledge of Soviet musical or political history. Unlike much concert music, his film music belongs to a story, told in the complex whole of moving images. The compositional processes for creating symphonies and creating film scores, however, can resemble each other, particularly in light of Soviet Russian perspectives on musical process. Under the broad concept of narration, as relevant to film studies and musicology, I engage possible ways in which Shostakovich's music inspires the desire the read stories by analyzing compositional processes and theories used in his film scoring. Shostakovich had a significant impact on the development of the film composer in Soviet Russia: his predisposition to the imagistic in his music allowed him to be a successful film composer in his time, and his approaches to technique, form, style, and codes for concert music, such as the symphony, were transferred to formulate an approach to scoring for films. Musical codes were part of this formulation, and demonstrated how film music was an amalgam of a borrowed musical past; they were also symbiotic with audiences' expectations, and the aesthetic concerns of directors and composers. I begin with the concepts that Shostakovich, film directors, and sound designers employed, and were common to Russian musical culture—the idea of *intonatsiya*, and the "symphonic," often known as *symphonism*, as applied to his film music. These and other concepts were at the heart of discussion about intelligibility in film music, and defining successful musical narration within certain cultural-political constructs. Some of these processes may explain why audiences, even today, hear images and stories in his concert music.

MUSIC AND CODE

The concepts of *intonatsiya* and *symphonism* resonate with film studies and film music of the past century. The concepts trace back to Boris Asafyev and his writings beginning in the late 1910s. These ideas permeated Soviet musical life, and have a long history in musicological discussion in both Russia and the West.[12] *Intonatsiya*, which can be translated with caveat as "intonation," is the embodiment of a musical concept; it can be a melody (and *melos* in the Asafyevan sense), rhythm, timbre, harmony, interval, or any other musical event.[13] This concept resonates with other loaded ideas such as code, *topos*, style topics, cue, sign, or trope—all of which represent different but related methodological traditions.[14] Since Asafyev's complex and myriad writings on these subjects have a long history, and connections have been made between his theories and Russian composers such as Shostakovich, my main objective is to draw together some of the highlights of Asafyev's concepts with contemporary film theory to illustrate Shostakovich's musical designs for cinema.[15] When I use the word "code," or on occasion the phrase "code complex," I simultaneously evoke the multiplicity of these traditions, but with an emphasis on Russian musical thought. In a sense, the idea of *intonatsiya*-as-code has a natural relationship with Shostakovich's film music, one fraught with many embedded contexts as well.[16]

Intonatsiya correlates well with film (and music) because codes connect audience and composer; in this period, Soviet film was a highly prized item, where practitioners were beholden to notions of a specific communication between listener and creator. Asafyev referred to these shared codes as an "intonational reserve," a kind of contract between listeners and creators, as a "dictionary" of the era—strikingly similar to a kind of *polistilistika* (polystylism) that permeated the 1920s.[17] This "vocabulary" is developed over the course of time to become "accumulation of musical ideas, often no more than fragments, which is crystallized in the collective consciousness of people within a given epoch and environment, and which represents the totality of all previous musical experience of that epoch."[18] This "intonational reserve" is shared between genres, as Asafyev explained, and unrestricted to simply a symphony or sonata. David Haas summarized it best:

> Asafyev's incorporation of the *intonatsiya* into a system of sound relationships allows for some degree of interdependence and interaction between *intonatsii*

[plural of *intonatsiya*] which would be sacrificed should any one of them be taken out of its context and frozen into a series of pitches. In fact the Asafyevan *intonatsiya* always requires a context, wherein it will be susceptible to change and can become the subject of the listener's process of interpretation within one work or between works.[19]

For music for cinema, this "intonational reserve" was often summarized in early film music manuals. Silent film practice often dictated that pianists improvise from their own internal musical dictionaries, or orchestras read from compilations created by their directors. When these manuals were beginning to be published in the early twentieth century, in many countries, a snippet of a musician's soundscape for film became ossified.[20] These manuals provide, though only in part, a peek into the musical decisions that these practitioners might have made in their era—a partial reflection of an era's "intonational reserve." In Russia and the early Soviet Union, such practices were under discussion as they were elsewhere, and manifested in similar manuals for practice, which often included charts with suggestions on how to accompany a film, as seen in figure 1.1.[21]

Such film codes are certainly of the same language from which Shostakovich and other contemporary composers/pianist-accompanists had drawn. For my discussion, I refer to this "intonational reserve"—one built on the histories of concert and film music traditions—again with the word "code" or the phrase "code complex," with the Russian contexts in mind. Asafyev's volume *Intonatsiya* post-dates the film scores that I discuss here (it was published in 1947), but his thoughts and observations were apparent before then: *intonatsiya* was seeded in writings from the teens forward and in his previous volume, "Musical Form as Process" (1930).[22] The concept, therefore, matured over the course of several writings.[23] Shostakovich's early scores appeared in an opportune time for the development of Soviet socialist realism and ongoing discussions of the changing purpose of music and art. To think of his approach to codes in the context of Asafyev's *intonatsii* seems fitting; Shostakovich's music was undoubtedly communicative, regardless of the concept of socialist realism. The associations evoked by his use of codes, or *intonatsii*, resonated beyond his film scores as much as those codes continued their previous meaning or associations. Shostakovich's film music was interstitial, continuing code traditions from opera and melodrama into cinema, and crossing regions, just as his music does today.[24] In the epilogue, I illustrate how these codes permeate music today often in terms of timbre and tempo, and how audiences continue *intonatsii* of their own.

Symphonism is part of Asafyev's discussion of music as process, and *intonatsii* play a role in the development of *symphonism*. The intonations of an

Начало	Конец	Содержание картины—надпись	Колич. мин.	Название музыкальной пьесы
		„Сборищ не допущу, в револю- цию играть не позволю".—Рабо- чие берут камни.—Бросили ка- мень в губернатора, оборвали рукав губернатору.—Взял пла- ток.—„Не расходись, — пугают только". — Сигнал. — Залп.—Па- ника. — Бегут. — Залпы — уби- тые.—Казаки—нагайки. —Девоч- ка плачет.	—	
		2 часть (9¹/₂ м.).		
11 ч. 12 м. 50 с.	11 ч. 16 м. 20 с.	3) В кабинете губернатора.— Волнение.—„Заготовить донесе- ние в Петербург".—„Зачинщиков выловить, довольно миндальни- чать".—Девочка плачет.—Доне- сение. — Убитый ребенок.—Гар- мошка.—Губернатор в детской.— Девочка отвернулась. — Гувер- нантка отошла.—„Оставьте меня, убийца детей".—Ушел.—Губер- натор один в комнате. — Гар- мошка.—Мертвый ребенок.—Гу- бернатор с куклой.—Бинокль.	3¹/₂ м.	3) Скрябин. „Мечты".
11 ч. 16 м. 30 с.	11 ч. 22 м. 20 с.	4) Заводы молчат.—Женщина рыдает у трупа—воспоминания.— Рабочие.—„Не ходи, ребята, с губернатором нам говорить не о чем".—„Не слушай его, губер- натор все может".—Губернатор в детской.—Утро.—Рабочий с гар- мошкой.—В участке.—Провока- тор и полицеймейстер. — „Угово- рил—пошли".—Улица. —Пьяный рабочий с гармошкой.—Гувер- нантка смотрит в окно.—„Так как же это случилось".	6 м.	4) Калинников. Антракт к 4 акту из муз. „Царь Бо- рис".

Figure 1.1: A fragment from a chart of suggested cues.
From D. Blok, and S. Bugoslavsky, *Muzïkal'noe soprovozhdeniye v kino* [Musical Accompaniment in the Cinema] (Moscow: Teakinopechat, 1929).

era, its musical dictionary of sorts, are the stimuli that contribute to larger narrative strategies and structures, and how a given work unfolds. *Intonatsii*, or codes as I refer to them, are part of *symphonism*; that is, the art of the development of music unfolding in time, as opposed to a prescribed and rigid schema. *Symphonism* is a form-as-process, and can result from the jux- taposition of ideas, or *intonatsii*. My discussion builds on some of Asafyev's ideas about form-as-process and *symphonism*; I do not examine just whether a film score is episodic or continuous, but importantly, the way that music relates to image and audience to create a fluid narrative within a given work.

THE EARLY SCORES

The central chapters of this book examine six of Shostakovich's early film scores as case studies for narrative in his music. These scores range from 1928 through 1936 and include *New Babylon* (1928–29), *Alone* (1931), *Golden Mountains* (1931), *Counterplan* (1932), *Youth of Maxim*, (1934–35), and *Girlfriends* (1934–36), overlapping with the Cultural Revolution and the official development of the socialist realist aesthetic in the arts.[25] Each score receives its own chapter and addresses Shostakovich's own categorization of his early scores as symphonic or fragmented. His first open statement on the symphonic quality of his scores started with *Alone*: "I always tried to find unified development . . . I always tried to seek a unified idea, which I was not especially successful at in the film *Alone*; it had no unified symphonic development; it had individual numbers . . . I was unable to achieve unified development."[26] This film, and this point of view, applies to three of the scores (*Alone, Counterplan,* and *Youth of Maxim*). This group of film scores was composed and designed in a way that appeared fragmentary, yet they still maintained cohesion, a sort of *symphonism* in the way that the music and image created the story. The other three scores (*New Babylon, Golden Mountains,* and *Girlfriends*) were sometimes labeled as symphonic, depending on the objectives of the film team. For Shostakovich, *symphonism*, or the symphonic, often referred to continuity in the rhythmic sense or as unified by melody or code. *Symphonism* for the directors and sound designers with whom Shostakovich worked often referred to that same continuity, and also to genres, forms, and styles of concert music. The differences in approach to the creation of these scores was often governed by the overall project and its contexts—some directors preferred less music, often in the form of short songs or segments of music they could manipulate, while others wanted continuous music or underscoring. Ultimately, this division between symphonic and fragmented was arbitrary—it mostly referred to the kind of involvement Shostakovich had with the film score, more than its perceived unity. Yet, such a division was an aspect of Shostakovich's approach to narrative construction, and was a construct that revealed the film team's negotiation with industry politics, technology, and changing aesthetic concerns for scoring.

Each chapter includes a case study of the text, that is, examination of form, organization, thematic/harmonic design in edited scores, music manuscripts, and the soundtracks of extant films all within the contexts of director/composer collaboration, the censorship or allowances allotted by the film industry, and the cultural politics of the time. The analysis of each case study is narrowly focused on understanding musical narration, showing how music participates in narrating the film's story. Since the score, as part of the overall sound design, is seen as an integral part of the larger cultural-political process of creating the film, the music manuscripts, internal studio documents, unpublished film scenarios, personal writings, and other unpublished and published documents by the directors and composer are therefore analyzed together to illuminate the reciprocity of the film product and its entanglement within studio politics, and more broadly, the art politics of the Cultural Revolution and ossifying of 1930s socialist realism.

Such a discussion of the cultural politics in film music centers on the debate about formalism and socialist realism and the place of these aesthetics in the arts. Folding in reception, therefore, aids in understanding how the industry, film/sound workers, and audiences negotiated music for film. Several indicators, such as the Soviet press, internal studio documents (memos, letters, and notes from committee meetings), and personal writings by directors, actors, and Shostakovich, each contribute to understanding how each film came to need music in some form, how the studio anticipated audience response, and how the audience reception affected studio politics. Each chapter, buttressed by the above cited archival documents, therefore folds together layers of reception and narrative analysis to situate each score in their political contexts and in the repertory of Shostakovich's music.

New Babylon (*Novyi Vavilon*, 1928–29, dirs. Grigory Kozintsev and Leonid Trauberg), discussed in chapter 2, was Shostakovich's first film score, and was composed during the final years of silent cinema. The score contains nonstop music from beginning to end, similar to the film accompanying practices of the time where continuous music was heard throughout the showing of a film. The approach to the content of the music, however, differed considerably in the eyes of the directors and composer. Instead of accompanying images as they appear, Shostakovich delved deeper into the meaning of those scenes using music to add to or lead the image. He theorized this approach in his 1929 article about the film score, referring to two principles that guided his compositional processes.[27] The close attention and care that he paid to the score failed in the end—the film was premiered in a time when the new Soviet film was hotly debated, and nothing appeared to satisfy the critics; and the score was performed badly due to lack of practice, copying errors, and cinema-house and film studio politics. When performed synchronously with the film, that is, in an ideal situation, this score bears the closest resemblance to continuity in his symphonies, and is best described as contemporaneous *symphonism* given the approach to form and repetition, and the use of quotation, allusion, and codes. Such an approach would usually be improvised by a cinema pianist, but instead was carefully and thoughtfully created as a continuously sounded score.

Alone (*Odna*, 1929–31, dirs. Grigory Kozintsev and Leonid Trauberg), the subject of chapter 3, was, as Shostakovich stated, composed in numbered segments that resulted in a fragmentary score.[28] This fragmentary approach was likely the result of two major issues: the striking number of changes to the scenario and the directors' desire for a "musical" film, that is, a score that attempted to behave similarly to sound-on-film. The music composed by Shostakovich was part of a sound whole; the symphonic, as he defined and/or controlled it, was therefore impossible. To unify the score, Shostakovich used recurring motifs and timbres as codes, which participated in musical narration. This was particularly heavy-handed because the final product was a partial talkie, and thusly relied upon music to express meaning that was typically evoked by speech. Each of these codes spoke to the nature of a character or issue in the film such as the exoticism of the Oirat villagers or the boorishness of the antagonist, or the village chairman. Contemporaneous reception shows that these codes were only partially effective, and that current politics regarding formalism and socialism, that is, how to make a film "intelligible to the millions," were becoming a greater consideration in the topic of films, and in the application of the emerging sound technology.

Golden Mountains (*Zlatïe gorï*, dir. Sergey Yutkevich, 1931), examined in chapter 4, was created between *Alone* and the future successful song-scored film *Counterplan*. The film reflects the continued preoccupation with the balance of songs and underscoring, and the intent to satisfy the demands for an intelligible Soviet film while establishing a successful language for film music. Similar to *Alone*, *Golden Mountains* uses a central song-motif that permeates the score, following the protagonist Peter and his development from apolitical peasant to engaged urban socialist. Unlike a later successful song-score to *Youth of Maxim*, there is substantial original underscoring. In addition to a song-motif, Waldteufel waltzes and urban romances are used to typify the bourgeoisie, and original underscoring is used throughout to highlight the actions and build suspense. The result was a score that balances song and original scoring with a tendency towards *symphonism*, which was a recipe for an overwhelmingly tepid success. Overshadowed by *Counterplan*, *Golden Mountains* was never canonized and, therefore, was almost forgotten when compared to Shostakovich's next score.

The score to *Counterplan* (*Vstrechnyi*, 1932, dirs. Fridrikh Ermler and Sergey Yutkevich), the subject of chapter 5, was considered fragmentary by some because the sound design was developed around a single newly composed song by Shostakovich, named "Song of the Counterplan." It took

Shostakovich almost a dozen sketches before he finalized his anticipated Song, which acts as the musical frame of the film. The Song leads the action as a leitmotif, and leads the characters through the story about the transformation of a positive hero in the context of the trials of a steel factory.[29] Less original underscoring occupies the score compared to Shostakovich's earlier ones, but is placed well to narrate the action; that is, this kind of underscoring was designed to be "unheard," and therefore had more in common with emerging full-sound films of the early thirties in Russia and in Hollywood.[30] Other significant musical moments in the film involve pre-composed revolutionary songs, such as "Partizanskaya" ("Partisan's Song"); or ambient sound, suited to depict the working-class characters or the sounds of factory. Regardless of the skillful attempts to unify a rather piecemeal score, the overwhelmingly positive reception of the film focused primarily on "Song of the Counterplan," which had much to do with the mythology and promotion of the film as socialist art imitating socialist life. The score was more complex than it seemed: in addition to "Song of the Counterplan," there was original underscoring, ambient sound, and the other borrowed songs that were repetitive (as with recurring motifs), strongly associational, or designed to be realistic (as with ambient sound design), acting as multivalent codes that "invisibly" narrate what appeared to be just a film with a catchy song. The Song took on a transnational life several decades after the film, including a reemergence of the Song in a film score during the Second World War, with its lyrics rewritten by the composer Harold Rome. This and other manifestations speak to the use of music as propaganda between Soviet Russia and the United States, demonstrating how a song became a code complex for multiple political purposes.

Chapter 6 provides a study of *Youth of Maxim (Yunost' maksima,* 1934–35, dirs. Grigory Kozintsev and Leonid Trauberg), the first in a film trilogy about the transformation of a young Bolshevik. As a song score, it continued the same logic of *Counterplan,* but relied far less on originally composed music.[31] Directed by Kozintsev and Trauberg, this film was their first success after the studio proclaimed *New Babylon* and *Alone* to be failures. The film used familiar pre-composed songs as narrative devices, much like *Counterplan,* as recurring motifs that were associated with specific characters. Maxim, the central character of the trilogy, is associated with the song "Krutitsya, vertitsya shar goluboy . . ." ("Whirling, twirling blue ball . . .") that follows his development into a proper socialist throughout the trilogy. Songs, including "Whirling, twirling . . ." unite the score and the trilogy overall, operating as recurring motifs. Unlike the other fragmentary scores, *Youth of Maxim* used remarkably little underscoring, resulting in one section of originally composed music by Shostakovich—his single

direct contribution was for the Prologue that opens the film. In addition
to this contribution, however, Shostakovich's influence and indirect work
with the directors peered through other musical choices in the film. Several
musical moments throughout the film betrayed the same techniques
and approaches to music-image relationship with which the director-
composer trio had experimented beginning with *New Babylon*. In the wake
of *Counterplan*, *Youth of Maxim* was received as a hit, and contributed to the
trend for song-score films with positive male heroes in the 1930s. It proved
to be a much needed success for Kozintsev and Trauberg after *Alone* and
New Babylon.

   Girlfriends (*Podrugi*, 1935–36, dir. Leo Arnshtam), discussed in chapter
7, was Leo Arnshtam's 1936 debut as a film director. It was Shostakovich's
third working experience with him, since Arnshtam had worked as a sound
designer on *Golden Mountains* and *Counterplan*. The score was composed
in numbers, which was similar to *Alone*. Yet, this approach suited encapsulated individual moments or scenes, as seen in *Alone*; as well as more
continuous sequences, where quoted musical ideas are interwoven into the
score to comment on the characters and their development over the course
of the film as seen in the scores to *Golden Mountains* and *New Babylon*. The
film centers on three young girls, who are mentored into becoming politically conscious *Komsomolki* by the time of the Civil War. The theme of the
film was intentionally crafted to show the strength of the Soviet woman,
as Maxim Gorky claimed the Soviet system would in his 1934 speech to the
Writer's Union, and reflected serious changes to women's lives and health
in the mid-1930s.[32] In comparison to his previous scores, Shostakovich
favored strings heavily throughout in a style reminiscent of Hollywood film
scoring, writing some episodes for string quartet—his first contribution
to the genre for film.[33] The score and the film thusly feel melodramatic due
to moments of resonant codes that referenced the early romance/woman's
film, a kind of "feminizing" of the film's characters. The score simultaneously referenced musical codes of war, situating the women within the
context of a war film. This variety of codes accumulates throughout the
score to represent the girls as independent, yet vulnerable and feminine
in contrast to previous representations of women in Soviet film. As such,
elements of the scenario and score simultaneously pointed to prior trends
in radical feminism, as they also reflected current and more conservative
socio-political trends in women's rights. The private reception by filmmakers, studio workers, and Joseph Stalin, and public reception that made it to
the press in February 1936 responded to this Soviet take on earlier radical
feminism. This press supported the idea that this was one of the first Soviet
chick flicks, and lauded it as an example of a woman's film in the wake

of the January 1936 *Pravda* attack on Shostakovich's opera with another female lead, *Lady Macbeth of Mtsensk District*.

Each of these six scores is uniquely situated in contemporaneous cultural politics and provided Shostakovich with the opportunity to experiment with moving images. Through these experiences with early cinema, he was able to negotiate the new path for the Russian film composer. These films, their scores, and their political contexts, therefore, provide a window into understanding how Shostakovich became a composer for early Soviet cinema, worked with film directors who would become celebrated in their time, and navigated the cultural politics and burgeoning demands for the intelligible Soviet film. More broadly, these studies provide new insights into his compositional processes, and the relationship between his film scores and his concert music. Examining musical organization in the form of codes, for instance, and how Shostakovich borrowed from non-film genres while working with the musical material of the Western musical past, suggests the plasticity of codes, and why audiences are inspired to construct their own narratives when listening to his concert music. In the epilogue (chapter 8) of this book, I review the case studies of these films, and discuss how codes similarly persist into a specific form of participatory multimedia. Specifically, I reflect on how audiences have constructed responses to Shostakovich's music in audiovisual media, such as YouTube videos of war images in montage set against his Eighth Symphony and Eighth String Quartet, and how pop artists sample Shostakovich's Seventh Symphony for satire and political commentary. Such reception illuminates how audiences hear certain musical ideas and codes that, for them, transfer between cinema and concert music much in the way Shostakovich described in his own writings on film from the 1920s to the 1950s.[34]

Debates over music and meaning persist, revealing variable approaches to musical aesthetics and ways of hearing. This book examines Shostakovich's work in early Soviet cinema while complementing those debates by interrogating three interlocking levels and types of narrative or narration: the narrative of Shostakovich as a composer, how musical narration operates in a given film, and how audiences respond to and participate in narration—and our expectations that lead to reading Shostakovich's music broadly, and the transference of musical elements such as codes. The intersection of these levels is what potentially mediates the musical narrative of a film through the Self, remediated through various technologies including film and social media such as YouTube. The way Shostakovich is heard, the way Shostakovich approached composition to maximize his popularity, and how audiences today construct narratives to his music is part of this debate. Understanding his approach to film scoring, his relationship to the

Soviet cinema and the demands for intelligibility, and his role as one of the first Soviet Russian film composers is one way to illuminate how he conceived musical narration in film, dealt with the plasticity of musical elements, and may explain his general intelligibility and popularity. Seeing and hearing his film music repertory may open up the Shostakovich-as-concept question, and provide another way to understand both his role in the world of Russian film music and the phenomenon of his enduring popularity.

CHAPTER 2

⌒✧⌒

New Babylon (1928–1929)
and Scoring for the Silent Film

*N*ew *Babylon* (*Novyi Vavilon*, 1928–29, dirs. Grigory Kozintsev and Leonid Trauberg) was Shostakovich's first exploration in cinema, and one of the most debated of his film scores. It was also his first symphonic score, which embodied his initial principles about film scoring that continued throughout his film music career. Unlike his score to *Alone* (1929–31, dirs. Grigory Kozintsev and Leonid Trauberg), the score to *New Babylon* was intended to have continuous music from beginning to end, similar to early cinema practices when music was heard throughout the showing of a film. Departing from the practices of piano- and orchestral-accompanying, Shostakovich and the directors, Grigory Kozintsev and Leonid Trauberg, approached the music differently. Symphonic in conception, at least in terms of fluidity and theme, Shostakovich sought a deeper engagement of music with image than what he believed was expressed in silent film accompaniment. His 1929 article outlined these thoughts, and demonstrated a clear approach to code by taking snippets of song along with multiple quotations and integrating them with newly composed material, and therefore engaging a topical history of Western music.[1] Such diversity and complexity made the score a difficult read for the unprepared orchestras that premiered his work. The film and its score were met with significant resistance throughout the process, and they failed, primarily because of the shifting contexts for the new Soviet film, and the composer's role in the industry.[2] Over the course of the twentieth century, the film's score has drawn greater appreciation, and has been celebrated for its unique integration of musical quotes and allusions into a style reminiscent of the concert symphony. This approach resembles much of Shostakovich's later work for the concert stage as well as his music for cinema, and resonates with his later claims of *symphonism* in his film music.

Inspired by Karl Marx's *The Civil War in France*, Kozintsev and Trauberg created a story based on the Parisian Commune of 1871 that acted as a metaphor for the proletarian struggle of the late twenties.[3] Their primary aim was to provide a positive portrayal of the "dictatorship of the proletariat" through comparison with a corrupt French bourgeoisie. The result was a historical drama and proletariat lesson that attempted to educate and entertain its viewers—a tall order in a time when few Soviet-made educational films existed, the majority of which lacked the entertainment value of a Charlie Chaplin or Harry Piel film. The comparison of the bourgeoisie and the Communards is achieved through character typage, a technique common to such films of the time, including *Battleship Potemkin* (1925, dir. Sergey Eisenstein). Such typing partially defines the two central characters of this eight-part, or eight-reel film: Louise, a saleswoman at the New Babylon department store who later becomes a passionate Communard; and the soldier, Jean, an average peasant-farmer who finds himself enlisted in the National Army to fight in the Franco-Prussian war and the battle against the Communards.[4] Although initially apolitical, both characters become involved in opposite sides of and act as typed-representatives of the "class war." Meanwhile, a romantic relationship slowly unfolds between Louise and Jean, but it is unfulfilled. Instead, Louise and the Commune are defeated, and the last scene shows Louise's death sentence. Still employed by the army, Jean does nothing but watch her judgment and execution by firing squad at the Père Lachaise cemetery while digging her grave. Although the remaining members of the Parisian Commune are finally executed along with Louise, they are celebrated in this film as a symbol of working class struggle.

The story of the Parisian Commune was well known by the late twenties, and has been referred to as the "official mythology."[5] As film scholar David Bordwell notes, historical films with popular topics such as *New Babylon* had "predictable *fabula* with unpredictable narration."[6] The innovation of *New Babylon* would therefore be found in its presentation, not in its well-known story. The presentation built upon aspects of Soviet montage of the twenties, exemplified by directors such as Eisenstein, Lev Kuleshov, Kozintsev, and Trauberg. Typically, their approaches to montage involved the fast-paced editing of different and juxtaposed shots in order to force the viewer to make immediate decisions about the content of the images. This form of presentation epitomized a kind of kinetic intensity, which was a common and effective approach to propagandistic and modernist films of the time, notably those of Eisenstein. In *New Babylon*, such editing can be found in the First Part, where four separate locales and their respective characters are introduced through crosscutting. The New Babylon store, a train station, a cabaret, and images of the workers' space are juxtaposed at a frenetic tempo to emulate the pacing of the mob of customers at the store, the activity at the train station and the cabaret, and the fast pace of the workers. As a result, the crosscutting creates comparisons that reveal the bourgeoisie as greedy, gluttonous, smug, and in support of the war, while the workers simply slave away to produce goods for the consumers. Although Soviet montage technique was generally regarded as modernist by 1928, this approach to editing was presumably intended to be "intelligible to the millions"—a catchphrase that epitomized the official position of Sovkino, the state organization for cinema. Although "intelligibility" was a buzzword that had variably understood meanings, this particular film appeared to achieve this directive in part by establishing the groups of characters or individuals that would develop over the course of the film to represent either side of a class war, even despite its engagement with aspects of modernist film style.[7]

The score, like the film, was also intended to be "intelligible," and to meet the recent demands in film policy. As a response to the 1928 Party Conference demands that highly qualified musicians be used for film scoring,[8] the Lenfil'm studio branch of Sovkino[9] specifically set out to hire a talented composer in Leningrad. They emphasized a need for a proper musical scenario, and indicated that the directors were looking for their own local composer as early as August 1928.[10] The directors and studio eventually agreed on Shostakovich for *New Babylon* particularly because he was a young professional composer of international repute, and one of the "most talented and interesting young Soviet composers" of his time.[11] At this point, Shostakovich had already experienced worldwide success with his Symphony No.1 (1924–25), and had finished his Symphony No.2, "To October," formerly known as the *Symphonic Dedication to October* (1927).[12] But despite their respect for Shostakovich, the members of the studio administration were somewhat unsure of his skills as a film composer, and decided to meet with musical directors from local cinema houses to discuss how a musical scenario would be made. Among these directors, film-theater director and compiler Mikhail Vladimirovich Vladimirov was present; and as the current chairperson of the musical sector of *Lenark'a*, (Leningrad Association of Cinema Workers), he signed the meeting's report.[13] After much discussion, Lenfil'm decided to hire Vladimirov as a consultant to ensure a "competent showing" of the score.[14] Shostakovich had already met the fêted figure in his first trip to Moscow in 1924, when he was eighteen years old, and he excitedly relayed his impression of the film theater director.[15] Although the studio felt the need to have Vladimirov assist the young composer, Kozintsev focused less on the politics of the studio and more on how he and Shostakovich musically fit together.[16] After reportedly having seen a rehearsal of *Nose*, an opera that revealed the composer's ability to musicalize the grotesquerie of Nikolay Gogol's story, Kozintsev decided that Shostakovich would be the perfect composer for *New Babylon*.[17] Shostakovich's first film score was thusly overseen by several interlocutors, adding to the tensions that eventually arose during the premiere of the film.

SYMPHONISM AND SHOSTAKOVICH

Shostakovich envisioned the score as a symphonic work, one that sounded continuous music from beginning to end. This thinking allowed the score to be conceived along the lines of a dramatic symphony, where themes and sections of music might function programmatically, as with late nineteenth-century works such as symphonic poems. Shostakovich outlined these thoughts in his first essay on film music, "O muzïke k 'Novomu Vavilonu'" (About the Music to *New Babylon*), published days before the premiere.[18] In it, he opined the state of music for films, and outlined in some detail his approach to musical meaning and organization in his score. After the discussion of his famed "two principles," Shostakovich concluded, stating that the score maintains a "continuous symphonic tone" despite the great amount of musical material.[19] His primary goal was to create a score that was "in the rhythms and tempi of the film and to augment its impact."[20] Codes, often in the form of borrowed music, played a part in that continuity, and resonated with the intent of the directors.

In parallel, Kozintsev equally discussed the score in symphonic terms, though with a different definition. He described it thusly:

> The episodes were formed in a bundle of feelings and thoughts as parts of a visual symphony. Each of these first and foremost has distinguished emotional [and] rhythmic character. The sinister scherzo [for] the collapse of the Second Empire; slow and sorrowful andante (siege of Paris); the gleeful theme of liberation (of the Commune); the stormy melody of the struggle; the requiem of the end. Thus, the real contour of the conception gradually appears.[21]

Although Kozintsev's musical conceptualization of the film-as-symphony refers to the dramatic tone of the work, it has some resonance with

Shostakovich's notion of his score as symphony, if only on a superficial level. Shostakovich wanted to maintain musical continuity that he associated with the symphony as a genre. What results is a continuous approach to the music's form built from disparate material that directly mirrors the action, the pacing and editing, character development, and emotional content in every reel of the film. Some reels reveal editing techniques such as crosscutting that requires the music to be fragmented and quickly edited in a montagist manner.[22] In order to maintain continuity, Shostakovich employed the use of recurring motives. He briefly listed the tunes that he quarried for his themes used throughout the score.[23] Employing the term "leitmotif," referencing a nineteenth-century Wagernian practice simultaneously with contemporaneous film accompanying practices, he claimed to use the "dances of the epoch (waltz, Cancan)," "melodies from Offenbach's operettas," and "French folk and revolutionary songs," of which he names the "Marseillaise," "Ça ira," and "Carmagnole."[24] He also borrows from himself, which he fails to note, notably from his theater piece *Bedbug* (1929). Although the pulling together of various musical material may at first seem hodgepodge, Shostakovich used the motifs to maintain continuity by connecting them closely with plot turns and character development. This continuity is contingent on his self-created "principles," which he outlined in his essay.

Shostakovich created principles, as he discussed them, as a response to a lack of unity and content in cinema music, which he described as *khaltura*. He protested against such musical hackwork in the cinema, where pieces of music were cobbled together to illustrate the film.[25] He declared, "Lack of space does not allow me to write further about so-called film music manuals (musical bits for tears, uprising, corrupt bourgeoisie, love, and so forth). I will say one thing: that this is such hackwork [*khaltura*], if not worse."[26] Instead of *khaltura*, he suggested that music should reflect and be guided by the individual film, striving for the portrayal of the "inner meaning."

This desire for music that had "inner meaning," that is, was more tailored and meaningful for a specific film, was echoed by the directors. Kozintsev wanted to avoid similar *khaltura*. As he related:

> Our thoughts were the same: not to illustrate the frames, but give them a new quality and range. The music should be composed to go against the action of the film, revealing the inner meaning of the occurrences. That was not the only thing we thought up! The "Marseillaise" should shift into *La belle Hélène*, great tragic themes contrast with bawdy cancans and galops.[27]

They agreed to avoid a film accompaniment style commonly used at the time, which depended upon the use of film-music manuals or cue sheets for individual improvisation or orchestral compilations in place of an original score; and instead wanted to create music that was particular to the film. This resonated with contemporaneous interest in synchronizing sound and film, as indicated in the "Statement on Sound" from August 1928. This Statement, which sought to theorize a role for sound in film that would allow the integrity of the Soviet montage style to be preserved, called for a synthesis of image and sound, or in the authors' words, "counterpoint."[28] Music critics later clarified this Statement, adding that a "film composer" would be needed to ensure that music and sound are integrated into the film in an organized manner that would lead to an "organic composition of visual and sound image."[29] Kozintsev, Trauberg, and Shostakovich were aware of these arguments, and their discussions of a specially composed score for *New Babylon* answered in part the spirit of the Statement's request.[30] This approach also aligned with the objectives of the studio, who wanted a composer especially for the film and wanted to move toward a goal of a new cinema where music would play a significant role.[31]

Shostakovich's principles were his answer to creating music that engages images and avoids *khlatura,* and thusly evoking Kozintsev's "inner meaning."

> The only correct path was to write special music, as it has been done, if I am not mistaken, in one of the first instances with *New Babylon.* When composing music to "Babylon," I was guided least of all by the principle of mandatory illustration of every shot. Mainly, I began from the principal shot in each sequence of shots. [Take] for example, the end of the second part.[32] The primary moment is the attack of the German cavalry on Paris. The part ends with a deserted restaurant. Total silence. But the music, despite the fact that the German cavalry is not shown on the screen, comes from the cavalry all the same, reminding the viewer of the impending menacing force.[33]

Shostakovich's two main "principles" were similar to ideas about music's role in sound film that would permeate most film theory across the world in the decades to follow, such as Siegfried Kracauer's oft-cited notions of parallelism and counterpoint.[34] The first, Shostakovich's "principle of the shot/scene," can be summarized as continuous music over potentially rapid editing, which embodies the overall meaning of the shot or scene; while the second, his "principle of contrasts," however, implies that he follows the rhythm of the film, that is, its editing style, instead of the scene's tone or mood. The "principle of contrast" also implies that music specific to a character or a shot should be contradictory to the central mood of the scene. The theorizing of these "principles" released Shostakovich from "musical-illustration," an approach typically used in silent film accompaniment or for orchestral compilations. He provided several examples of each principle, including the one above, while discussing borrowed music and its intended meaning. These principles are served by multiple codes throughout the score, manifesting as song and style quotations.[35]

Appropriate to the film's story and in keeping with current theater and music practice, Shostakovich used French songs to support the idea of a class war. As he claimed in his essay, he used the revolutionary song "Ça Ira," which appears in part 4, to support the Communards. In this scene, the Communards are attempting to sway the soldiers to their cause; and the tune anchors the meaning of the story's events. [36] When the soldiers meet them, and the Communard women offer them milk to drink, the tune appears only with brief harmonic preparation and in a contrasting key and mode (C major). In the scenarios and extant versions of the film, the subtitles read, "What great guys, what handsome guys" coinciding with the manuscripts and a cue in Manashir Yakubov's edition, published by DSCH (hereafter referred to as the DSCH edition) "The soldiers are given milk to drink."[37] After the soldiers express a lack of desire to join the Communards and continue on their way, this revolutionary tune abruptly ends—the tonally sunny moment shifts— and fails to reappear for the remainder of the film.

The "Carmagnole" as a code operates differently in the score, appearing as a recurring motif, and often in reference to battle. Its associations are more complex—it appears firstly in connection with the bourgeoisie as they abandon their work on the new operetta and head to Versailles prior to the battle with the Communards. The quotation is positioned just between these two symbolic events—the failing of an operetta and the move to Versailles to observe the battle—and clearly played in the French horn and trumpet, suggesting a militaristic topic.[38] Similar to instrumentation in the score to *Alone*, the horn as a topic evokes the revolution, as does the context for the song.[39] The second appearance of the "Carmagnole," in the strings in part 5, offers a different meaning, by coinciding with the scene where the Communards are proclaiming their happiness at their newly found freedom. Its penultimate appearance, stated twice, surfaces in the battle scene—once when the Communards receive news that the army (representing the power of the bourgeoisie) has broken through the barricade; and again in an interesting layering with the "Marseillaise" as the two groups engage in battle. As the Communards discuss their impending loss, the tune sounds in the horns as in its first appearance, and is heard in the trumpet and trombones (see Example 2.1a). Just minutes later, the "Carmagnole" sounds in the trumpets as the horns and trombones play a fragment of the "Marseillaise." The quotation of both songs lasts only three bars and ends

Example 2.1a: Excerpt from "Carmagnole" in its first appearance in the battle scene (brass only).

Modified from Manashir Yakubov, ed., *Dmitry Shostakovich: New Collected Works*, vol. 122, "The New Babylon" [*Dmitry Shostakovich: Novoye Sobraniye Sochineniy, Tom 122*, "Novyi Vavilon"] (Moscow: DSCH, 2004), 379, mm.63–64.

Example 2.1b: Excerpt from "Carmagnole" and "Marseillaise" in the second battle scene (brass only).

Modified from Yakubov, *Dmitry Shostakovich: New Collected Works*, vol. 122, "The New Babylon," 399, mm. 215–217.

three bars before the score edition indication "Battle."[40] (See Example 2.1b.) After the "Battle" indication, parts of the "Marseillaise" and "Carmagnole" are fragmented and developed, as are the rhythms implied by the tune; a kind of symphonic development akin to a Beethovenian symphony.[41] The triplet rhythms used in the variation of the "Carmagnole," as seen in measure 216 of the DSCH edition, and the dotted eighth-note anacrusis of the "Marseillaise" used throughout the score (see Example 2.1b) become the musical fodder that Shostakovich used to create the rhythmic dynamism that propels that battle scene. After the whole statements of the codes, only occasionally do recognizable fragments of them surface; the focus instead is on the rhythmic drive of this scene, using those rhythms originally belonging to the songs, and eventually symbolizing the Communard's defeat.

The "Carmagnole" makes its final appearance at the end of the film, over the images of Louise's final utterances to Jean ("We will meet again") and the phrase "Vive la Commune!" spoken aloud by another worker via

Example 2.1c: Excerpt from "Carmagnole" in its last appearance (winds only).
Modified from Yakubov, *Dmitry Shostakovich: New Collected Works*, vol. 122, "The New Babylon," 528, mm.149–150.

intertitles. According to the extant manuscripts, this statement of the "Carmagnole" is the last music heard as the film ends.[42] (See Example 2.1c.) This final statement of the "Carmagnole" emerges in a stable key area (E-flat major followed by A-flat major) in contrast to the slow-moving, tonally unstable music of part 8 that appears earlier to parallel the mood of the chiaroscuro images and the defeat of the Commune.[43] Of the French revolutionary songs, this prominent placement of the "Carmagnole" represents the Commune's revolution, a common symbolic transfer used to signify the Russian revolutionary spirit that was expressed in theater works in the 1920s.

Within the film, this "Carmagnole" code accumulates meaning through visual association with the plight of the workers and their cause. It first appears with the bourgeoisie moving to Versailles, signaling the onset of the battle; it is later associated with the Communard's happiness and eventual defeat. The layers of association seem clear—the "Carmagnole" cues revolution, even though it is a failed one in the case of the Commune, as it cues the hope that a revolution can bring to a newly formed state. Since this sentiment was reiterated throughout the late teens and twenties in Russian theater and film, it is understandable that the directors and composer would select a musical parallel to the French revolution.

In addition to the "Carmagnole," the two other aforementioned songs—the "Ça ira" and "Marseillaise"—were also used in proletarian musical organizations through the twenties to signify revolution.[44] The histories of these songs are entrenched in the history of the French revolution and the story of the Commune. "Ça ira" and "Carmagnole" were both created in the 1790s, and used as rallying cries by participants in the revolution, particularly the *sans-culottes*, or disenfranchised urban militants.[45] Proletarian groups in Russia similarly used these three songs, and associated the radical militant meaning of these tunes with the underclass and democratic ideals.[46] The militant histories of these songs are further reinforced by the timbral choice—Shostakovich prominently featured brass instruments for the majority of their appearances to evoke a specific association. The layering of the "Carmagnole" with the "Marseillaise," with the latter being the national anthem of France, adds value: they create layers of meanings to be read, and an association with a successful revolution. Although it seems a natural choice, Shostakovich was working within a history of musical and historical codes, and adding to these codes a new layer of Russian revolutionary spirit typical to the time, place, and media.

The "Marseillaise" was famously heard during the French Revolution, even more so than the "Carmagnole" and "Ça ira." Shostakovich emphasized its use, placed it most prominently throughout the score in the "most unexpected contexts," and treated it like the other revolutionary borrowings.[47] The first and last statements, appearing in parts 3 and 7, are distorted, out-of-tune, and fragmented. In both instances, the rising major second and the perfect fourth leap are altered in the opening phrase, resulting in the creation of a minor second and tritone, and therefore creating a "wrong-note" impression (see Examples 2.2a and 2.2b).

At these musical moments there are indications in the DSCH edition such as "Surrender," which correspond to the Guard's demand of the Communards' weapons; and a final scene where the bourgeoisie brutally beat the Communards after their defeat and before their execution. In both instances, the music was written for wind instruments, with a prominently heard solo bassoon for the first appearance, and upper wind ensemble with full orchestral accompaniment for the last.[48] Bassoon, often used as a comic and grotesque instrument in past symphonic poems such as *Also sprach Zarathustra* (Richard Strauss, 1895–96), is a grotesque choice for this statement of the "Marseillaise."[49] Such a timbral choice consciously contradicted the setting of the central and only instance of the full statement of the "Marseillaise" in the denouement of the film.

This full statement of the "Marseillaise" at the denouement is the only instance where it appears as a complete song, and it was strategically placed in part 5 when the bourgeoisie gather at a bar in Versailles to await the beginning of the battle.[50] An actress, who appeared earlier onscreen in the film's operetta, hops upon a chair and leads the bar crowd in a rendition

Example 2.2a: Excerpt from distorted "Marseillaise" in part 3.
Modified from Yakubov, *Dmitry Shostakovich: New Collected Works*, vol. 122, "The New Babylon," 209, mm.159–161.

Example 2.2b: Excerpt from distorted "Marseillaise" in part 7 (winds only).
Modified from Yakubov, *Dmitry Shostakovich: New Collected Works*, vol. 122, "The New Babylon," 488, mm.150–152. At this point, the "Marseillaise" appears in the winds with support in the strings and brass (in measure 150) and continues (until measure 165), and eventually blends into the orchestral fabric through subtle variation.

of the French song, with lyrics in intertitles and the song in full orchestral statement marked "Marseillaise" in the DSCH edition and manuscripts.[51] (See Example 2.3.) At this point, the song is diegetic; although it is a silent film, it is heard within the diegesis and sung accordingly by its characters. This rendition of the "Marseillaise" certainly emphasizes the placement of this film in its time; such a practice of visually representing music was common to silent cinema. It was an expected practice to encourage the viewer to imagine the actress's voice, and the voices of the bourgeoisie in the bar amidst the orchestral statement. The entire text of the song is relayed through intertitles in quotation marks, cut with images of the

Example 2.3: Excerpt from the "Marseillaise" and the bar scene (winds only).
Modified from Yakubov, *Dmitry Shostakovich: New Collected Works*, vol. 122, "The New Babylon," 343, mm. 261–263. A full tonal statement of the "Marseillaise" begins in full orchestra with winds excerpted here for clarity. This statement continues and then is layered over a quotation of Offenbach's Cancan. A fragment of the "Marseillaise" returns again (see measures 317–321 in the edition), with a change in scene.

singer, non-diegetic inserts of trumpets and cannons, and faces from the bar crowd. The non-diegetic inserts, reminiscent of Eisensteinian practice, reinforce Shostakovich's music and draw together the potential historical meanings of brass instruments, war, and national anthems.[52]

Such a culmination of the images of instruments associated with war, musical and otherwise, enables the "Marseillaise" to operate as a complete code at this climatic moment right before the Battle of the Commune. Significantly, Shostakovich had reserved the use of trumpets and French horns for this particular statement of the "Marseillaise." Up to this point, the fragments of the tune had been played by the strings and the winds. The first phrase of the full statement is with orchestra, one of the few moments of the film that utilizes every instrument of the ensemble; while the second phrase is reserved for brass quartet only, before returning to the full orchestra to finish the statement.[53] It is throughout this statement that the intercutting of trumpets, cannons, and the bourgeoisie force a viewer to associate brass instruments and the "Marseillaise" together, binding music (and the idea of it) to the image in a space between diegesis and non-diegesis (a "fantastical gap").[54] Kozintsev wrote that he edited this scene to specifically create a web of meanings to signify power, national identity, and war; and eventually the brutality of the bourgeoisie.[55] The "Marseillaise" therefore is completed as a code of the bourgeoisie

Example 2.4: Excerpt of layered "Marseillaise" and Cancan (horns, trombone, and upper strings only).
Modified from Yakubov, *Dmitry Shostakovich: New Collected Works*, vol. 122, "The New Babylon," 349, mm.286–289.

and their power, lacking any irony, and foreshadows their victory over the Communards.

The univalent sincerity of the "Marseillaise" as bourgeois code is challenged, however, after the first full orchestral and brass statement of the song. The horns, which have been associated with battle and war throughout the score, begin a second statement of the tune in C major layered over a string rendition of Jacques Offenbach's Cancan in B-flat major from *Orphée aux enfers*, both of which dissolve into a variation based on both quotations (Example 2.4). As Kozintsev reminded, "great tragic themes contrast with bawdy cancans and galops."[56]

According to Trauberg, Shostakovich was encouraged to layer the two tunes, and in response to this request, he used instrumentation (brass versus strings) and key (bitonality) to differentiate between the melodies, calling attention to their differences and their meanings, while creating a musical transition from the statement of the "Marseillaise."[57] The music of the Cancan enters as images of Paris "the gay" and "the carefree"— intertitles reused from previous scenes—are intertwined with images of cancan dancers' legs cut from earlier reels of the film. Such intercutting is a continuation of the editing style from the previous statement of the "Marseillaise," and it anchors the images on the screen by referring to earlier scenes of the partying bourgeoisie.[58] The editing of these recurring images with these musical quotations builds upon the "Marseillaise" code, and suggests irony and grotesquerie already firmly associated with the bourgeoisie; that is, the Cancan belittles the associations of the sincere national pomp of the "Marseillaise" when visually intercut with the frivolity of the bourgeoisie of the film, and musically layered with a dance quoted from an opera equally received as parodic in its time (one of the "dances of the epoch" about which Shostakovich wrote). The directors and composer, who insisted on an ironic and negative depiction of the bourgeoisie, were intent to make the collision of these meanings clear. The enmeshment of Offenbach's dances and French national songs indicated their choice to distinguish the character types and themes of the film, which ultimately functioned as codes that index historically embedded meanings and symbolism.

As he indicated in his article before the premiere, Shostakovich borrowed songs and styles from the epoch to be used throughout the score. The French songs were sometimes layered with other tunes (as with the "Marseillaise" and the Cancan), or he used quotations from past concert music to characterize or symbolize themes, issues, or characters. Waltzes and galops were among the dances/rhythms that Shostakovich selected in order to depict class tension and characterization of the workers and the bourgeoisie. Of the two styles, the galops were employed in the first half of the film, while the waltzes permeated the score throughout.

Kozintsev frequently wrote about the galop as an important musical idea for the film—musically, visually, and formally—which resonates well with Shostakovich's own predilection for the code in his other works.[59] Kozintsev employed this galop to capture the qualities of the bourgeoisie in the first reel, emphasizing how contradiction and "visual 'alliteration'" underscore the themes of this film:

> The frames not only engage semantic synthesis, but many elements of the plastic arts (distinctive visual "alliteration"): lace on the counter and soap suds in the washtub of the laundresses; the dancing galop and the rotation of the day in the store; the fog of the garden and the steam of the laundry. The similarity of one element clashed with another in contrast: the abundance of "sales" with the emptiness and the poverty of the [workers'] shops.[60]

The alliterative images that Kozintsev listed are entirely visual, with the exception of the galop. He realized the visual counterparts of the "dancing galop" and the "day in the store" through crosscutting between the cabaret and the New Babylon store. Shostakovich found a direct musical realization to Kozintsev's visual crosscutting and emulation of its structure by using musical blocks, each of which represented the chaotic New Babylon store, the train station attendees, and the cabaret; and each of which contained the same busied galops every time these images appear throughout part 1. These musical blocks correspond to events in separate locales, including Louise and the busy store, the Manager deciding on Louise as his "dessert," and Louise receiving an invitation from the Manager.[61] The events as they correspond to musical sections appear as follows in figure 2.1.

Although they contain different sections of music that seamlessly elide into each other, both the "Train Station" and "The New Babylon Store" have the features of a galop, that is, $\frac{2}{4}$ meter with offbeat rhythms.[62] "The New Babylon Store" is a newly composed galop with the rhythm normally associated with that style. The "Train Station" section is a galop by rhythm and by association—it has the same melody and key, offbeat rhythms, and meter of a musical number titled "Galop" from his contemporaneous satirical theater work, *Bedbug* (1929).[63] The "Train Station" in *New Babylon* has the same melody in the same key (G major), $\frac{2}{4}$ meter, and offbeat rhythms that are also used in this "Galop."[64] Shostakovich likely used this number in *New Babylon* because it contained the same surface features that signify its style; a common approach that he applied to his theater and film music of this time.[65] This particular theater piece was also satirical, much in the way Shostakovich characterizes the bourgeoisie in *New Babylon*, suggesting that the composer regarded the galop not as a rhythmic style that historically grew out of the waltz, but as a popular dance style and rhythm that could lend itself to satirizing the antagonists of the film. Coupled with images of the cabaret and the partying bourgeoisie, the galop takes on a rowdy, superficial, and elite meaning that appears oppressive in comparison with the images of the workers managing the busy demands of the shopping bourgeoisie at the store, and thereby complementing Kozintsev's attempt at "visual alliteration." This mad dance of a galop eventually becomes a code to represent the greed, gluttony, and oppression of the bourgeoisie.

[A] Train station → **[B]** New Babylon Department Store and its customers → **[C]** Manager (Boss) → **[B]** New Babylon Department Store and its customers → **[D]** Saleswoman (Louise) → (Invitation to the Ball) → **[B]** The New Babylon Store and its customers → **[A]** Train Station

Figure 2.1: Part 1 in blocks as it corresponds to events in the film. This part is symmetrical and self-contained, corresponding to a block form, which can be shown as ABCBDBA. Both A ("Train Station") and B ("New Babylon Store") recur, acting as structural signposts throughout the part. This form breakdown includes the "Invitation to the Ball" as part of "Saleswoman," that is, part of D.

The waltz was another of the "dances of the epoch" that Shostakovich exploited as a code throughout the score, serving as an example of his "principle of contrast" and a complement to Kozintsev's attempt at contradiction and "alliteration."[66] There are only four instances where waltzes appear in the manuscripts and the edition. Three of them are musically different from one another, while the fourth is a repetition.[67] Of these three waltzes, two are quotations from preexisting works. In each instance the waltz serves as a cumulatively building code to signify the rottenness of the bourgeoisie and the final defeat of the Communards.

The first two waltzes, the second of which is a restatement of a fragment from the first, are associated with scenes where the bourgeoisie dine, celebrate, or prepare for their operetta. The first instance of a waltz appears in part 2 and contains subsections, some of which are quotations from Jacques Offenbach's *La belle Hélène*; while the brief second appearance of a waltz in part 4 borrows from a subsection in part 2, thereby acting as a recurring motif.[68] The initial appearance, and subsequently the second, of this waltz is an Offenbach quotation. Beginning with the trombone entry, corresponding to measure 94 in the DSCH edition and continued by the strings in measure 102 forward, approximately one third of the way into the entire waltz section of part 2, Shostakovich quoted directly from the Entr'acte of the beginning of act 2 in *La belle Hélène*, a scene in Helen's apartment.[69] (See Example 2.5.)

Shostakovich chose this music, which is from the second part of the first phrase of Offenbach's Entr'acte, to evoke the decadent dancers and drinkers of bourgeois Paris in the 1870s. Since Offenbach's operas and operettas from the 1860s and 1870s parodied the conventions of opera and mythology, and were subsequently chastised for being musically "decadent," the prominent use of a famed quotation from *La belle Hélène* reinforces the socialist critique of the bourgeoisie in the film.[70] Hence, this particular waltz begins the building of the waltz-as-code throughout the film. By the end of the film, this waltz participates as part of a generalized waltz code.

The third waltz continues to reinforce the link between bourgeois decadence and the larger concept of the waltz within the context of the film. It builds upon the Offenbach quotation with another quotation, again from Shostakovich's contemporaneous theater work, *Bedbug*.[71] This quotation, identical to *Bedbug* and in the same key (D minor/G major), appears in part 6, where the bourgeoisie are shown in Versailles.[72] Eric Roseberry writes that Shostakovich drew upon the waltz and galop as general ideas in *Bedbug* to critique bourgeois culture.[73] Within *New Babylon*, this third appearance of a waltz is written to accompany images of the bourgeoisie waiting for the Battle as if it were an operetta performance. They are reclining and

Example 2.5: Excerpt from *La belle Hélène* quotation (horns and trombone entry only).
Modified from Yakubov, *Dmitry Shostakovich: New Collected Works*, vol. 122, "The New Babylon," 95, mm.94–99.
The trombone begins the quotation from *La belle Hélène* (see measure 94), but the full statement is restarted and finished by the strings (see measure 102ff).

watching the human players in the Battle, with opera spectacles in hand, which accentuates their indifference. The three waltz statements combined, both borrowed from the satirical works *La belle Hélène* and *Bedbug*, further build the waltz code as a socialist critique of bourgeois decadence and wealth.[74]

The fourth and last occurrence of the waltz is Shostakovich's first example of the "principle of contrast." In part 6, when Jean meets Louise on the barricades and confronts the bourgeoisie as they applaud him from Versailles (again, as if watching a battle-as-operetta), Shostakovich related that the soldier is "filled with despair," while the music builds into a "frantic" and "obscene" waltz.[75] This waltz is Shostakovich's creation, but by this point in the score the general signifiers of an Offenbach-styled waltz, or of most waltzes—triple meter with emphasis on the downbeat and seemingly periodic phrases—are strongly associated with the bourgeoisie (see Example 2.6).

Shostakovich's music hints at the exaggerated and contrastive use of the waltz at this moment in the film, which adds to the perception of irony and the grotesque, or more specifically what Esti Sheinberg calls the "satirical grotesque."[76] The satirical grotesque, as defined by Sheinberg, expresses contempt as well as horror and disgust. In many of Shostakovich's works, Sheinberg notes that the composer distorts dance genres to become relentless, clumsy, and heavy, creating a violently grotesque presentation of a musical idea.[77] Similarly, the sarcastically triumphant waltz of part 6 that Shostakovich described in terms of contrast is overly celebratory, disinterested, and banal, as indicated by the intense volume and full texture of the orchestra in combination with the image of the bourgeoisie applauding Jean in the Communard battle as if he were a player in some distantly observed operetta (see measures 516–543 in the DSCH edition). The

Example 2.6: Excerpt from Shostakovich's waltz (winds only).
Modified from Yakubov, *Dmitry Shostakovich: New Collected Works*, vol. 122, "The New Babylon," 455,
mm.516–518. The brass and strings, not seen in this rendition, double the winds and flesh out the orchestral
sound; they also add to the emphasis on beats 2 and 3 as typically found in waltzes. For a printed full edition,
see Yakubov, through measure 543.

The bourgeoisie applauds the soldier.

textural buildup and harmonic tension/resolution (a common V/V–V–I cadential pattern, with ten measures of dominant pedal) precede this waltz and also contribute to the banal triumph of this final waltz statement.[78] In combination with these aspects, the tune appears relentless because of its seemingly symmetrical but uneven phrases (7+14+7), which are delimited by cadential and melodic structure and constant repetition.[79] The first phrase contains symmetrical rhythms and repeated melodic ideas that encourage two-measure groupings, with an initial first measure that stands alone. The second phrase consists of fourteen measures that fluctuate between two- and three-measure groupings, throwing the phrase structure off balance. The final phrase returns to the seven-measure format, with predominantly two-measure groupings, and a final, independent measure.[80] The outward symmetry and internal asymmetry creates a simple, well-ordered waltz statement that also evokes exaggeration and relentlessness making this section satirically grotesque rather than a plain statement that the bourgeoisie have won the battle. Two ideas emerge from this satirically grotesque contrast that closes the waltz code: the victory of the bourgeoisie and Jean's own internal crisis. Similar to the galop, the waltz-as-code is part of Shostakovich's method of capturing the internal state of a character, and propels the viewer/listener to identify with the Communards, taking this score beyond the usual "illustration" of standard compilation scores.[81]

In his article about the film, Shostakovich discussed his borrowing of French songs and Offenbach quotations, but he only mentions one other of his borrowings from the concert music tradition. In addition to his borrowing from *Bedbug*, he also quoted from other composers, citing specifically music for piano. The piano was an important instrument in the silent era, often being the only instrument for accompaniment in small theaters. Since Shostakovich was expected to write this score to be played with orchestra and for piano, it would be reasonable to borrow from the pianistic tradition, particularly if it suited the narrative of the film.[82] There are two instances where he cites well-known pieces for piano. They operate as integral musical commentary, and more subtly, reflect an essential use of an instrument that was already a staple in music for silent film. I consider this evocation a subtle reference to the role of the piano in cinema of the teens and twenties. Generally, it is a kind of code, albeit a truly subtle and easily overlooked one.

The first reference to the piano as a significant aspect of the film's narrative is the most subtle. Shostakovich wrote,

> An interesting method is used in the Fourth Part. There is a rehearsal of the operetta. The music plays a rather well-known exercise by Hanon, which takes on different nuances in relation to the action. Sometimes it has a gay mood, sometimes boring, sometimes terrifying.[83]

Shostakovich varied the "well-known exercise by Hanon,"[84] which was likely borrowed from one of the piano exercises from the *Virtuoso Pianist* by French composer and pedagogue Charles Louis Hanon (1819–1900).[85] It also slightly resembles a motif from Act I, no.3 of Offenbach's *La belle Hélène* known as the "Song of Oreste," though in this case, it is more likely a quote from Hanon.[86] This section of music correlates with cuts between dancers at an operetta rehearsal and an officer in the countryside, and operates as a small section within the whole variation form of the fourth part.[87] (See Example 2.7.)

The section begins with the cue "People dance at a rehearsal," with rhythms, intervals, and melodic contour most similar to Hanon's exercises numbers two and three from the *Virtuoso Pianist*, and somewhat similar to the "Song of Oreste."[88] Midway through the section, the tonal center shifts from C to E-flat (measure 7 in Example 2.7) at the point where the designation "Officer smiles" appears in the DSCH edition. This cue corresponds

Example 2.7: Excerpt from the fourth part, Shostakovich's variation of the "well-known exercise of Hanon."
Modified from Yakubov, *Dmitry Shostakovich: New Collected Works*, vol. 122, "The New Babylon," 225, mm.44–51.

to a cinematic cut to images of the countryside, where the officer smiles at his soldiers while they prepare their cannons. Shostakovich discussed his music as having contrasts, meaning that his music follows the nuances of the action, as revealed in the film editing that corresponds to this section, rather than to the overall tone or action of a scene. His discussion of this specific section is within the context of a reel of the film where there is a juxtaposition of scenes of the soldiers in the countryside (who eventually meet the Communards) with scenes of the operetta rehearsals. The result is a montage between two different groups of people in two different locales, both of which eventually decide to relocate to Versailles.[89] As I have written elsewhere, this moment represents a musical equivalent to montagist filmmaking in the United States and Soviet Russia in the twenties, as it is also reminiscent of the crosscutting technique that Kozintsev used to create the "alliterative" comparisons between the shop and the workers in part 1.[90] Shostakovich wrote his music in a montagist manner to suit the rhythm of the editing. The cutting between "different moods," that is, musical styles in this moment and overall section of part 4 therefore suggests a direct influence of the cinematic montage techniques of the period on Shostakovich's music.[91]

Shostakovich's choice of Hanon's music as fodder for this variation set is out of place with his other borrowings, reflecting neither a French revolutionary topic nor contemporaneous satire. Yet, Shostakovich wrote that this quotation was "well-known," potentially to any classically trained pianist. Such exercises for piano, particularly of Hanon, fail to appear in Soviet film music manuals from the 1920s, which suggests that Shostakovich was probably regarding this music as well known to trained pianists or general audience members who had piano lessons in their youth. What is peculiar about this statement is the assumption of pianistic knowledge; the majority of the pianists playing in Russian cinemas in the teens and twenties were trained outside of the conservatory.[92] Some of the more famous *pianist-illustrators* were musicians from a different, separate realm than that of the conservatory, having worked in theaters and popular venues.[93] Hence the emphasis in Shostakovich's contracts for the score to *New Babylon*: the studio wanted a composer of "international repute," one that was conservatory trained, and one that would establish a new tradition in film scoring.[94] Such a statement amidst the documents of his hiring quietly stated a new turn in film music, and a desire for a differently trained professional. Shostakovich's choice of Hanon, therefore, subtly suggests a preference for the piano, the primary instrument of cinema musical practice at that time, although masked in variations suitable for the film's narrative. In short, he took an idiomatic pianistic idea as material for experimenting with rhythm, image, and meaning in this new medium of film scoring; an extremely subtle way to reference the old cinema tradition while starting a new one.

The last instance of piano-as-code carries through it several histories as it narrates the end of the Commune in part 6 during the Battle of the Communards. Towards the end of the battle, when the defeat of the Communards looms, an older man sits at a piano and begins to play as the Commune burns to the ground. In extreme contrast to the battle raging around him, immediate cuts to the intertitles show in quotation marks a title "Oh, How I Love the Time of Cherries," which refers to a French popular song often titled, "Le temps des cerises." This song has specifically signified the Commune since its publication in 1885 by Jean-Baptiste Clement and Antoine Renard as "La chanson de la Commune" (The Song of the Commune), and was sung by Communards.[95] Baptiste, who fought in the Battle, wrote this song and noted that its inspiration was a young female medic named Louise, a woman who has been conflated with the famous female Communard and fighter Louise Michel.[96] The original song lyrics refer to the battle and to the Commune throughout, being a "Time of Cherries," referring to the coming of spring as a metaphor for liberty.[97] Almost two decades later, the song was parodied and further politically refined as the "Time of Crisis" (Le temps des crises) by Jules Jouy.[98] It was silent film practice to cue specific musical ideas in the film through intertitles, allowing the accompanist or orchestra to fill in the music, a kind of cueing of the accompanist; scoring the song "Le temps des cerises," a song sung by Communards, would have been the likely choice. Shostakovich, however, chose differently, and failed to mention this quotation in his article, where he discussed his other borrowings. Instead, Shostakovich obliged with Pyotr Tchaikovsky's "Old French Song" from *Album for the Young* (*Detskiy al'bom*, op.39, 1878), a cycle created during the time of the French Commune.

There are multiple ways that Tchaikovsky, the piano, and this specific musical piece interact within this film. Tchaikovsky's "Old French Song" is appropriate in title and musical content for this contrastive moment in the midst of energetic music for battle; the song is lyrical, simple, and with a medium tempo, signaling a contemplative moment in the middle of the struggle. It firmly creates *ancrage* in this moment of calm, where the song, with its French implications and contemplative mood, correlates with the piano onscreen.[99] It was common practice in early Soviet film to use the piano as an anti-revolutionary icon to symbolize tsarist Russia; in this case, it could be easily read as a symbol of the bourgeoisie.[100] Tchaikovsky was sometimes conflated with the image of the piano as a representative of pre-Soviet musical traditions, and he was a composer often cited in film music manuals throughout the 1920s.[101] Taken altogether—the simplicity and calm of the song, its title, its composition during the time of the Commune, the iconicity of Tchaikovsky as an oft-cited composer in early silent cinema, and the iconicity of the piano as an instrument in Soviet films and its clear use in accompaniment in early cinema across the world—this moment in the film can be read to signify the resignation of the Commune and its defeat, powerfully indexed between the French and Russian past and the Soviet utopic present-future. The result is the musical anchorage of the image of a Communard playing a piano in a burning Commune to the sounds of a pre-revolutionary composer and the resulting resignation and defeat of the Commune depicted on the screen. This clever choice of music for these images acts as a code and ironic commentary (a Communard playing an 1878 Tchaikovsky piece on a piano during an impending defeat) that reinforces the victory and oppression of the bourgeoisie.

RECEPTION

The reception of the film's codes and score's innovations as a whole was generally poor, leading to the eventual canonization of this film as a failure at its premiere. The failure occurred because of multiple reasons. Writers and critics over the course of almost a century, however, have claimed it was because of Shostakovich's music and its resulting effects—lack of rehearsal, musical complexity, and copying errors.[102] Although musical events surely were partly to blame, contemporaneous arguments about the appropriate "Soviet" quality or intelligibility of cinema equally applied to *New Babylon*.[103] As a result, its reception was complex and varied. As Kozintsev retrospectively related in his book *The Deep Screen*, there were multiple points of view on the usefulness, intelligibility, and success of the film.[104] The variety of opinions about the content and the style of the film revealed that critics, film workers, and the public at large were still unclear as to whom the cinema served and what was "intelligible" and permissible in Soviet cinema.

Musicologist Yuli Vaynkop related one of the technical and cinemapolitical reasons surrounding the failure of the premiere. He wrote,

> An overly enthusiastic cinema entrepreneur was too hasty in sounding the alarm about Dmitry Shostakovich's music to the film *New Babylon*, by ascribing the film's failure to the young composer's supposedly unsuccessful music. This classical maneuver of shifting the blame to someone else's shoulders should have met with the appropriate rebuff, particularly since this accusation is supported by many cinema conductors deprived of "royalties" for their musical-illustrational compilations due to the presence of a ready score . . .[105]

In the documents for hiring Shostakovich it was clear that an interest in complying with recent trends in music for original films, and a lack of trust motivated the studio to hire Vladimirov to supervise the young composer. The studio's claim that Shostakovich was new to the film music profession, and that Vladimirov would be an appropriate mentor, was only part of the situation.[106] Vladimirov was an established conductor at the *Picadilly* Cinema, had been the director/conductor/composer/compiler at the cinemas where *New Babylon* would be premiered, and was closely involved with Lenfil'm in the supervision and review of their musical scenarios for other films.[107] Although Vladimirov's stance on Shostakovich's hiring is unclear, it is clear that the studio changed their minds about Shostakovich's hiring and added Vladimirov at a later date to supervise the composer.[108] It is therefore highly probable that Vaynkop was correct—Vladimirov's and other conductors' livelihood was directly affected by the new shift to original scoring ("ready score"), and it was suspected by Shostakovich and others that Vladimirov had a hand in sabotaging the score.[109]

Vaynkop did, however, credit Vladimirov for attempting to give the score proper play. He related,

> This music is played horribly everywhere, although to be fair we should say that M.[ikhail] V.[ladimirovich] Vladimirov (conductor at the *Picadilly* cinema) treated it with more care than the rest, achieving the most piquancy and expressiveness and the fewest mistakes and [least] tempo confusion.[110]

Others also related that the performances at theaters in Leningrad and Moscow were unsuccessful. Leo Arnshtam related how badly Shostakovich's music was performed, claiming that the composer ran from theater to theater only to find that orchestras were nearly destroying his score.[111] Shostakovich himself wrote, in a letter to Ivan Sollertinsky, how he feared that he would be maligned by cinema management.[112] This fear was grounded in both perceived jealously and threat, and by certain other factors. Since the music was given to theater orchestras, like those of the *Picadilly* and *Gigant* cinemas only days before the premiere, conductors were generally unable to rehearse the orchestras well.[113] Orchestras such as these were unaccustomed to performing specially tailored scores of this level of difficulty, leaving much work to be done on the part of the conductor. If the conductor refused to comply, the results would be disastrous. Vladimirov was expected to conduct the score better than most because of his contract with the studio. And he did, at least initially; according to Sovkino, the score was performed well for the first week at *Picadilly* and *Gigant* theaters.[114] Other cinemas, however, had difficulty. Even though the studio wanted to delay the film's showing due to Shostakovich's illness, it pushed ahead anyway, aware of mistakes in Shostakovich's corrections, especially to orchestral and piano parts sent to other cities.[115] Shostakovich had sent parts to Moscow, but considered them inadequate; he wrote to Moscow director Ferdinand Krish about the Moscow premiere, with details on how to improve the score's and film's showing.[116] Other conductors and cinema managers may not have received similarly close attention and were not required to oblige with a serious preparation of the score.

Prior to the premiere, and under circumstances where the orchestra appeared prepared and the conductor compliant, Shostakovich's music was well received and deemed "intelligible" by studio officials. The administration of Sovkino screened the film almost a month before its premiere, approved the music, and strongly recommended that Shostakovich's music be performed well with the screenings of the film. As Sovkino related,

> This music is distinguished by its considerable closeness to the style and rhythm of the film, by great emotional strength and expressivity. The effect of the picture is greatly heightened. Furthermore, despite the originality and freshness of the form, the music is sufficiently simple and can be appreciated by the mass viewer.[117]

After the film's premieres in Moscow and Leningrad, most critics found the film score to be successful in fulfilling the Party's directives for the new Soviet film. As reviewer and one of the Lenfil'm studio heads M. Gartsman claimed, "Dmitry Shostakovich carried out the instructions of the Party assembly: his music is an integral part of the film. And we will add, one of the best parts."[118] The idea of the music being "one of the best parts" is further supported by surveys taken by Sovkino at workers' clubs that I found at the Gosfil'mofond archive.[119] Most of the audiences at these clubs enjoyed the film and its music, ranking the music alongside their usual favorites: cinematography and the performance of the actors.

These reviewers also noted Shostakovich's use of codes throughout the score. One reviewer praised the composer for his ability to evoke the ideology of the film specific to the historical era through French revolutionary songs, such as the "Marseillaise."[120] Critic and musicologist Kliment Korchmaryov, however, panned the score, citing the "primitive presentation of the borrowed material" as the least of the score's problems. He complained,

> Shostakovich, a very talented person, came to this work without enough care; he obviously wrote the music hurriedly, [and] as a result of that, it emerged uneven in quality and style; among the simple, even primitive presentation of the borrowed material (the Marseillaise, Carman'ola [sic], fragments from the operettas of Offenbach), there was much muddled atonal music, which was difficult to perceive. The most successful music [belonged] to the first part, where the composer emphasizes the dynamics of the film language well. Unfortunately, the

extraordinary technical complexity in both the orchestral parts and especially in the piano [score] would prevent the performance of this generally interesting work in the provinces.[121]

Korchmaryov's mixed review was one among several that considered the score "muddled," "atonal," "formalist," "aestheticist," "art for art's sake," and, therefore, modernist and unsuccessful as a Soviet film.[122] This language continued into the thirties, when film music critic Ieremiya Ioffe discussed the score to *New Babylon* in connection with the "formalism" and "constructivism" of the late twenties.[123] Despite the attempts by Shostakovich and the directors to create a symphonic work full of era-appropriate codes, the film's style was received by many critics as unsuccessful, codifying this film's reception as wholly negative in the decades to come.

Similar offshoots of these debates continued decades after the premiere, and after the film had fallen into obscurity. In the 1980s, conductor Gennady Rozhdestvensky found some score fragments in the Russian State Library in Moscow, and compiled the score into a suite that he released both as an audio recording and as an accompaniment to the film.[124] Since the film existed in multiple versions after its immediate premiere (due to re-editing by cinema theaters because of censorship and theater needs), fitting even the original score would be difficult. Cropping a suite, consisting of partial fragments of the score, proved even more fraught with problems. After Rozhdestvensky, film enthusiasts across the world started making their own compilations of the existing music and film, resulting in varied versions of the film and score recorded together and released publicly. The film, therefore, currently exists in multiple editions, some with Shostakovich's music and many with compilation scores often consisting of pieces by Wolfgang Amadeus Mozart, Fryderyk Chopin, and Camille Saint-Saëns. The "Ur" edition appears to be the Gosfil'mofond cut, which is housed in their archive in Belye Stolby, Russia. Many other European cuts exist: the British Film Institute (BFI) made a copy with a compilation score that is still in circulation in the United States; BACH films in France also circulates a copy with a compilation score; Cinematique Suisse has the German export version, which like the BFI version, has extra shots cut out due to national censorship; Marek Pytel has made a version of *New Babylon* from fragments of the Gosfil'm and the Cinematique Suisse versions, edited with Shostakovich's Suite to *New Babylon*; and most recently in December 2006, Frank Strobel synchronized Manashir Yakubov's 2004 edition of *New Babylon* score (from the *New Collected Works*) with the Gosfil'mofond cut. Of these versions, the Strobel appears to be the most current and authoritative, since it uses the edition of the film that remained in the Soviet Union (not edited for export) and the most complete version of New Babylon score that is currently extant and published.

The multiplicity of these versions demonstrates a nexus of cultural politics around the regard for silent film as a heritage or tradition, and the desire to showcase the first film score of a major composer. The creating and re-creating of this film demonstrate the problems inherent in representing silent films and original scores as sound films, not to mention the negotiation of technological changes. Some of the recreations of the score and film are personally or politically motivated—to either defend modernism of the period or Shostakovich's reputation as an early film composer.[125] In this process, particularly of the past twenty years, mistranslations and misrepresentations of the film have arisen. The mistranslation of a passage in Shostakovich's article about New Babylon, for example, has been freely circulated across Europe and the United States for almost thirty years, until a recent correction. Instead of reading it as "exercise by Hanon," it was read as "galop," leading some critics and enthusiasts across Europe to misinterpret the music in that section of the film.[126] This mistake, and the multiple aforementioned renditions of the film, has bearing on reading codes—re-editing the film and its music greatly affects the rhythm, tempo, symphonism, and of course, content of the score. Although it is not my objective to do an analysis of each version of the films and their scores that are available, suffice to say that such re-editing and reinterpretation has led this film and its score to exist in multiple versions, allowing for endless reinterpretations of the score and its reception over the course of the past eighty to ninety years.[127]

New Babylon was Shostakovich's first film score, and first experience working with the Soviet film industry. It was also a proving ground for new techniques, and an opportunity for him to apply a symphonic, continuous approach while maintaining some of the traditions of silent film practice. Codes surely can be found in the score since his approach emulated some of the silent film practices of borrowing music to evoke characters or ideas. His ability to meld together the codes, match them closely with the content and rhythm of the images, and maintain a continuous symphonic tone was a first for him and for Lenfil'm studio, both of which attempted to create a new tradition of film scoring. This film is a window into silent film practices and the cultural politics of hiring a concert music composer into a heretofore popular medium. Shostakovich's use of codes, therefore, resonated with film practice, as his approach to symphonism resonated with concert music. A contentious film and score with a muddled history, New Babylon represents many firsts for the composer, the directors, and the Sovietization of the film industry.

CHAPTER 3

༚

Alone (1929–1931) and the Beginnings of Sound Film

*A*lone (1929–31, dirs. Grigory Kozintsev and Leonid Trauberg) was Shostakovich's second experience with film scoring, following on the heels of his first, *New Babylon* (1928–29). Both films were attempts at being socialist and propagandistic in terms of plot, and shared a similar modernist approach to technique. *Alone* was a first in ways different from *New Babylon*, however; it was Shostakovich's first quasi-sound film, and first experiment with the balance between sound, composition, and image. The film's uniquely transitory position, being caught between the end of silent film and the advent of sound-on-film, and between modernism and "intelligibility," sets it apart from *New Babylon*. It offered Shostakovich a new challenge in terms of integrating his music with the story and discourse.[1] This same distinctiveness offers a kind of complexity and multiplicity found in the spaces between sound and image. Examining the several layers between the film, its music, its viewers/listeners, and Shostakovich unravels how codes operate within and beyond this film. Coupled with the technological shift between sound and silents, these layers, when peeled apart, show multifarious levels of narrative process.

Codes are a method in which Shostakovich managed to unite a score that was forced to be fragmentary instead of symphonic in approach. Unlike *New Babylon*, a film score that used codes within a larger narrative structure that Shostakovich deemed symphonic, *Alone* has a fragmentary score, written in "numbers," because of the quasi-sound nature of the film. In order to balance spoken word, music, and ambient or sound effects, the score had to be written in designated numbers and inserted when needed. Both the drafts of the scenarios and the musical manuscripts show a consistent movement between setting and resetting the music in various parts of the eventually finished product. Symphonism, in the manner that Shostakovich desired, was simply impossible for this new kind of film.

Unity was achieved, however, through his peculiar approach to codes in this film score. Whole sections or songs were sometimes repeated as numbers themselves, while some recurring motifs occurred within numbers, or between them within reels of the film. On a smaller level, timbres, instrumentation, and borrowed motives/songs unified the score according to the film's characters or subsidiary ideas, adding another layer to the musical narrative, and relating to the various subtexts of the images and the subthemes of the storyline.

The submotivic level, that is, the smaller codes, therefore act as the glue that connects the main themes and subthemes of the film (socialist building, realism, ethnography, the pagan/non-Soviet), pulling together what would otherwise be a visually/aurally fragmented film. Although it seemed an effective structure for a film that would be received as appropriately socialist and entertaining, the reception was mixed. This structuring of the film narrative through code failed to save the film's perceived unity, and reviewers tended to see the film as complex (read: too modernist to be socialist) and ineffective as a believable socialist story. The modernist means to a socialist end was nonetheless felt in the various levels of narrative, musical and cinematic, and represents the transition to sound cinema. This transitory technological state shares certain traits in common with other periods of remediated sound such as the beginning of film, the advent of the music video, and the iPod. How audiences heard then, and how they may hear today are related through the interstitiality of those codes, on smaller and larger narrative levels.

SYNOPSIS

The title, *Odna* or *Alone*, refers to a young woman, played by Yelena Kuz'mina, a recent graduate from the Pedagogical Institute in Leningrad.[2] The first half of the film concentrates on her anticipation of her new life after graduation. The film begins with her rising out of bed, ecstatic and happy, preparing for the day. She later meets her fiancé, with whom she travels around the city, gazing through store windows at china sets and picking out new furniture and other fixtures for their future home. Dressed in white, a color chosen specifically by the directors, these two lovers prance around the city in ecstasy, hanging off trolleys covered in white flowers, and playing instruments and metal pots in department stores, while the main leitmotif of the film, the song "Kakaya khoroshaya budyet zhizn'" (How Good Life Will Be), plays in the background.

The mood, color palette, and the music of the film shift as the young woman leaves her fiancé temporarily to inquire about her teaching assignment. Until this point in the film, she had dreamed of teaching in the center of Leningrad, as shown in a daydream scene where she is instructing attentive students in newly remodeled classrooms. Teaching in the city would allow her to settle into her new married life. She arrives and discovers that she will be sent to teach children in the Altai region in Siberia, far from her dreams. She leaves the building with the intent to complain about her assignment and request a new one in the city. She makes her way to Ministry of Education and is confronted by another woman who expresses admiration of Kuz'mina's assignment in the Altai, wishing that she too could better serve her country. Kuz'mina then telephones her fiancé, who responds indifferently to her dilemma. After her conversation with her fiancé and coming into contact with an "anti-socialist," she decides with some hesitation that she will take the job in the Altai.

The second half of the film opens with a serene landscape shot of the Altai mountain region, reminiscent of Aleksandr Dovzhenko's films.[3] With a fade out, then fade in, we see Kuz'mina arriving in the Altai, lukewarmly greeted by the local people. She states, through intertitles, that she has arrived to teach the children of the village. With her arrival and settling in, the viewer recognizes through sparse statements and the actions of the villagers that there is conflict over the shepherding and trading of the sheep between the people of the village and the *bai*, or the owner of the land.[4] Kuz'mina unknowingly has arrived in the middle of a "class war."

The next section of the film shows Kuz'mina's attempts to teach the children of the village, despite their obligation to learning their daily village duties. With much resistance from the *bai*, Kuz'mina manages to teach the children for a brief time before becoming deeply involved in the villagers' conflict. This change in her character, her decision to teach in Siberia away from home, and her involvement in defending the villagers against the *bai* signals a turning point in the film. She has developed beyond bourgeois urbanite and has become a representative builder of the socialist dream. For her interference and initiation of a riot of the oppressed villagers, the *bai* orders a driver to leave her in the mountains to freeze to death in the wilderness of the Altai as she leaves to seek help for the villagers.[5] The villagers rescue Kuz'mina and take her to the village while sending a message to Leningrad to come and retrieve her. The "airplane from heaven" arrives, to take the nearly dead Kuz'mina home.[6] As the plane leaves, the villagers comment on the fate of Kuz'mina, who is assumed to recover upon returning home.[7]

A NEW KIND OF FILM

Alone was a new breed of film, as was its score, particularly in the context of the Cultural Revolution. By 1931, some of the first sound films were introduced to the public, including *Alone* and Dziga Vertov's *Enthusiasm* (*Symphony of the Donbass*). These sound films premiered in midst of the Cultural Revolution and the first Five-Year Plan (1928–32), when the arts were enmeshed in the shift towards a socialist realist aesthetic that would officially begin by 1934. Film became a contentious art form. Seen as the "most important of all of the arts," it became increasingly apparent that the medium would become a space for the negotiation of state politics and progressive art.[8] Coupled with changes in technology and shifting perceptions of modernism, film became the arena where political battles for the public's affiliation with the state would take place. Music faced similar challenges, and in film it became an important point for debate over the role of arts in politics.

Because of these contemporaneous politics and changes in the arts, film was required to be a constantly changing medium. Early experiments in the 1920s by directors such as Sergey Eisenstein and Lev Kuleshov challenged and later established film as a formidable visual art that had the power to persuade. Later regarded as modernist, the techniques exemplified by such directors came under fire, and a new kind of rhetoric in the form of declarations began to surface in the latter part of the decade. The creation and reception of *New Babylon* was an example of this rhetoric, and was symptomatic of the changing nature of arts and politics. Sovkino, the state organization for cinema, stated that film needed to be "intelligible to the millions"; and music for cinema, including *New Babylon*, needed to follow this guideline as well. The reception for *Alone* was similarly evaluated, as either "intelligible" to the public or too "formalist," that is modernist, to serve the millions.

Through the course of the scenario's development and the eventual move towards hiring Shostakovich for work on the film score, the directors faced a certain tension between their objectives and the studio's push for a properly socialist film. After *New Babylon*, a film about the general heroics of a people set in the historical context of the Parisian Commune, Kozintsev and Trauberg were encouraged by the studio to create a realist film that examined the inner workings of a person's mind.[9] Together with the popularity of the concept of the construction of the individual, to borrow the proletarian language of the time, the directors fashioned a scenario around a heroine.[10] Initially inspired by a newspaper article, this scenario focuses on a politically apathetic individual who transforms into a proper socialist citizen after facing multiple challenges in the Altai region.[11] How this individual grew, and whom she encountered to achieve that development, changed over the course of several versions of the scenario. Several male characters were gradually added throughout the story as prompts for her development.[12] It was clear that the studio wanted an individual who would stand out, as opposed to the individual who represented the masses; her psychology and her process became a central focus of the film's scenario, which appealed to the directors' objectives of avoiding typage.[13] Initial scenarios had Kuz'mina engaged in debates with pagan/non-Soviet characters, with equal amounts of dialogue between them. Over multiple revisions, many new characters were added, the pagan/non-Soviet characters were only represented visually and with little dialogue, and Kuz'mina was made a central character.[14] This choice, to focus on the individual hero(ine) instead of an individual as mass stereotype, presented tension between the modernist inclinations of the directors and the studio's new directives for socialist film.[15] The combination of the two resulted in a film and score that appears somewhat schizophrenic, and retrospectively transitional in a time when the socialist film, its hero(ine), and film music were being redefined.

In the contemporaneous literature about *Alone*, the polemics of the film were entangled in the perceived shift in the directors' film style as much as in the shift in redefining the representation of modernist technique (discourse) in socialist content (story).[16] Their earlier films had been "eccentric" in their definition, an era-appropriate "slap in the face." By the time of *New Babylon*, they had begun to engage historical themes redefining the individual character. Kozintsev in particular was searching for a new approach to avoid the montage editing and character typage found in the work of Eisenstein and Vertov, typage being one approach upon which certain studio heads insisted.[17] Such approaches, which for him had "outlived their usefulness," failed to reveal the inner world of the character and create a realism that he ostensibly sought.[18] As the scenario grew into a more complex story where individual characters were made to be more sophisticated, Kozintsev sought greater realism in the storyline while using familiar modernist techniques. This approach signifies the seeming contradictions of the time, where modernism flourished just enough as early traits of socialist realism were being formulated. Interpreted as a form of "austere realism," the film and, consequently, its score, held greater complexity, where agitational-propaganda, new socialism and realism, and modernist aesthetics coexisted.[19]

ALONE WITH SHOSTAKOVICH

Alone was the first film in Russia to be conceived as a true sound film. Kozintsev specifically requested Shostakovich as the composer to this new sound film, with the intent of continuing his working relationship with him.[20] Early scenarios, dating from the early summer of 1929, showed that the directors intended for music to play a significant and ambitious role in the film.[21] In terms of settling on a composer, the studio agreed to discuss Shostakovich's hiring beginning in July 1929, the time when more complete versions of the scenarios were written; after much debate, they offered the composer a contract by that September.[22] Specific instruments, sounds, and kinds of music were already being discussed by the directors as indicated in scenarios dating from July 1929, coinciding with the beginning of the discussion of Shostakovich's hiring (see Figure 3.1). Sometimes specific music was indicated for a moment in the film (as in the beginning where Kuz'mina prepares for her day to the sounds of a far-away *sharmanka*[23]); at other times, an abstract description of a music would evoke an idea complementary to the image.[24] It was clear that even before Shostakovich was officially hired, the directors regarded sound and music as integral to the film in it earliest conception. They also had specific codes in mind for certain scenes, and appeared to work with the composer on giving the music a strong narrative role in the film.[25]

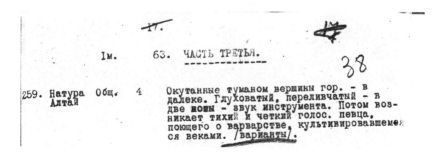

Figure 3.1: Manuscript fragment from initial scenario. The fragment reads: "Mist-shrouded mountain peaks—in the distance. Muffled, iridescent—two notes—the sound of an instrument. Then a quiet and clear voice arises. The singer sings about barbarity which had been cultivated for centuries."
Source: Lefil'm archive, TSGALI SPB, f.257, op.16, d.192.

The directors finally went abroad in September 1929 to shoot the second half of the film in an Oirat village in the Altai region.[26] Their intent was to capture enough footage of the villagers as a scenic background to the ideals put forth in the film. This intent was thwarted several months into the process, when the directors had a change of heart.[27] Meanwhile, Shostakovich was officially hired, and began work on segments of the film. He composed the music for this film in fragments, akin to a number opera. Unlike *New Babylon*, where he favored a symphonic approach, Shostakovich provided numbers atop the segments for each scene, and wrote more than necessary to be arranged at a later time. Some of these sketches/orchestral parts made it into the final film, such as the one that I found in 2008 in the Lenfil'm archive; while others, a few sketches from *Alone* that came from the numerous newly discovered manuscripts found in the Glinka Museum Archive in 2004, contained numbers that did not appear in the final version of film.[28] Given the approach to the score, such segments could be easily excised from the film at a later date. Shostakovich considered this approach anti-symphonic. He wrote in retrospect,

> I always tried to find unified development, so there would not be a tavern scene followed by something completely different. I always tried to seek a unified idea, at which I was not especially successful in the film *Alone*; it had no unified symphonic development; it had individual numbers: No.1—a rushing tram, No.3—a playing barrel-organ, and so on, but I was unable to achieve unified development.[29]

Although he preferred to write in a symphonic approach, one that he deemed more continuous as in the case of his previous film score, he acquiesced to this number approach for *Alone*. Such a method was ultimately necessary considering the multiple challenges the directors faced to overcome the limitations in the promised sound equipment, and inability to properly record voice.

Similar to other film composers of the time, Shostakovich organized his contribution to the score by theme in a leitmotivic manner. The central song, "How Good Life Will Be," operated as Kuz'mina's motif throughout, although other motives took on associative significance in relation to characters, ideas, and places. This was the primary way in which Shostakovich could unify the film, since his desired symphonic method was impossible. In combination with found sounds and ethnographic recordings that were added by the directors, the overall sound design built upon associations, which created various levels of meaning throughout. Codes are part of this associative accumulation, and intertextually operate throughout the film.

There are several modes of narrative in *Alone* that constitute the discourse, or design, of the film. Slower editing than found in the films of modernist colleagues like Eisenstein and Vertov, carefully chosen color schemes (varying shades of blacks and whites), long shots versus quickly edited close ups, and numbered musical segments play integral roles in this design. These segments, or musical numbers, which contain fully composed songs, careful instrumentation/timbre, and/or ethnographic recording, can be read as a nexus of histories, ideologies, and meanings within and external to the film. Within *Alone*, these musical numbers contain several kinds of music that I define as codes, including songs and singular musical aspects. Songs act as clearly defined codes in their structure, containing multiple musical facets that constitute a whole even as they reference other histories and traditions. Singly defined codes, such as a kind of instrumentation, or a motive that is only rhythmic or melodic, can also be intertextual but musically unidimensional. Framing these musical numbers as open codes allows for a more nuanced approach that operates beyond systems as well as within, and avoids defining them as singly defined pieces.

Newly composed or borrowed songs are significant proponents of the film's narrative, particularly the song "How Good Life Will Be."[30] Kozintsev stressed in his writings how this song served a narrative role in depicting the naiveté and expectations of Kuz'mina in the first half of the film.[31] He considered this song to be multivalent and ironic, and to represent the character's unarticulated and trite desires.[32] For Kozintsev, this song also coincided with specific visual effects and cues. In the first appearance of the song, Kozintsev directed the cameraman Andrey Moskvin to shoot the beginning of the film, including the costuming of the young couple, entirely in white. This proved to be a difficult task for contemporaneous cinematographers.[33] This brightness was designed, he wrote, to depict the "nonstop smiling" of young people building their new lives; a carefully crafted ironic commentary on bourgeois lifestyles in a pro-socialist storyline. The harsh brightness of the *mise-en-scene* and lighting paired with the music built this song into a code, one that was generally received as "parodic," and sometimes regarded negatively by critics because of its perceived irony in the context of the character's rebuilding.[34] For him and with Shostakovich's participation, this musical code participates equally, if not leading much of the narrative in these scenes.

The song's first appearance, rooted in the first half of the film, enacts the story of Kuz'mina life before her transformation. In a montage of city scenes, including the couple shopping, riding trolleys (see Figure 3.2), and the ridiculous playing of instruments in department stores, the

Figure 3.2: The couple on the tram with instruments.

structure of the song converges with the editing. The song is repetitive (see Example 3.1), with one line of text repeated throughout.

The song is organized in a block form, and was performed with a professional singer in a *bel canto* style. The rhythm evokes a slow galop, a style and rhythm that Shostakovich consistently used in his music for theater and the concert hall.[35] The overall style and structure of the song resembles his theater music—it is self-contained and uses a full but small predominantly string orchestra with brass acting as punctuation, particularly to match the scenes where horn players appear on screen, hanging off the trams. This similarity to his theater music is unsurprising—a different segment from this score (a "march") was also used in his contemporaneous theater piece, *Hamlet*.[36] Although this song was newly composed by Shostakovich, its approach is familiar and the outcome effective. The combination of musical and cinematic narrative creates a complex, a kind of "syncresis," rendering the intended irony of the scene potent, and strongly building Kuz'mina's character as opposite of the film's projected socialist ideals.[37]

The song's next appearances continue to build on the narrative associations that Kozintsev and Shostakovich rendered in its first appearance, and at pivotal points of Kuz'mina's transformation. When Kuz'mina receives her assignment, for example, "How Good Life Will Be" appears a second time. At first resistant to the new offer, she fights for a position in the city, and wins it. Wandering into the hallway considering her new life, she begins to have a change of heart. An older "anti-Soviet" character appears and commiserates with her, driving her to realize that she wants to go to the Altai. At that point, the song appears in the original key area, accompanied by an overdubbed statement of the song's brief text. The good life implied by the song, with its ironic context, begins to shift with this scene—Kuz'mina realizes what a good socialist life might be, and the first half of the film concludes with her realization. Although there was no change to the music (it was simply cropped to fit the shot), another layer of meaning is folded into the code of this song.

The final appearance of "How Good Life Will Be" finishes the accumulation of meaning in this code. As Kuz'mina stands in the village advisor's home hoping to persuade him to defend the villagers against the *bai*, the song is heard and signals the moment she acts in the interest of the villagers thereby completing her transformation. Still unchanged yet shortened for the scene, the song builds meaning from its context instead of musical revision. This song is the musical equivalent of Kuz'mina, and transforms in response to the contexts of the film. "How Good Life Will Be" may still remain an ironic commentary, as Kozintsev asserted; yet it takes on a sincere twist to depict a good life as a socialist one. The song, therefore, is constructed along with her character transformation: it remains unchanged in musical content, yet flexible enough to accommodate a sincere and an ironic reading.

There were practical reasons for this multivalency and needed flexibility of the musical content. The film had multiple revisions from its original scenarios indicating a tense negotiation between the directors and the studio. Originally, the film had focused on two characters, the shaman and Kuz'mina, and showcased a debate between them over the role of state politics in the Soviet periphery and converting the peoples of those outlying regions to the current socialist system. Over many revisions, new characters were added, but the basic structure remained the same. This initial set of scenarios was written prior to the directors' trip to the Altai region. During and after their trip, the scenario significantly changed. As indicated from a lengthy letter in the Len'film archive, Trauberg wrote that the directors were having a change of heart about their scenario plans.[38] Instead of making a fiction film, he argued for a culturally sensitive documentary film that would reveal the Oirat lifestyle. Trauberg was interested in a film that depicted Oirat culture less as a backdrop for socialist endeavors and was instead an ethnography of a Russian-Siberian-Altai sub-culture. Trauberg's lengthy letter showed a shift in perspective about peoples on the periphery of Soviet Russia and a desire to delve into individuals and their cultural differences as a form of upholding the socialist agenda—viewing them as a mass worthy of justice and attention. According to the studio responses, this idea went over badly.[39] Trauberg's request for a change in film type,

Example 3.1: "How Good Life Will Be," beginning only (tenor with upper strings only).
Transcribed from the film and modified from Yakubov, *Dmitry Shostakovich: Novoye Sobraniye Sochineniy, Tom 123, "Muzïka k kinofil'mu 'Odna',"* [*Dmitry Shostakovich: New Collected Works*, vol. 123, "Music the Film *Alone,* Op.26"] (Moscow: DSCH, 2004), 35, measures 93–100.

from fiction to documentary, was flatly rejected and the remainder of the memo demanded that they come back to Leningrad immediately. The directors returned shortly thereafter, and the scenarios were subsequently revised. The final scenario and film product still contained a varied crop of characters, more specifically "typed," but with occasional and inconsistent attempts at individual character development. The shaman's character was reduced, significantly, to a non-speaking role and appears only twice and only in connection with non-Soviet paganism. The Oirat villagers were used more as a backdrop, with occasional speaking roles. Compared to the earliest scenarios, however, the villagers were significantly more active, were filmed with attention to detail, and were made into heroes at the end of the film along with Kuz'mina. Despite the studio's rejection of their documentary inclinations, the directors still managed to fold in a culturally sensitive and aware depiction of this Oirat village, and to incorporate these depictions to create a fiction film bordering on a documentary film in terms of style. This attempt at a fair depiction resonates well with Kozintsev's later declarations of the realism of this film and the ethnographic quality of his few recordings.

The code of "How Good Life Will Be" is closed at the end of the film, when the text of the song, without its usual accompanying music, is intercut with images of Kuz'mina being loaded on a plane to Moscow. The music is new; and with a full orchestral sound and fanfare common to film of the time, it accompanies a montage of smiling Oirat faces juxtaposed with Kuz'mina and the plane. Even though the song "How Good Life Will Be" is replaced, the concept carries through and finishes the narrative of a good socialist life while leaving Kuz'mina's fate open. Kozintsev considered this ending unsatisfactory and false, but provided no reason why he considered it so.[40] There is no evidence as to why Shostakovich failed to reprise the "How Good Life Will Be" musical code at the end; yet the two aspects, the concept and the song, are at this point inextricably linked. The repetition of the song throughout would have guaranteed that linkage in the audiences' minds. A full orchestal "epic" sound was chosen instead, a qualifier used to identify a code akin to a full orchestra in Hollywood Golden-Era film scoring, one that never surfaced in Shostakovich's film music before, but potentially can cue a Hollywood-style happy ending with which he was familiar.[41]

Other songs operate similarly to "How Good Life Will Be," though with entirely different references. The song "Konchen, konchen tekhnikum . . ." ("Graduated from the institute . . .") is a borrowed musical tune, and has only newly appeared; I found a later version of it in the Lenfil'm studio archives.[42] This song was eventually scored for soprano, clarinet, flute, and light strings, but appears here as an orchestral part (*partitura*) fragment (for oboe) as a single melody (see Example 3.2a). I found this fragment on the *verso* of an English horn part in a loosely organized stack of orchestral parts, ordered by number. Compared to earlier sketches, the published edition, and the soundtrack, these parts appear to be earlier orchestral versions, some of which were used for recording sessions: some are page fragments, while others are more complete numbers; and the stack overall revealed a few different types of handwriting—likely that of copyists, and performers' additions. Many of the numbers do not specifically align with the exact numbers of the final version of the film, yet some of the music contained within them was the same or similar. This particular oboe sketch was noticeably displaced thanks to the difference in musical content from the other pages in its section, and the different pen color and handwriting. Interestingly, the oboe is left out of the final version of this number (the only wind instruments used are clarinet and flute), and neither the wind instruments nor strings have the primary melody. The melody, in both this

Example 3.2a: Shostakovich's sketch of the oboe orchestral part for "Konchen . . ." (first two lines).
Source: Lenfil'm archive, TSAGLI SPB, f. 257, op.16, ed. khr. no.2025, 69 ob.

sketch and the final soundtrack, skips in intervals of a third with a limited range and nursery rhyme sing-song quality, and is Shostakovich's recomposition of the urban ditty, "Chizhik-Pyzhik."[43]

In its final version for voice, clarinet, flute, and strings, the song introduces the viewer to Kuz'mina who rises out of bed bouncing around her apartment and getting ready for the day (See Example 3.2b). This song is generally accepted as a children's tune akin to "Pat-a-Cake" and sometimes referred to as a nursery rhyme.[44] It was also used in Nicolay Rimsky-Korsakov's opera *Golden Cockerel*, when King Dodon is forced to sing a song to Queen Shemakha.[45] Within the context of the opera, the king's choice of the song is interpreted as rebellious; and given its children's culture contexts, it seems absurd.[46] In the 1930s, Shostakovich would have known its connotations as a children's song and from the *Golden Cockerel* and rewrote it with this new text in mind, a text that reiterates Kuz'mina's elated state and preparation for her anticipated new life after graduation. (See Example 3.2b) He may have been motivated to choose this song to create an ironic commentary, since its history as a simplistic and potentially absurd tune correlates to Kozintsev's intention for this scene and for the overall opening of the film. The director described it as the "parodic-naïve" dream life of Kuz'mina and intended this part of the film to be ironic.[47] Because of Shostakovich's contrafactum, and slight rewriting of the music "Konchen . . ." can be read as parodic-naïve when aligned with the frivolity of the scene.[48]

Even without the history of "Chizhik-Pyzhik" as a children's song, its contour, melodic jumps, and sing-song quality group it with other similar song types, and lends this scene a silliness that evokes the character's state of being. Furthermore, Shostakovich appears to have reused "Chizhik-Pyzhik" in "Critics" from *Satires* (1960), a set of songs based on the poems by famed satirist Sasha Chorny.[49] Gerard McBurney also makes a case for hearing a version of the ditty in *Moscow, Cheryomushki* (1959), suggesting it is one of many parodied songs that Shostakovich borrows.[50] This song,

Example 3.2b: Shostakovich's "Konchen . . ." (partial) as it appears in the film.
Transcribed from the film and modified from Yakubov, *Dmitry Shostakovich: New Collected Works*, vol. 123, "Music the Film *Alone*, Op.26" (Moscow: DSCH, 2004), 10, measures 6–11.

therefore, carries a history of multiple ways of hearing: it can be interpreted as ironic in several contexts, and regarded as a multivalent code.

Another borrowed song that acts as a code, in this case referring to socialism and to the Altai locale, appears in Shostakovich's underscoring in the second half of the film. When Kuz'mina realizes that the children are unable to come to school she takes the schooling to children, who are forced to work in the field. During her session, she sits with them and teaches them about the *kulak* resistance during collectivization using Soviet newspapers. To keep from freezing, she then invites the children to dance in a circle, at which moment the music shifts instrumentation (low strings and clarinet to flute) and key/mode (from D-flat minor to F major) into a recognizable reference to a Civil War song known as "Marsh Budyonnogo" (March of Budyonï). This reference is cemented for the viewer/listener when the intertitles appear with the phrase "Konnaya Budyonnogo" (cavalry of Budyonï), which syncronizes with an eighth-note pattering of the tune that more clearly resembles the original song, as well as evoking connotations of the known Civil War hero.[51] The content of this well-placed song creates an apparently effective connection to the idea of socialist building in the Altai, since critic Kliment Korchmaryov, who negatively reviewed the film score overall, considered the song to be an "especially impressive" moment in the score.[52] This song, well-known throughout the twenties and associated with socialism, was still seen as appropriate musical material to cite in a film score, as indicated by

Korchmaryov's review.[53] The appropriation of the music to the "March of Budyonï" acts as a code of a recent Soviet past, and was received as a positive rendering of socialist construction during this moment in the film.

The final song that acts as a code in *Alone* resembles "How Good Life Will Be" in its accrual of meaning through recurrence. The song, titled by film music critic Ieremiya Ioffe as "Russian Lot," repeats three times throughout the second part of the film: firstly introducing images of the Altai, and lastly images of the advisor's wife and child.[54] In its first occurrence, where images of the snowy Altai winter are shown in a long shot, the melody is scored monophonically in piccolo flute, and immediately segues into the overdubbed acapella voice of the tune. This song bears a slight resemblance to Russian village music in its changing meter (triple-duple), melodic contour, and limited range. It was said to be written by Shostakovich, though it does not appear in any of his known manuscripts.[55] The text is sparse but appears to be a kind of lullaby, which is appropriate since the scene shows the wife singing to a baby. Words like "Sudarevo" and "Sidorom" are names of the child and the father, followed by words such as "my little child" ("dityatko").[56] Sudarevo is also a place in Russia; the text could also be referring to the child as a person of that region (see Example 3.3).

With the musical aspects and sparse text, the folk are signified as pre-Soviet and rural along with images of the frozen Altai and meager surroundings. The later appearances of the tune are underscored and are further associated with Kuz'mina and the Altai, solidifying a connection to the land and the folk. Such a potentially pre-Soviet nationalist connection was espoused by Kozintsev as part of their attempt to depict the Oirat and Altai as realistically as possible. In terms of narrative function, this song encapsulates the character of the land and creates a sense of isolation and rural life to which Kuz'mina responds. Such a characterization builds on the dichotomy of rural/urban and pagan/Soviet, which was the crux of the film's thesis. The code of the song and its transformations resonate with the characteristics of an everyday folk song, as opposed to a newly created folk song designed by contemporaneous state composers.[57] Such a musical choice—to compose a song that resembles a folk song instead of copying out a pre-existing tune—resonates with the directors' agenda and initial attempt to create a documentary film.

Specific instruments and their timbres were used as codes of their own throughout the film according to the directors and the composer. From the earliest scenarios, the directors had intended to use specific sounds to illustrate scenes. In a scenario from July 1929, shown in Figure 3.1 above, several cues indicate instruments and voices in relation to the shots.[58] At the

Example 3.3: Excerpt from Shostakovich's "Sudarevo . . ." from the film. Transcribed from the film and modified from Yakubov, *Dmitry Shostakovich: New Collected Works*, vol. 123, "Music the Film *Alone*, Op.26" (Moscow: DSCH, 2004), 105, 6–13.

beginning of the third reel, the cue sheet indicates a shot of the "Nature of the Altai," and against it, two notes on an instrument being played with a voice rising out of it, singing of ancient times.[59] The invention of the musician with his instrument was, therefore, part of an exoticist creation of a nearly mythic Altai. Although the scenario changed dramatically before the completion of the film, this scene correlates with a scene from the final film that opens with the *akïn*, or village bard. This bard is shown singing and playing on his *dombra*, a stringed instrument typically used in the Altai region, to the villagers as they shear the sheep.[60] Shostakovich's response to this indication was unique—instead of indicating a *dombra*, he chose a harp with French horn. The horn begins the scene, undulating in two notes a third apart, where the harp enters shortly thereafter, also moving between two notes, a half-step apart. Although Shostakovich was clearly amenable to scoring for folk instruments as indicated by his manuscripts,[61] it is likely that recording a *dombra* would have been an impossible choice given the restrictions in the recording technology that the directors faced, particularly since the directors were unable to take any recording equipment to the Altai.[62] Instead, Shostakovich's use of harp is a creative choice, since it is the only solo stringed instrument of the orchestra with significant volume that could timbrally match the *dombra* when plucked. The French horn, historically associated with the outdoors and war in countless European examples, is also a fitting choice to pair with the harp. The histories and the sounds of the harp and horn then conflate with the images on-screen. Although potentially jarring—European instruments and their codes combining with a "folk" instrument of the Altai region played by a single bard—the pairing echoes the paradoxes of the film. Attempting realism and a culturally aware approach to this regional group, the creators still had to rely on European histories, in this case audibly heard. The codes—the image of the inaudible *dombra* and singer merged with the audible French horn and harp—create a tension between creator/ethnographer and subject embodied in the film, and reference the story's tension between urban/rural and Soviet/pre-Soviet.

The hurdy-gurdy tune originating from the first half of the film is another code that signifies the urban side of the dialectic formed within the film's story. Kozintsev had expressed that the urban/rural, Soviet/pre-Soviet, and dark/light were the film's primary dichotomies. The first half of the film was designed as sunny and naively optimistic, and the second half as dark and difficult. These dichotomies were intended to be multivalent, however, and the directors sought to complicate these perceived opposites throughout the film. The hurdy-gurdy code participated in this creation of nuance, beginning with the opening scene of the film. As Kuz'mina prepares for her day, and after the appearance of "Konchen, Konchen . . .," she opens her bedroom curtain to see a hurdy-gurdy player (*sharmanka*) on the street. The tune sounds in an off-screen orchestra, a choice that was made because of sound limitations, and acts in this scene as part of the city soundscape.[63] The tune reappears, however, twice more—once at the office where she receives her assignment and lastly in the Altai as she settles in to her new home. At the office, the hurdy-gurdy code appears in a succession of repeated motives, accompanying her statement to the assignment officer that she would rather be in the city to create her new life. The tune appears in the exact same key, yet the instrumentation has changed to an actual "hand-organ" and the player is nowhere on-screen. The choice of hand-organ in place of orchestra— in this case, over images of Kuz'mina's pleading—operates as a signal of her optimism and anticipation that was witnessed in the first scene of the film. This is the "parodic-naïve" about which Kozintsev wrote. Even in the earliest scenarios for the film, it was clear that the *sharmanka* was associated with Kuz'mina's inner thought process and with the city.[64] The sound of hand-organ replaces the image of the hurdy-gurdy player in the beginning of the film, providing enough of the code to cue Kuz'mina's emotional state.

This emotional state is further reinforced in the last appearance of the tune. While Kuz'mina settles in to her new hut (*izba*), a series of recurring motives sound. As she begins to unpack, the same alarm clock from the beginning of the film rings, followed by the hurdy-gurdy tune in a minor mode instead of its original major mode (C major–C minor). On screen, Kuz'mina performs her exercises, referencing a Soviet upbringing, and begins to daydream about teaching her new class as the hurdy-gurdy code sounds in the off-screen orchestra. Here the music is heard in the diegetic space of her mind—a kind of imaginary soundscape—as opposed to source sound in the diegetic space of the film. Although the tune never crosses into the diegesis again, the music carries the symbol. The code signifies the city life that she has carried with her to the Altai; for Kozintsev, he thought it to be a "real-life" symbol—"a reminder of her thoughtless past," and one that was associated with the character from the earliest scenarios.[65] The hurdy-gurdy code, therefore, has multiple layers that accumulate over the course of the story and into the second half of the film. It is a symbol of the city, of an urban mindset, and of Kuz'mina's original naïve intentions that follow her into the Altai. As Kuz'mina transforms according to the narrative design of the story, the hurdy-gurdy code disappears and is replaced by others, such as the "How Good Life Will Be," which signify her new "good" life.

Timbre plays a strong narrative role in the film, where specific sound colors and instruments form their own codes built on a history of tone color. In certain moments, these timbres become recurring motifs. One motif that evocatively uses timbre as narration, which operates as a code in the second half of the film, is the motif of the village chairman.[66] This character is one of the main villains and enemies of the state, and participates in blocking Kuz'mina from fulfilling her duties. The code appears in three places in the film—when the chairman awakes lazily in his hut to hear Kuz'mina advocating for the children of the village; when he, the *kulak*, and the *bai* meet to discuss the purchase of the villager's sheep; and when the chairman speaks to the people about preparing for Kuz'mina's burial.[67] The initial appearance of the code follows the "Russian Lot" lullaby, where Kuz'mina finds the chairman in his home accompanying himself with obnoxious snoring. After being awakened by Kuz'mina, the chairman is accompanied by what Kozintsev calls a "symphonic snore," which enters with a dirge-like motif in the contrabassoons and low brass (see Example 3.4 and Video 3.1).[68] ▶

This example consists of a half-note undulating motive accompanied by glissandi in the low range of the trombones, musically picking up the actor's snore and using it as an ostinato throughout the remainder of the scene, where the chairman denies Kuz'mina any help with her situation Kozintsev described it thusly:

> In the severe winter cold, the teacher ran to the hut of the village advisor. . . The early glow of the samovar, the woman with the lifeless face, the monotone swing of the cradle; on the stove a person sleeps on a sheepskin coat. . . The snoring, at first usual, mundane, was the only sound of the scene; then the snore became louder, started to burst and whistle (we invited a special imitator) and finally, the whole creation of symphony orchestra joins in a hoarse wheeze, turning his loud snore into a kind of prehistoric animal. The teacher begs and pleads, tears appear in her eyes, but slowly and heavily the musical action gathers strength, growing into a symphonic snore.[69]

Example 3.4: The snoring chairman.
Modified from Yakubov, *Dmitry Shostakovich: New Collected Works*, vol. 123, "Music the Film *Alone*, Op.26" (Moscow: DSCH, 2004), 113, measures 4–8.

The following appearances of the chairman's code are musically identical, with one exception: in the second instance, where he meets with the *kulak* and the *bai*, the trombone glissandi are omitted and instrumentation slightly scaled down. The third instance, where the chairman declares to the villagers that they must give up their livelihood, the code returns in full to underscore his speech, and thusly fully codifying his status as an enemy of the state. This meaning of the code was noticed by contemporaneous critics such as Mikhail Cheryomukhin, who believed that the music of the "snoring" scene and its suggestive trombone glissandi effectively captured the "savage, lazy mug" of the character of the village chairman.[70]

This "symphonic snore" finds a parallel in other narrative works by Shostakovich, namely two of his operas. *Nose*, for instance, also uses music to express the physicality of the imagery. The first time the main character, Kovalyov, appears he is sleeping, and his snoring is accompanied by violin and trombone—a similar orchestration and texture to the snoring scene in *Alone*.[71] Another opera, *Lady Macbeth of Mtsensk District*, includes a similar code to express the physical. The trombone glissando played by the orchestra during Sergey's and Katerina's sex/rape scene led an American critic for *The New York Sun* to dub the music "pornophony" in 1935.[72] These trombone glissandi abound in the two operas and the film, and propose something boorish, lazy, or sexual. For Shostakovich, Kozintsev, and contemporaneous listeners, the trombone glissandi have that evocation, acting as a timbral-musical code.

Such an idea was labeled "leittimbre," a commonly used concept in Russian music scholarship and one that Asafyev discussed in regard to his *intonatsii*; it suggests that timbre acts as a strong musical code akin to that of a melodic/harmonic code.[73] Ioffe suggested that Shostakovich's music, including the chairman's code, operates according to leittimbre, that is, using instrumental colors to evoke an association as would a recurring motif.[74] Kozintsev similarly related that Shostakovich was the inventor of the association of certain instrumental colors with characters throughout the film.[75] This trombone glissando thusly resonated with audiences of *Alone* and the two operas, cueing a history of its leittimbral associations.[76] The meanings of this glissando are understood similarly today, yet the specificity of the meaning relies on context, in this case, the moving images. Cheryomukhin contended, as I argue here, that this leittimbre code is active part of the *syuzhet*, or discourse of the film.[77] Like the other codes, this one drives the narrative, signifies the contemptible character of the chairman, and pushes the story to the breaking point of revolution.

Other leittimbres function similarly throughout the film, yet with less melodic continuity. The trombone glissandi and their association with the village chairman, according to Cheryomukhin, were part of a category of low-range instruments that he associated with the Altai and the *bai* throughout the film.[78] Kozintsev had clearly drawn a division between the bright first half of the film and the dark second half of the film in terms of color, shooting, and story. Music served a similar function. Music for the Altai, particularly opening scenes throughout the second half, consists of minor-mode linear layering of solo wind instruments including oboe, bassoon, and flute, which contrasts with the bright tonal homophony of the first half. The first shot of the second half of the film, for example, consists of underscored solo oboe and flute. The music for the *bai*, accompanying the image of him speaking to Kuz'mina and other characters, is similar to the music for the Altai, suggesting a connection between the land and the character. Yet, the Altai music consists of either 1) an accompanied half-step undulating line and solo bassoon or oboe and horn, or 2) a scalar melody that ends in a long trill (see Example 3.5).[79]

The music for the *bai* is usually played by one or two solo woodwinds, accompanied sparsely in either steady eighth notes or a drone scalar in ascent and descent, and has grace note or Scottish snap hiccups, almost "leit-gestures" (see Example 3.6).[80]

Example 3.5: "Music for the Altai" (bassoon and strings only).
Modified from Yakubov, *Dmitry Shostakovich: New Collected Works*, vol. 123, "Music the Film *Alone*, Op.26" (Moscow: DSCH, 2004), 74, measures 1–5.

Example 3.6: One example of the *bai*'s leit-gesture (oboe only).
Modified from Yakubov, *Dmitry Shostakovich: New Collected Works*, vol. 123, "Music the Film *Alone*, Op.26" (Moscow: DSCH, 2004), 101, measures 10–14.

These specific instruments and quasi-motifs appear in three moments throughout the second half of the film: 1) when Kuz'mina introduces herself to the village advisor; 2) when the *bai* enters the classroom to intimidate Kuz'mina and take the children into the field to help shepherd the sheep; and 3) at the end, when they argue over the fate of the sheep and the villagers. For Kozintsev, these codes, less melodic and more timbral, reinforced the power of the *bai* and act as his "old and rattling voice."[81] This "rattling" served as a contrast for Kozintsev's bright part of the dialectic, that is, a sharp contrast to the new good socialist life that Kuz'mina was building for herself and the villagers. Contemporaneous critics referred to the *bai's* linear melodies and instrumentation as "atonal wandering," directly participating in the rhetoric that critiqued contemporaneous modernist endeavors in music and film as formalist and unintelligible.[82]

Although the melodies were different, the instrumentation links the two codes of the *bai* and the Altai. The texture, instrumentation, and "atonal wandering" contribute to the exaggeration and physicality that makes the *bai's* leittimbre/leitmotif seem grotesque, particularly when it is intended as substitute for his unheard voice. The reception of the low-range instruments as signifiers of the Altai and *bai* was similar to the reception of the chairman's code, suggesting a broader link between the Altai, *bai*, and chairman, and thusly suggesting that such instrumentation was grotesque and designed to oppose Kuz'mina and her ideals.[83]

Since the recording technology for the film failed to be sophisticated enough for recording voice and creating synchronized speech, with the exception of one example, the music had to be written to carry more of the narrative.[84] As a result, specific numbers of Shostakovich's score needed to take on near-vocal qualities. Viewers of the film, such as Ioffe, argued that instrumental music can operate as a metaphor for speech and vocal timbre, and described Shostakovich's music as "imitating speech" in an almost onomatopoetic manner.[85] Using the melodic woodwind lines of the *bai* as an example of musical metaphorical speech, Ioffe argued that the *bai's* music imitates the speech intonation and general emotions of the character, and the timbres, accents, and rhythms of the "intonational-vocal image" of the person.[86] In other words, the music acts as a narrative replacement for speech, a kind of musical typage.[87] It allows for coding the *bai's* speech as a code based on timbre and general musical characteristics (hiccups, linearity, etc.) instead of a recurring melody or harmony, and thereby evokes the "rattling voice" that Kozintsev illustrated to depict the *bai* as a kind of state enemy. The music therefore acts as a code and as a bridge between diegetic and non-diegetic space—closing the fantastical gap—and driving the story with this unusual combination of instrumental timbres and grotesque image.[88] The codes, made of timbral associations, are a kind of musicalized speech.

Using the orchestra to create musical speech was an attempt to deal with the limitations of the sound technology, a technology that was initially promised to the directors. Realism was sought, and was displayed in many ways—through the desire for speech, pre-recorded found sounds for effects, and ethnographic recordings. As revealed in Shostakovich's manuscripts, the composer shared a similar perspective. In the portfolio of newly discovered manuscripts, a few previously lost numbers from the film were found, many of which indicated instruments that would have been difficult to record with the contemporaneous sound technology.[89] Among these were numbers that were never used in the final version of the film. These specific numbers were titled or included instrumentation that indicated that Shostakovich was considering folk instruments possibly native to the region of or neighboring regions to the Altai.[90] One early sketch, for example, had the handwritten word "*rozhok*," a kind of pastoral Russian horn, while another was for *balalaika*, both of which were made for specific moments in the film associated with the Altai. The *rozhok* manuscript (Figure 3.3), an early sketch with the indication at the top "4th part, No.3," has the same contour and intervals as the "Sudarevo" song in the final soundtrack to the film; the word "*rozhok*" was written at the bottom of the manuscript and in a different pencil. This sketch indicates three instruments (English horn, timpani, and contrabass), with the melody in the English horn moving primarily in thirds and fifths.

The indication at the top refers to the reel and number of this sketch; it does not appear in the final film, but it does have qualities that connect it to the Altai music of the third and fourth reels. Since Shostakovich was hired when Kozintsev and Trauberg were still extensively revising and re-editing the scenario and indicated a desire for realism in terms of sound in those scenarios, it is fitting to see Shostakovich write "*rozhok*" at the bottom of this manuscript as a potential substitute for or parallel to the orchestral instruments, particularly the reedy English horn. It also resembles Shostakovich's treatment of orchestral instruments that appear in connection with the Altai (oboe, English horn, French horn, bassoon, and other brass) in the final version of the soundtrack. In terms of melodic contour, intervals, and instrumentation this manuscript easily could have been part of this section of the film, especially since it closely resembles the "Sudarevo" song that did appear in the final soundtrack.

Neither the *rozhok* nor *balalaika*, however, had the sheer force of a relatively similar Western orchestral instrument such as the trumpet (or cornet, for which Shostakovich wrote in this score), English horn, or modern strings.[91] Nonetheless, it shows Shostakovich's attempt to accommodate the desire for a folk-nationalistic emphasis—a kind of ethnographic, or folk nationalism (or "realism" to use Kozintsev's word) that the directors sought—very early in his compositional process.[92] It also supports the narrative that relates how Shostakovich and the directors were convinced that nuance could be recorded with the contemporaneous technology, a desire

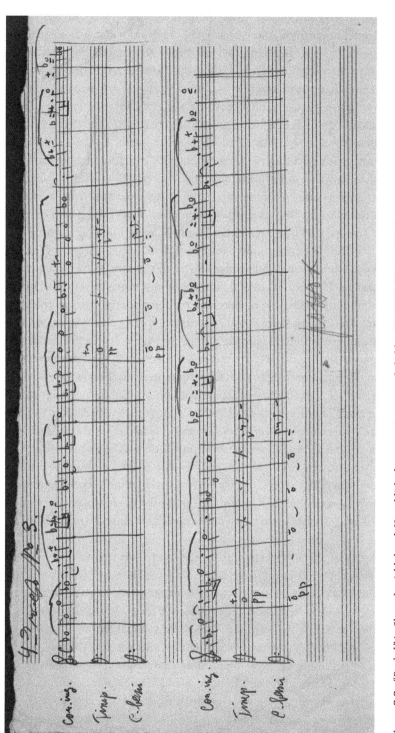

Figure 3.3: "*Rozhok*" in Shostakovich's hand. Unpublished manuscript currently held in VMOMK f.32, No.2290.

that was relatively unfulfilled. Even though some of these sketches were likely rejected because of sound technology restrictions, it was clear that the composer was engaged or at least charged with engaging a kind of ethnographic realism that Kozintsev so intently outlined in his writings about the film and in early scenarios.[93]

Using instrumentation and timbre as a significant part of narrative device was an attempt at realism that resulted in music that acted as symbolic codes. Kozintsev and Shostakovich also sought a kind of realism through integrating ethnographic recording with composed music. Similar to the use of harp and horn for the *dombra* on-screen, the creators, particularly Kozintsev, wanted a way to depict the shaman as "real" and "authentic."[94] In order to do this, Kozintsev shot images of the shaman in the Altai and transported him back to Leningrad to record him performing an actual ritual with the new sound equipment, which they dubbed over the images.[95] This audiovisual code is used twice in the film. It firstly appears after Kuz'mina arrives in the Altai, and gazes at a horse skin draped on a pole, a symbol of protection in shamanism. She then approaches the village chairman. During their initial conversation, they are interrupted by the shaman's music, which is made visible through a cut to the image of the shaman healing a sick woman. After a return cut to the chairman and Kuz'mina, he explains to her that what they hear is the old, pre-Soviet ways. This crossing of the diegetic space with an overdubbed ethnographic recording blurs the line between the two spaces in a way similar to the musicalized speech of the *bai*. The difference, however, is the authenticity of the recording. Kozintsev prided himself on presenting the shaman as real, part of the many "real-life symbols" for which he strove to represent in the film.[96] The second appearance of the shaman's music confirms Kozintsev's assertion. After Kuz'mina speaks with the chairman, she walks to her new *izba*, and starts to think of her city life. Kozintsev related,

> The sound part was difficult enough. The simplest sounds received their own development in the scenario, [where] living sounds grew into real-life symbols.[97] Every morning a barrel-organ played in the courtyard where the young woman lived (as was customary at the time). Shostakovich composed a "galop" (it was recorded onto a reel); the barrel-organ theme then shifted into an orchestral arrangement. The light-hearted city melody went with the young woman, as though accompanying her, to the distant village: a reminder of her thoughtless past. The sound fabric of the episode of the teacher's arrival was complex. The young woman was settling in, unpacking her things; suddenly the alarm clock went off, and then the tune of the distant city barrel-organ was heard. A tambourine's crude strikes and the hoarse cry of the shaman (a genuine recording)

invaded the merry motif. A device for threshing corn pounded and squeaked (a genuine recording), and then as if stitched into the sound fabric, a woodwind phrase arose—the voice of the *bai*, composed by Shostakovich. The voice, rattling and senile, appeared several times in the film, [and] became stronger and grew in power.[98]

After the ringing of the alarm clock and entrance of the hurdy-gurdy tune, the "reminder of her thoughtless past," the shaman's music intrudes on her daydream as indicated by her sudden turn towards the window.[99] The shaman's music here is further defined as an opposite to Kuz'mina and her city life. Instead of interacting with the hurdy-gurdy code to create a harmonious effect, the shaman's music overlaps along with hammering and pounding sounds creating cacophony (see Video 3.2).[100] ▶ This musical layering, or montage, continues over a montage of images of the shaman, villagers working and children playing, and the horse skin. This musical/visual scene embodies the dialectic of the film—of village/city, Soviet/pre-Soviet, pagan/urban, dark/light—and reinforces the directors' desire to create a realistic representation of the villagers. In some ways, it can be read as a fetishizing of the folk Other, a depiction of the folk to the folk, which later became the method for representation of folklore under the doctrine of socialist realism.[101] The shaman's music nonetheless represents the pre-Soviet way of life that the directors had wanted to portray in a documentary fashion while shooting in the Altai. It can also be read as a code that resonates with other forms of ethnographic recording in films of the 1920s such as *Storm over Asia* (Vsevolod Pudovkin, 1928), which also displayed images of everyday life in Central Asia, and were edited to create a fiction film.

This ethnographic recording also resonates with other codes that the directors/composer chose to signify the "real" or "authentic." The music of this recording is from an actual healing ritual, and has similar contour to and traits of music in this region, particularly those of the Altai Mongols and Turks.[102] It consists of overtone singing, together with the chanting of the shaman and hand drum. Overtone singing also appears in another shot of the Altai in the second half of the film, thereby codifying an association with the land and its people.[103] Such music would have been familiar to Soviet urban dwellers of the time, since the Altai was a romanticized region, and many films had been shot there.[104] Although the specific qualities and contexts of the music may have been misunderstood, it would at least be familiar to listeners of the time, and recognized as Oirat or Altai. The shaman's music, therefore, carries a meaning of rural and Eastern, in itself a kind of code that would resonate contemporaneously. It is "real" in the way that Kozintsev intended, though its use in the film was simultaneously symbolic in its montagist presentation and operation within the film's dialectics. This symbolism was apparent to viewers at the time. Critic Korchmaryov expressed, in the midst of a raging debate on formalism and burgeoning socialist realism in cinema and music, that the scene was one of the "defects" of the film because it was symbolic instead of "real."[105] The code of the shaman, intended to be "real" and objectively representative of the Oirat yet used symbolically as a code in the film, therefore resonated with Soviet audiences at the time.

Codes work as a narrative force throughout *Alone*, unifying what would otherwise be a fragmentary score. These codes are variably expressed: as full songs that are newly composed or borrowed from popular culture, or as instrumentation and timbre. Each of these codes interacts as part of the narrative structure, guiding or sometimes leading character and story development. Embedded in these codes were the objectives of the directors and the composer; they constantly revised the film and its score throughout the filmmaking process because of the changing politics at the film studios and their view of peripheral Others. Socialist content with a modernist spin, a desire for documentary-style filmmaking, and a conscious consideration of the role of the Oirat villagers form a fiction film that attempted to relate to contemporaneous politics. Set against burgeoning sound film technology and its complications, this film became the center of debate in many cinema circles, and enjoyed a mixed reception. Today, it entertains as an artifact of early sound film, with its musical codes lost in what is often perceived as poor narrative development.[106] The strength of the score's narration lies in its reliance on musical codes, indexing the world of the film, current politics, and the history of musical style and gesture.

CHAPTER 4

⌒⌒⌒

Golden Mountains (1931)
and the New Soviet Sound Film

Caught between the transitional film *Alone* (1929–31) and the incredibly successful *Counterplan* (1932), *Golden Mountains* (dir. Sergey Yutkevich, 1931) was an example of the mixed politics of sound film on the cusp of a codified socialist realist style in filmmaking. Similar to *Alone*, the sound design and original music borrowed upon aesthetics from the 1920s, while forging a style of sound film that would epitomize the "intelligibility" of socialist realism. Shostakovich used codes that were borrowed and original, and unified them in a symphonic score that was similar in continuity to *New Babylon*, but with consideration for the emerging sound technology. He relied on unique coding choices to depict the film's story, going as far as to include unusual instruments such as the Hawaiian slide guitar. The approach to sound design in this score, shared in part with sound engineer Leo Arnshtam, was unique in its combination of ambient techniques and melodic writing; a song was exploited as the central motif of the film, yet various kinds of sound and music were implemented to attempt some semblance of realism.[1] Similar to questions of aesthetics and technology encountered during the creation of *Alone*, the scoring to *Golden Mountains* revealed an extension of modernist inclinations of the 1920s and an attempt to incorporate newer socialist aesthetics. Although seen as an initial success, it was nearly forgotten after the overly hyped *Counterplan* was released almost a year later.

Overshadowed by the monumental success of *Counterplan*, a film with the first successful song-score by Shostakovich that garnered a mythical reputation over the course of the Soviet era, *Golden Mountains* never achieved a canonical status. Even with its primary song, "Kogda b imel zlatïe gorï" (If I Only Had Golden Mountains) which remained a recognizable urban folk ditty throughout the twentieth century, it still was relatively neglected. One of the reasons that it failed to become a significant film in the Soviet canon was because it attempted a symphonic approach with "formalist" elements, instead of the newly favored song-oriented approach that was about to become endemic to popular Soviet film. With such innovations, the film and its score became an example of burgeoning aesthetics and methods of sound-on-film design, the shifting power of the film industry and its politics, and instability of Soviet aesthetics in the early 1930s.

Along with *Counterplan, Golden Mountains* was produced in a time of politico-aesthetic uncertainty and remarkable change in sound technology. At this time, the Soviet film industry was becoming more concerned with how sound cinema should evolve, especially during the gradual move from partial to full sound films in the early thirties. With criticisms resembling those of Ippolit Sokolov—criticisms that revealed his dislike of partial sound films and their potential formalism—critics were still focusing on the industry's lack of organization and its crisis.[2] In early 1931, the reborn journal *Proletarskoe Kino* (Proletarian Cinema), formerly *Kino i zhizn'* (Cinema and Life),[3] complained of these issues, urging a "socialist reconstruction" and establishment of a "correct political line" that in theory would attempt to get rid of any "bourgeois method" in cinema.[4] Over the course of 1931, an argument over what was proletarian versus Bolshevik became more prominent. This argument seemed to be focused on issues of documentary film and its ability, or lack thereof, to participate in "socialist reconstruction."[5] This fight between what has been described as separate interest groups led in part to the 23 April 1932 reorganization of cultural organizations such as RAPM, RAPP, and ARRK.[6] In the midst of this "reconstruction" and "reorganization," several sound films were released, including *Alone*, Dziga Vertov's *Enthusiasm* (Symphony of the Donbass, 1931), Sergey Yutkevich's film *Golden Mountains* and Fridrikh Ermler's and Arnshtam's *Counterplan*.[7] Needless to say, the arguments over the proper use of sound technology and its relationship to form and content, and the composer's role in the creation of the soundtrack, implicitly and sometimes explicitly still continued in the discussion of the relative successes and failures of these films.[8] The next two fiction films for which Shostakovich wrote music therefore presented a similar set of issues that began with *Alone*—defining realism, naturalism, and the evolving prototype of the socialist realist film.

PRODUCTION

The production of *Golden Mountains* was particularly messy, and resulted in multiple versions that were required to satisfy the needs of both silent and newly emerging sound theaters, which was typical for industries and theaters that were attempting to changeover from silent to sound films. According to Tatiana Egorova, Yutkevich began shooting the film around the time that *Alone* was being shot, in 1931.[9] Archive materials, however, provide a different account. A document from Gosfil'mofond shows that Yutkevich submitted the first version of the film's scenario on 6 March 1930, with the name of the film "Metallozavod," or "Metallurgy Factory."[10] He resubmitted a revision of this scenario a few days later with the title "Shastlivaya Ulitsa" and with some changes to the overall plot.[11] It is possible that Yutkevich began shooting sometime in 1930, after the scenarios were approved, but there is no other evidence at this time to show that he began shooting in that year, or in 1931, therefore casting doubt regarding the shooting schedule of the film.[12] Regardless, a sound version of the film was finished and shown for the first time on 6 November 1931 at the *Khudozhestvennï* (*Art* Theater) in Moscow, the only theater equipped for sound at that time.[13] A silent version of the film was also released in 1931; and a new revision of that version was finished in 1937, to be released in 1939.[14] According to an *montazhnï list* (editing sheet) that I examined at Gosfil'mofond, the original silent version had six parts and was 1757 meters long, presumably shorter than the first sound version of the film. The sound version was also rereleased, presumably with significant changes to the film and soundtrack in 1936.[15] Arnshtam wrote that he removed "over half of the film" and rewrote the scenario, but does not explain the reason for the cut.[16] John Riley claims that the film originally existed in 3583 meters, 131 minutes, and was cut down to 2605 meters, 90 minutes; a cut of over one-third of the film.[17] If Arnshtam's and Riley's claims are correct, then it seems that at least four versions of the film (both sound and silent) exist or had existed. The second sound version of the film released in 1936 (approximately 90 minutes) appears to be what remains available today, and is the version that informs this discussion.[18]

The process of creating the music and recording the sound was typically challenging for the early 1930s. According to Shostakovich, he wrote the scores for *Golden Mountains* and *Counterplan* in 1931.[19] Sof'ya Khentova supported this claim, stating that he wrote the score for *Golden Mountains* in the fall of 1931.[20] This time frame seems likely, since he had finished the score to *Alone* in spring of that year and was busy with several other projects through the summer and fall, including *Declared Dead* and *Lady*

Macbeth of Mtsensk District. In a few months, Shostakovich produced a score for the film and a suite that were performed around the time of the premiere of the film. The score, which is partially extant in manuscripts and in the soundtrack (phonogram) of the film, was written in approximately eight parts, corresponding to the organization of the film in seven parts and a finale.[21] The film score in partial *partitura* (orchestral parts) appears to be an orchestration of the piano score.

Similar to manuscripts of his earlier scores, these manuscripts show details of Shostakovich's process, including his thoughts on orchestration, timing, and character entrances and instrumentation. His piano score especially shows his working out of timings, characters and their relationship to music, and instrumentation. He often notated which event occurred in the score along with a fragment of music, such as "Peter runs," when the character runs from Vasily's house, or "The Death of Vasily," when Vasily is dying. Some of the more interesting notes in the manuscripts concern instrumentation. He spent some time experimenting with different "folk" instruments such as the *balalaika, dombra*, and *bayan,* and with other uncommonly used orchestral instruments such as the harp for earlier parts of the film score, which appear to correspond to the lavatory scene and Peter's epiphany at the end of the film. The harp appears in the orchestral score, while the other "folk" instruments appear or are mentioned earlier in the piano score. Of his scores to date, this was probably his most experimental in terms of instrumentation, featuring other uncommonly employed instruments such as saxophones and Hawaiian guitar that were popular in music-hall works of the time.

In addition to the different and extant versions of the film, the musical sources available today include a published version of the suite to *Golden Mountains* and manuscripts of this suite, and manuscript fragments and sketches from the original score.[22] The suite is the only published music from *Golden Mountains* to date.[23] A manuscript to the suite and partial sketches of the unpublished score are extant, and consist of fragments and a piano score. At least two *partitura*, one of the suite and one of a partial score are also extant.[24]

The sound production of the film was carried out differently from that of *Alone*, although not without its challenges. Yutkevich had stated that the film had to be "shot all at once," because there was no apparatus for rerecording the sound.[25] As a result, the speech, ambient sound, and the orchestra needed to be organized in such a way that everything could be recorded all at once. Yutkevich praised the sound operator Ilya Volk, who was, in his opinion, crucial in balancing the multifarious sounds of the film. He states, "The labor of the sound director I. F. Volk was wonderful. He amazingly 'orchestrated' for cinema the *balalaika* with percussion and French horn, barrel-organ, and orchestra with organ."[26] Although successful, such balance was particularly difficult, since cameras still produced loud sounds that could be picked up by the sound recording equipment. To resolve this issue, Arnshtam also claimed that the camera had to be housed in a box the size of a "small coffin" that was airtight and upholstered with a "thick layer of felt."[27] This box-like construction around the camera also was used in *Alone*, illustrating how directors such as Yutkevich were still coping with sound recording issues in the latter half of 1931.

SYNOPSIS

Similar to *Alone*, the plot for *Golden Mountains* is a product of its time and a prototype for socialist realist films, particularly ones centered on the lone male hero. It focuses on the development/conversion of the apolitical individual towards the socialist cause, the construction of the Soviet state, the class "war," and the abolishment of pre-revolutionary ways. Set in 1914, the film begins with an oil field workers strike in Baku that, as the viewer discovers by the end of the first reel, is running parallel to a similar workers' strike developing in St. Petersburg. The first reel finishes with a shift in locale to show the Bolshevik Vasily imploring Petersburg workers to fight for the freedom of the Baku workers, thusly setting up the following reels, which depict the oppressive life of the factory workers in Petersburg under the son of the factory's owner. The members of the pre-revolutionary bourgeoisie are depicted as villains through alcohol and religion, while the factory workers are portrayed as victims that are eventually pushed to revolt. Amidst these characterizations, the protagonist, Peter, is a rural farmer who becomes a revolutionary after witnessing the oppression of his colleagues. Initially, Peter is unwittingly manipulated by the bourgeoisie through the gift of a pocket watch (which plays a recurring waltz) and alcohol; but after witnessing the Bolshevik Vasily's arrest, Peter is moved to act on behalf of the workers. The film ends with Peter confronting the factory boss and initiating a riot that morphs into an incremental growth of a workers' revolution years later, all of which is depicted in an editing style strongly reminiscent of Eisenstein's and Pudovkin's films from the 1920s. A last shot of Peter marching with the workers reinforces the permanence of his conversion to the appropriate cause, and metaphorically links the Petersburg strikers with the Baku strikers, as reinforced by an intertitle.

THE SCORE

The score to *Golden Mountains* was labeled a symphonic score, yet exhibited some similar traits and extended many of the experiments and music/
image relationships of its immediate predecessor, *Alone*. Unlike *Alone*,
however, where a few bits of "live" speech were sprinkled throughout,
Golden Mountains was regarded as a true "speaking" film with a score that
was symphonic in approach.[28] Arnshtam considered it an enormous task to
fit the speech, sound effects, and what he referred to as "blocks" of music
into the film.[29] As in *Alone*, *Golden Mountains* was a score with musical
"numbers" composed to correspond to the numbers of a scene or its parts,
the "blocks" to which Arnshtam referred.[30] In contrast to *Alone*, the pauses
between numbers work well within the film, since these pauses give way
to speech or other sounds around which the composer had to negotiate;
the blocks of music in the score were, therefore, part of the natural state
of the soundtrack. Shostakovich never complained of *Golden Mountains* as
being block-like or lacking in continuity. His scoring instead contradicts
this claim. Shostakovich worked closely with Yutkevich and the sound
team (including Arnshtam) to create an integrated score.[31] The composer
used recurring musical ideas and sectional development, and incorporated
his musical score into the overall sound design, including various sound
effects and synchronous speech while necessarily considering the changing relationship between sound and image—an approach that he would
continue to use for his scoring in the 1930s.

To further elaborate on the meaning of his definition, Arnshtam simultaneously claimed that the score was "symphonic" in its use of closed
forms, a seeming contradiction to his assertion of a fragmentary "block"
score. He wrote,

> What streams of great symphonism music can bring to cinema! . . . in "Golden
> Mountains" we used great symphonic forms, where many parts of the film could
> become parts of the symphony; in the film there is no music for filling any sort
> of emptiness.[32]

Arnshtam considered the score "symphonic" in two ways: 1) in the sense
that Shostakovich imported symphonic forms such as the fugue, or used
unifying characteristics or ideas in the music, such as leitmotifs; and 2) in
the sense that the film and its form resemble the structure of a symphony.
In the former sense, Arnshtam used the term "symphonic" to indicate
genres, techniques, or styles that borrow from the classical tradition; in
this specific film, those include fugues, motifs, and general underscoring.

The latter sense, the film-as-symphony, resonates with similar assertions by other directors that films have comparable developmental potential to a musical symphony.[33] Years later and in comparison with *Counterplan*, Arnshtam considered this score symphonic in regard to its continuity and unity, that is, the manner in which Shostakovich wove his music into the overall narrative of the film.[34] The term "symphonic," therefore, takes on varying shades in Arnshtam's definitions and Shostakovich's approach, indicating both a borrowing of specific forms and codes from the concert music tradition, and a sense of musical continuity and unity.

Many of the discussions about the score to *Golden Mountains* focused on its unity or its division into "blocks." Following contemporaneous discussions of *Golden Mountains*, Egorova argues that Shostakovich had to cope with fragmentation resulting from the variety of sound sources in the film (speech, effects, and diegetic music), and was forced to create a film score that used unifying devices such as leitmotifs so that the film would appear continuous and "symphonic."[35] Egorova's claim of *Golden Mountains* as "symphonic," however, implies that this was not a consideration in his earlier films; Shostakovich had already used unifying techniques (e.g., codes) in earlier scores, such as *New Babylon* and *Alone*, and was already quite adept at creating a symphonic and continuous score. The use of the word "leitmotif" in this context also has possible connections to an increasing interest in Hollywood scoring in the Soviet Union more than to Shostakovich's desire to fill a void. *Golden Mountains* is, in some ways, a "musical" film like *Alone*. Yet the greater presence of speech, or rather the ability to actually better record speech, allowed for an opportunity for the kind of narrative symphonism that Arnshtam envisioned, as much as for the possibility of fragmentation and newer ways of approaching musical continuity.

The in-between space that *Golden Mountains* occupied in terms of silent/sound or music/speech, and the film's sound-on-film credentials were heavily debated throughout its production. Similar to *Alone*, the film was a pivot point for the ongoing discussion of the future of sound cinema. This crisis of sound film in the Soviet Union was a serious background for a meeting with Lenark'a at ARRK, where Yutkevich and Arnshtam defended *Golden Mountains* and its presumed modernist failings, including lengthy descriptions of their views on sound film.[36] In their discussion and defenses of their approach to sound, each talked about how they were seeking to integrate speech and sound, including music, and to maintain a solid sound design plan as a significant part of the film's scenario. The tone of Yutkevich's specific presentation, and of Arnshtam's defensive response to the criticisms lodged at Yutkevich during the meeting, indicated disagreements about how music and speech should appear in the new Soviet sound film.

Yutkevich envisioned a balanced work—much in the way that Arnshtam described in his writings, and the way that Shostakovich wrote his music as part of the whole—that gave equal importance to music, speech, and sound. Still deeply rooted in earlier modernist experiments with image and sound (citing Shklovsky, et al., Eisenstein, and the "Statement on Sound"), Yutkevich indicated a strong support for music in film as something more than "illustration." In fact, Yutkevich stated directly that he wanted to use musical genres and forms from "musical culture" to work in tandem with the sound design, and with the images. Instead of avoiding the fugue, for example, Yutkevich encouraged the use of such forms (and even instruments), and went to list instruments such as the organ, and forms such as the waltz, galop, polka, march, and so forth. Such a form as the fugue could find a place between the images, as part of editing and speech. It posed a challenge for them, particularly in creating "cinematographic montage" that gave attention to all components.[37] Regardless of the perceived success of this attempt to merge speech, sound, and music, it was clear that Yutkevich was attempting to put music on par with speech in the burgeoning Soviet sound film, allocating it an important and integral role in the changing field of sound cinema. Yutkevich, like the other directors with which Shostakovich had worked, valued the role of the music and the composer in the new Soviet sound film.

Notably, *Golden Mountains* was the first of Shostakovich's film scores that was interpreted as having a "leitmotivic system" by scholars and critics.[38] Arnshtam, many contemporaneous authors such as Ieremiya Ioffe and Mikhail Cheryomukhin, and later scholars such as Egorova and Khentova all use the term "leitmotif" in connection with this film, yet disagree in their classification of the film as more "symphonic" than his previous scores.[39] This desire to label the score was likely a result of the shifting perceptions of realism in film and in film music. Although these critics and scholars misunderstood the term "leitmotivic" in the strictest sense, this description implies that they regarded Shostakovich's earlier "formalist" films, such as *New Babylon*, as lacking a certain unity and "symphonic" organization. Such a shift in perception correlates with the current politics, and explains why the film was later received as a "formalist" mistake regardless of its immediate positive reception in 1931. Musical structure and use of codes were, therefore, issues at the forefront of the reception of this score.

Shostakovich used recurring musical ideas and segments, and localized development within episodes to integrate his music with speech, ambient sound, and action. Often described as leitmotifs, two of the central codes of the film operated in tandem with Peter's growth into a revolutionary.[40] The

Example 4.1: Horn melody of "If I Only Had Golden Mountains," as played in E-flat major in the overture to the film, sounding over the introductory credits. Author's transcription.

Example 4.2: A reduced version of the waltz tune that appears in the gift of the watch scene. The main theme is played by Hawaiian guitar (orchestral accompaniment excluded).

first is an urban song, "If I Only Had Golden Mountains" (Example 4.1), and the second is a waltz by Emile Waldteufel titled "Les Violettes" (Example 4.2).[41]

The waltz has greater prominence throughout the film and is used at various points of Peter's gradual conversion. Being a waltz, a genre that Shostakovich had previously used to illustrate bourgeois tendencies (e.g., in *New Babylon*), and authored by a composer known for his waltzes in Russia, this kind of borrowing was deeply seated in aural images of a nineteenth-century Russian past.[42] The "Golden Mountains" song, however, is limited to the first part of the film, often adopting the meaning that the urban drinking song (*zastolnaya pesna*) implies—the wish for "golden mountains," or more simply, a better quality of life. Both of these codes come to represent either side of the class war in the film. The waltz is associated with the negatively portrayed bourgeoisie, while the "Golden Mountains" song is associated with the workers. Each code exemplifies or underscores cinematic/musical techniques that are used to represent characters, and act as a commentary on the overall message of the film.

The waltz appears eight times throughout the film, four times as a fragment, serving as a continuous thread throughout the film that emphasizes the power of the bourgeoisie and Peter's eventual conversion to revolutionary (see Figure 4.1). Two of the appearances serve as significant turning points in the plot, while the others punctuate the action of the specific scenes, often diegetically.

Musical Idea	Type	Position of appearance (if recurring)	Event/Association
Golden Mountains song	Leitmotif, underscoring	First	Opening credits
Music – A (galop 1, with percussion solo)	Recurring, underscoring	First	Opening scene of Baku workers
Golden Mountains song	Leitmotif, diegetic	Second	Accordion player and girl
Bortyansky concerto fragment	Non-recurring, diegetic	NA	Diegetic choir sings concerto
Waltz	Leitmotif, underscoring	First	Religious scene/factory gala
Theme – B (string duo)	Recurring, underscoring	First	Opening of lavatory scene
Music – C (Chastushka)	Non-recurring, underscoring	NA	Lavatory scene
Golden Mountains song	Leitmotif, diegetic	Third	Lavatory scene
Theme – B (string duo)	Recurring, underscoring	(First)	Lavatory scene
Waltz	Leitmotif, underscoring	Second	End of lavatory scene
Waltz	Leitmotif, diegetic	Third	Son/engineer at the piano
Music – D (ABA′ music)	Recurring, underscoring	First	Transition between son at piano to factory
Waltz	Leitmotif, diegetic then underscoring	Fourth	Peter receives the watch; shows it to workers
Music – D (BA′ music)	Recurring, underscoring	Second	The workers disperse
Golden Mountains song	Leitmotif, underscoring – diegetic – underscoring	Fourth	Camera tracks into *traktir*; Peter sings the tune; return to underscoring (during dream)

Figure 4.1: Table of musical appearances in the *Golden Mountains*.

Musical Idea	Type	Position of appearance (if recurring)	Event/Association
Music – E (song in *traktir*)	Non-recurring, diegetic	NA	After Peters awakes, in *traktir*
Music – F (galop 2)	Non-recurring, underscoring	NA	Peter in hallway, interrupts meeting of workers
Music – A (galop 1)	Recurring, underscoring	Second	Meeting of the workers
Music – G	Recurring, underscoring	First	Opening of scene and Vasily's attack
Waltz	Leitmotif, underscoring	Fifth	Vasily's legs go limp, cut to master in *traktir*
Music – G	Recurring, underscoring	Second	Robbing of the unconscious Vasily
Waltz	Leitmotif, diegetic, underscoring	Sixth	Whistled by man entering home; sung by Peter; then moves into underscoring; then sounds from watch again
Waltz	Leitmotif, underscoring	Seventh	Police take Vasily away
Music – H (galop 3)	Non-recurring, underscoring	NA	Peter runs out of Vasily's home and to the home of the "boss"
Waltz	Leitmotif, underscoring	Eighth	Meeting the "boss"
Theme – B (string duo)	Recurring, underscoring	Second	Peter wandering
Music – I	Non-recurring, underscoring	NA	Peter begins riot and strike
Music – J (finale)	Non-recurring, underscoring	NA	Finale of film; images of workers gathering, marching; Peter marching with them

Figure 4.1: (Continued)

The waltz as a code represents the bourgeoisie, and is symbolic of oppression, which is presented in its first appearance. It opens the scene of the celebration at the factory, appearing as non-diegetic underscoring after the son of the factory boss, the engineer, leads a toast. The waltz is edited to repeat several times, coinciding with the hoorays of the factory workers. A subtle shift in the waltz's context takes place: the first appearance of the waltz initially complements the control of the owners over the workers, but takes on another meaning when the son-engineer leaves the factory. As he confronts the job seekers outside of the factory, among them Peter, the waltz continues to sound, acting as a sound bridge, as do the diegetic hoorays from inside the factory walls. The context of the celebration and affirmation of the power of the owners, accompanied by a full orchestra with brass instruments as the primary soloists, creates a counterpoint against the poverty of the begging peasants. This was noted at an internal Lenark'a meeting, where one of the participants, in some defense of appropriately used nineteenth-century music, claimed that this scene was "harmless comedy," and cited this "favorite waltz" as descriptive of the event and an effective musical representation of the bourgeois characters.[43] The use of the waltz in this counterpoint underscores the main message of the film, effectively introduces the waltz as a code that vilifies the owners while creating sympathy for the workers, and ultimately supports Yutkevich's argument that genres and forms from "musical culture" can be used in film scoring.

The code of the waltz builds as a symbol of bourgeois power throughout its next appearances. In the lavatory scene, when the master, the sidekick to the son-engineer, finds the workers congregating and discussing their situation, a brief repetition of an almost unrecognizable fragment of the tune appears in the underscoring to signal his entry. At this point, this non-diegetic fragment cues the implied presence of the bosses, and musically invades the space of the workers. Yet the full presence of the tune is only realized in the code's next appearance, this time in the diegesis. For the first time in the film, the waltz is materialized through the son-engineer, who plays the tune on the piano at the beginning of the fourth part, while he is concocting his "little idea"—an idea to manipulate Peter and control the other workers. Playing the waltz through and temporarily stopping to speak with the master, the son-engineer manages to complete a full statement of the waltz by the end of the scene, claiming the code as his own, and connecting it with its previous incarnations in the underscoring. Its diegetic performance signals that the son-engineer is consciously wielding this tune as his particular weapon. From this "little idea" forward, the waltz continues to be strongly associated with the son and his power over the workers.

The watch scene contains the central and perhaps most memorable use of the waltz-as-code. As the son-engineer gives the watch to Peter, the waltz appears in underscoring, with Hawaiian guitar playing the melody with the accompaniment of a string orchestra (see Example 4.2).[44] This music continues over images of the son, Peter, and the onlooking workers. The waltz stops in the underscoring, giving way to speech between Peter and the workers. As they talk about the watch and Peters opens it, the waltz (and its variations) in a music-box timbre is heard, sounding diegetically from the screen (see Example 4.2).[45] The watch and the waltz hereafter are a visual and aural object of the bourgeoisie's control over Peter.

The last appearances of the waltz reveal a shift in mood, to correlate with Peter's slow conversion to the revolutionary cause while evoking the potential destruction of the strike. Its fifth appearance is associated with Vasily, in a scene where he is attacked in an alleyway. Vasily is grabbed by one man, and hit on the head with a rock by Peter, all of which is shown in moderately quickly edited shots (although never showing the face of the victim) in Eisensteinian fashion. Never revealing his face, the only indicator of Vasily's consciousness is revealed in a shot of his legs. The waltz enters in underscoring only after his legs go limp, followed by an immediate cut to the master at the tavern. Appearing at the end this montage, the waltz, therefore, cues the momentary victory of the bourgeois owners over Vasily's revolutionary plans. The reappearance of the waltz continues to symbolize control over the workers, more specifically appearing in tandem with images of the elimination of the strike leader.

The exact fragment of the waltz that first appeared in the lavatory scene is restated when Peter sings it to a baby in Vasily's home, marking the code's sixth appearance in the film. It is also one of several instances where the music exists in the "fantastical gap" between diegesis and non-diegesis.[46] Peter begins singing a version of the fragment that appeared only in underscoring in the lavatory scene; Peter, therefore, should be unfamiliar with this specific musical idea, regardless of its derivation from the waltz. The character thus has insider knowledge of a fragment that has only been used in off-screen underscoring. This technique is familiar to Shostakovich: much like the snoring scene in *Alone*, a character initiates a sound, or in Kozintsev's words, "leads the image," that is taken up by the orchestra in the underscoring.[47] It that moment, Peter rereads the inscription on the watch aloud ("For diligence, from the boss"), and begins to realize the true intent of the gift. Disrupting his thought and the song, the police enter and take Vasily away; just as the master enters, the waltz appears a seventh time in non-diegetic underscoring—an aural parallel to and continuity of Vasily's attack scene.

The turning point and the final moment of Peter's conversion mark the final appearance of the waltz. After running out of Vasily's home after his arrest and to the mansion of the unseen "boss," Peter finally meets the owner of the factory and confronts him, speechless, with the waltz accompanying him in underscoring. Upon realizing that this boss is the same man who owned the factory for which he previously worked, Peter tries to attack him, only to be hauled away. During this moment the waltz appears in full volume and with a different character and instrumentation from its previous statements to exemplify both Peter's rage and his complete transformation. Instead of the original triple meter version of the waltz (see Example 4.2), the first few measures of the waltz tune are deconstructed in a Beethovenian manner—the tune is fragmented and played by the brass in strident triplets in duple meter, and then further fragmented and repeated while punctuated by a series of chords in the rest of the orchestra. Shostakovich's orchestral restate- ment of the waltz led Arnshtam to describe its use as "symphonic"; a form he considered typical for Shostakovich and representative of how the composer used "major symphonic forms" in the film.[48] In this sense, the tune becomes organically reconstructed to create an epic climax. Such a climax, with full orchestra and brass, finalizes the transforma- tion of the waltz from initial fragment and diegetic song to full orches- tral statement, acting in parallel to Peter's eventual revolutionary turn. The code of this Waldteufel waltz was constructed by Shostakovich and Yutkevich to therefore deepen and shift along with the authorial stance of the film—the bourgeois owners as villains and the workers as neces- sary revolutionaries. Yutkevich's idea of using "musical culture," a waltz in this case, is clearly exemplified in the transformative use of the code throughout the film.

The application of the song "If I Only Had Golden Mountains" is far more limited than that of the waltz, appearing only four times in the film (see Figure 4.1) and often in the foreground of the diegesis or as part of a more complex underscored scene. The song solidifies its central role in its first appearance, sounding over the credits (see Example 4.1). Similar to an overture in Golden-Era Hollywood cinema, it serves as an introduction and ties into the title of the film. In this overture, the tune appears in E-flat major in the horns, with full orchestral accompaniment, and it has an ABB+ coda form that is played twice over the credits. Although the song was a generally recognizable folk tune, the coda part of this form was newly written by Shostakovich; the ABB section is the same musical form as the original well-known song, on which Shostakovich based his version.[49] Shostakovich's first phrase (A) is a variation of the known song, while the second phrase (B) is nearly identical to most versions. Hence, Shostakovich recomposed a song/code that is similar enough to the original version to be recognized by its audience.

The opening scene of the film marks the next appearance of the song, as part of the diegesis, and is played by the accordion player. This musician, played by actor Boris Tenin, plays through several verses while flirting with the woman beside him and introducing a melodic variation of the tune. Because this song is traditionally known as an urban drinking song and has been transmitted orally, it exists in several variants; the general structure and contour of the song, therefore, is the main referent. These variants differ mostly in the first half of the musical phrase. In these initial appearances, the song operates as an introduction to the idea of the film, and establishes an association with and empathy for the workers. Using a popular culture reference such as this well-known *zastolnaya pesna* was a way that Shostakovich used music to draw the listener/viewer into the film and identify with the characters.

The lavatory scene contains the next appearance of the tune and several other recurring musical ideas as part of a scene complex (see Figure 4.1, Theme B). The scene begins with a theme for string duo (Theme B), which underscores the speech of one worker describing the illness and eventual death of his wife to the other workers. Reminiscent of the Altai theme from *Alone* in its texture, instrumentation, and slow rhythmic ostinato, this theme uses two string instruments, a *balalaika* and *dombra* (or mandolin and harp).[50] One instrument repeats an ostinato consisting of two pitches to accompany (a half-step apart), while the other plays an undulating tremolo melody. Theme B evokes a sense of desolation in its instrumentation and sparse ostinati, just as *Alone's* Altai theme represents the loneliness of the wilderness, accompanying the complaints of the workers. The instrumentation also evokes instruments that are associated with the working class, just as the piano was associated with the bourgeois factory owners earlier in the film. The return of this code at the end of the film, over the images of Peter running from the owner's house to the factory to initiate the strike, confirms its association with the workers. Theme B's placement in each scene suggests as association with the anticipation of and eventual workers' strike.

After the workers' complaints are heard, one worker begins to play "If I Only Had Golden Mountains" on harmonica. Instead of an exact sound match with a harmonica, however, the listener hears a *bayan*, playing the tune much in the same way as the accordion player in the opening scene of the film. In the context of the complaining worker, a dream of "golden mountains" implied by the song seems absurd in comparison to his dream for basic health care, but does reveal both an attempt to brighten the situation and comment on the sheer poverty and poor conditions of the workers. It can also be read as revolutionary in place of the typical meaning of a drinking song —the workers wish to have "golden mountains," which in this case, means better benefits and working conditions—the same requirements demanded by the workers in Baku, a episode that opened the film, and returns at the end. Simultaneously the codes of the "Golden Mountains" and Theme B act as cues, and in counterpoint to the images on screen, while unifying the film through repetition and associative meaning. Shostakovich, therefore, continued to employ his ideas of creating music that acts as a counterpoint to the action, while also providing a multivalent commentary that suits the anti-bourgeois message of the film.

The final appearance of the "Golden Mountains" tune, only midway through the film, occurs during the tavern scene with Peter and the master, and constitutes the most complex display of the song. The code is intricately woven into the fabric of the scene, appearing several times throughout: first in underscoring and then in the diegetic space. As the camera tracking leads the viewer into the space of the tavern to the table where Peter and the master sit, "If I Only Had Golden Mountains" is heard in the underscoring. The melodic shape, key (E-flat major), and instrumentation (upper winds and horns) of the tune in underscoring are exactly the same as the initial version of the tune that appeared in the overture over the opening credits. It ends, just before the master speaks. He requests that music be played and instantly the "Golden Mountains" song is played in the tavern, becoming diegetic, yet is still the same underscoring of the tune in the key of E-flat major with no visible diegetic orchestra. After some conversation, Peter drunkenly sings along with it, singing the last stanza of the known version of the song, that is, the AB part of the form, corresponding to the lyrics of "Za laski, rechi ognevye/Ya nagrazhu tebya konyem. Uzdechka, khystik zolotye/Sedel'tse shito zhenchugom" [For kindness, fiery speech/ I shall reward you with a horse. A bridle, a golden whip/A saddle embroidered with pearls], which clearly refers to wealth and the decoration of objects used in horse riding, as it does to dreams of gold.[51] This confirms its context as a true *zastolnaya pesna*. Just as Peter eventually passes out, the "Golden Mountains" song segues with a variation of the tune in organ, a choice Yutkevich undoubtedly preferred, again presumably heard in the diegesis of the tavern. It then slips into underscoring and follows him into his dream of his glorious horse, becoming a variation of the tune in orchestral accompaniment to his dreams of "golden mountains." (See Video 4.1.) ⊙ The shift from his singing to sleeping is cued in the music, where his singing along with the simplified wind instrumentation of the tavern music expands into a full orchestral statement that, towards the end of his dream, becomes dissonant and out of tune. The sourness of the music near the end of his dream also cues the viewer/listener to expect a shift in the action; in this case, Peter's waking from the dream. When Peter awakes, the "Golden Mountains" song ends in the orchestra and the music of the diegetic space has shifted to different music in the space of the tavern, a *tsyganshchina*-styled song for female voice and guitar.

This final appearance of the "Golden Mountains" song operates as a code that cues Peter's state of mind as it seamlessly moves between diegetic and non-diegetic space to immediately accompany his desires and foreshadow his future character development. The song represents Peter's wishes for "golden mountains," contrary to the desires of the workers: that is, wealth and recognition, resulting from his work in the factory. The meaning of the song within the entire film thus becomes clear at that moment—it exemplifies the dreams and aspirations of the character that are used by the owners of the factory to keep Peter in a state of ignorance and intoxicated by his own desires. Yet, the shifts in the music (instrumentation, diegetic/non-diegetic) that accompany his movement between his conscious and unconscious states follow his dreams of "golden mountains," and can be read as the souring of those dreams and as a potential foreshadowing of his eventual transformation.

This interweaving of speech, image, and song with underscoring, and movement between diegetic and non-diegetic spaces was particularly sophisticated in 1931, and a significant feat for Shostakovich and Yutkevich. Not only did Shostakovich demonstrate his ability to continue to apply and adapt his own theories of film music to sound film as he had in his two previous silent and quasi-sound film scores to *New Babylon* and *Alone*, he also managed to cue and exemplify the hero's present behavior and foreshadow his later transformation through subtle permutations and recompositions of known musical works. The celebrated "Golden Mountains" "folk" song, particularly as a contradiction to the bourgeois-signified Waldteufel waltz, therefore, has the potential to cue listener/viewer identification and assimilation, in Anahid Kassabian's sense of the term.[52] In other words, a worker would be encouraged to identify with the characters and their desire for a socialist future—a demonstration of how music toes the line of the studio's directives. As with *Alone*, Shostakovich's use of such an urban song taps into the cultural politics of the time: the burgeoning definitions and application of a socialist realist aesthetic and the inevitable exploitation of the "folk" in music as an aspect of socialist consciousness.[53]

As with *New Babylon*, galop rhythms and the musical sections created from them act as codes and pervade the score, often in tandem with scenes with action or anxiety. The central galop that dominates the score is from the opening scene with the Baku workers (see Figure 4.1, Music A). The galop is sounded over the images of oppressed workers, who eventually revolt; this was described by Ioffe as "full of anxiety and alarm."[54] Shostakovich begins with a technique that he used in *New Babylon*, one that Michel Chion refers to as "acousmatism."[55] Acousmatic music, when the viewer/listener hears a sound before seeing its origination or inspiration on the screen, is heard in the opening of the film, where a galop (Music A) sounds before the images of the horses and the Baku workers appear.[56] This is similar to *New Babylon*, where the galloping music of the German cavalry is heard before it is seen, alerting the viewer/listener, and initiating the associative meaning of the scene. In *Golden Mountains*, after the galloping horses are seen (thus "de-acousmatizing" the galop) and the images cut between the horses and the workers, the music is then associated with the struggle of the Baku workers.

After the acousmatic entrance, the galop continues, and moves in counterpoint with the images and their meanings at specific moments; this was the first instance of music/image counterpoint in the film, when the Baku workers are shown laboring with great difficulty (see Figure 4.1, Music A). Yutkevich credited Shostakovich with this contrapuntal innovation. He related,

> We were immediately convinced that he [Shostakovich] wrote in musical forms, consisting of counterpoint with the visual series. . . . Let's refer to the film *Golden Mountains*. [For] the galop [there] was shot of horses; then, when the workers haul the pipe, the representation went slowly—the [film's] theme was unusually heavy labor, but the music sounded energetic: the effect was staggering.

The galop-styled music then shifts to a solo percussive section over images of the Baku workers, who are moving a large and heavy pipe. (See Video 4.2.) ⊙ As one of these workers falls to the ground, the music comes to a halt with a cymbal crash. The shots that flash in quick editing emulate the last fuzzy images that the worker sees before falling unconscious, punctuated by bass drum and woodblock hits. This aural and visual kinetic technique momentarily evokes the character's point-of-view, while the rhythm, timing, and timbral shifts of the music correspond directly the rhythm of the rapid cuts, musically evoking the physicality of a fainting spell. This close mickey-mousing predates the "White Nights" scene in *Counterplan*, where Shostakovich closely imitates the screen action.[57] This example of the galop narrates a different meaning than the aforementioned scene from his next score would: this galop is interwoven into a musical section that viscerally reinforces the message that the workers are overworked—a staggering effect, as Yutkevich wrote—thus setting up the impetus for the strike and the class war of the film. This galop code is closed at the end of the film, when it reappears over crosscut images between Vasily speaking to the Petersburg workers and images of the Baku workers beginning to strike.[58] This galop, therefore, kinetically narrates the images of strike, and represents the impending and metaphorical union of the Baku and Petersburg workers at the end of the film.

Another galop appears in connection with eventual conversion to the cause, one that Yutkevich considered an important moment of music/image counterpoint. During a fade, Shostakovich wrote a second galop to acousmatically cue the beginning of the scene following the tavern dream sequence (see Figure 4.1, Music F). This cue continues over images of Peter and the master entering the hallway, and the moment where Peter interrupts the meeting of the strikers. This galop was borrowed from the first half of the "Transition to the Kitchen" from an earlier theater piece, *Declared Dead* (1931), another instance where Shostakovich borrowed from his contemporaneous theater works.[59] Similar to the opening Baku scene, the music cues the scene before it is visible, in this case alluding to the worker's strike. Yutkevich described this scene as a kind of counterpoint that echoes the principles set out by the "Statement on Sound." He wrote,

> It did not have illustration . . . This galop was used on the slowest part of the film when its hero the peasant Peter in painful meditation descends down the staircase: in this time the rapid repeat of the galop conveys the internal creation of the hero . . . S. Eisenstein, who, being in the U.S., presented *Golden Mountains* to American viewers [and] said that the film, with his point of view, corresponded to the claim, which he wrote about together with V. Pudovkin and G. Alexandrov: the principle of new applications of sound and music in cinema, [should] not be naturalistic, outwardly emotional element, but a symphonic, contrapuntal correlation with the visual series.[60]

According to Yutkevich, this borrowed galop was used as a counterpoint to the image to signify a change in Peter at an early moment of his slow conversion, that is, "the internal creation of the hero"—a musical equivalent to a character's point-of-view (POV) shot. This phrase, "the internal creation of the hero," is also complemented by Arnshtam's discussion of Peter's character and his "inner monologue," that is, a kind of voice-over-narration that revealed Peter's thoughts.[61] Arnshtam, Yutkevich, and Shostakovich were, therefore, deeply invested in aurally conveying the internal state of a character and in developing an equal and complementary relationship between sound and image as was debated in the late 1920s, either through "inner monologue" or through musical codes such as the galop. This codifies the galop as a code that acts acousmatically and in counterpoint in both instances of its use—in this case the Baku scene and the worker's meeting scene—connecting the galop with the theme of a strike, and humanizing the workers by musically depicting their internal states.

The codes of waltz, urban song, and galop all served as continuous threads throughout the score, operating in underscore, diegesis, or in the "fantastical gap." They also helped to unify the plot across scenes and episodes, thus creating an overall "musical continuity editing" that connected the music and images more closely, especially when accommodating speech.[62] For this film score, continuity editing means that Shostakovich wrote music that would smooth gaps that were produced by editing, such as fades or quickly edited sequences. He also was in a position to take advantage of the advancements in sound film technology, which allowed him the opportunity to have music seamlessly disappear, become "unheard," yet continue over speech and images. The waltz code in the first scene can serve as one example, where repetitions of the waltz provided a sound bridge sounding over images of the boss leaving the factory and speaking to the workers.[63] He also could accommodate speech by lowering the volume of the music as the boss addresses the new workers. Similarly, Shostakovich adjusted the volume of the ostinato of the string duo that continued under the speech of the workers in the lavatory scene, only stopping when "diegetic" music would begin (the *chastushka* and the harmonica player).[64] This approach to underscoring, one that allows music and speech to exist simultaneously, was new for Shostakovich. It was also an approach that he would revisit in his next score to *Counterplan*.

Shostakovich also used musical continuity editing to link, through underscoring, two scenes without speech. As the son-engineer finishes the waltz at the piano at the end of his "little idea" scene, the image fades out and then fades in, showing images of him walking through the factory to find Peter. The music, in this case a four-trumpet solo in the formula of a fanfare, creates a sound bridge by beginning before the fade and continuing into the next scene over the fade and over the images of the son-engineer in the factory. The music follows the action closely, and ends when he finds Peter and begins to speak to him. Shostakovich used what appears to be a three-part ABA' form; one that easily transferred to the suite version of the score (see Example 4.3).[65]

In this scene, the sound bridge provides a sense of continuity between two disparate locales. This and other instances throughout the film show how Shostakovich maintained a "symphonic" continuity, one similar to

Example 4.3: The trumpet fanfare that accompanies the son-engineer. This is the beginning of the A section (of ABA′) that corresponds to the transition of scenes, from the son at the piano to the factory.

Excerpted from the Introduction ("Vstuplenie") from the suite of *Golden Mountains.* Yakubov, *"Muzïka k kinofil'mam, partitura"* (Moscow: Muzïka, 1987), 117, measures 1–6.

Hollywood continuity editing at the time, by having music sound over potentially fragmented editing, particularly during fades.[66]

Shostakovich also developed material locally, within specific scenes, to create musical continuity. At times, he was required to compose by "number" and isolate the musical development to specific scenes.[67] With the codes of the waltz and the urban song, he used repetition and variation; while occasionally creating recurring sections of music, as with the Baku scene. For other moments, he developed non-recurring musical material locally, confined to specific scenes in the film. The BA′ sections of the ABA′ music used to accompany the boss walking through the factory, for example, only appear again at the end of the scene after Peter has accepted the watch and the workers disperse (see Figure 4.1).[68] Vasily's attack in the alley and the worker's strike at the end of the film constitute the two other instances of localized development. Both examples contain original music whose development is also confined to the scene and often consists of little variation.[69] The episode of Vasily's attack is the more significant example, which contains both recurring codes and silence—a great benefit of a true sound film.

The episode of Vasily's attack is punctuated with silence, carefully cued with the musical content. The music (see Figure 4.1, Music G) enters only when Vasily is hit over the head, again to reappear over an image of the fleeing thief/attacker, Peter's accomplice, as seen in the map in Figure 4.2.[70]

Silence ——— Music G ——————————	Ticking watch ———————→
Watch Vasily/prepare attack	Peter approaches Vasily
Waltz leitmotif, Music G ———————	Silence ————————→
Vasily attacked, images of master, attackers	Attacker robs Vasily
Music G returns —————————	Silence ————————→
Attacker walks away	Peter helps Vasily

Figure 4.2: Scene of Vasily's attack.

Music G is sparse, alternating between an ornamented ascending line in bass clarinet solo that sequences several times and fills in the space of a tritone, with a series of punctuated chords in the pairs of low winds (bassoon and bass clarinet) and other low wind accompaniment. The overall timbral effect is muddy and dark, emulating the tension and eeriness of the scene. It acts as the episode's ostinato, using timbre as the dominant carrier of meaning, similar to Shostakovich's characterization of the *bai* in his score to *Alone*.[71] Along with the silence, it alternates with other specifically diegetic sounds, or previously heard codes.

The sound of Peter's ticking watch, the music to Vasily's attack, and the fifth appearance of the waltz leitmotif are presented as a linear sound montage. This montage illustrates the nexus of Peter's hesitant involvement with the attack on Vasily, his connection to the master, and the bourgeoisie's desire to destroy Vasily and the strike. As in this episode, development across the film was relegated to codes and other musical recurrences, forcing Shostakovich to sometimes compose moderately developed localized sections of music that still manage to embody the larger issues in the film. This is probably why scholars such as Egorova consider the score symphonic, despite its apparent fragmentary approach.

Another method that Yutkevich and Shostakovich employed to create musical continuity was to collect "found" sounds and repurpose them as a natural extension of the diegesis. Using these sounds highlighted the film's sound capacity, adding to its realism—a quality debated and desired by the studio. The repetition of the church bells during the church ceremony and the cheering of the crowds during the opening factory scene, for example, add to the overall realism of the film, while narrating religion as a bourgeois necessity and characterization. The sounds of the train near the end of the film, when Peter begins the strike—and the sounds of wind, which accompany Peter as he runs to begin the strike—are both examples of found sounds that could be also read as a representation of the themes of industrialization and isolation in the film, and as an attempt to root the images metaphorically and realistically within the film.

The factory whistle, also a diegetically placed but overdubbed sound, acts both as a unifying element and a commentary on the action. It is employed twice in the film—once to indicate the changing of shifts at the factory in the beginning of the film, and again to initiate the beginning of the strike sequence at the very end of the film. This whistle bookends the film, and transforms in meaning in its last appearance, similar to the primary song in *Alone* ("How Good Life Will Be"): initially, it calls the workers to their daily tasks, but later it calls the workers to strike. The diegetic realism of all of these sound effects encourages viewers to assimilate and identify with the film, as did the other codes. These found sounds also satisfied the studio's directives for appropriate realism—a way to comply with an aesthetic push towards socialist realism—while it also encouraged a sound continuity that mirrored Shostakovich's employment of musical continuity.

When Egorova called *Golden Mountains* "symphonic," her claim seemed to rest on her discussion of the leitmotifs (and as, in my words, codes) in the film; while "symphonic," as used by others, including Shostakovich himself, meant that a score was more developed and unified by methods that would weave music into the overall sound design of a sound-on-film work. The borrowed material of the codes (the Waldteufel waltz, "Golden Mountains" song, galop from *Declared Dead*) and the newly composed music creates continuity depending upon the organization and action of a scene or episode. Notably, the borrowed codes of the waltz and urban song were foregrounded more than in his previous scores; they appeared more frequently and at crucial meaning-laden moments throughout the film (the gift of the watch, Peter's dream in the tavern, Peter and the baby, and so forth). The other underscoring and brief allusions were set in the background and integrated into the musical fabric of a scene. Each of these approaches acts as models for the impending design of future Soviet sound films, where music can take on foreground, middle-ground, and background roles akin to Hollywood cinema of the same time. This symphonic approach is therefore a result of necessity, and adaptation to sound-on-film.

The question as to why *Golden Mountains* was deemed more "symphonic" than previous scores, particularly ones that used music as the primary carrier of meaning, is therefore a result of the interaction of image, speech, and music rather than resting on any of the three aspects alone. Unlike *Alone*, the music/image relationship in *Golden Mountains* was fluid and continuous, that is, perfectly timed with speech entrances and exits, with no superfluous pauses, and with the rhythm and timing of the editing, as indicated in the manuscripts. For the section of music for the attack of Vasily, for example, Shostakovich crossed out "2.30 sek," (2 minutes, 30 seconds) indicating even more exact timings for parts of a scene than in previous scores.[72] Although less of the music was repeated and written in a number-oriented manner as in *Alone*, what Shostakovich and the sound designers achieved was presumably the most perfect union of music, speech, and sound effects in film at that time. To discuss Shostakovich's "symphonism" in the case of *Golden Mountains* requires recognition of the fusion of image and music, rather than a discussion of a "pure" musical text essentially separated from the image. *Golden Mountains* therefore marks a shift in the perception of Shostakovich's film music, rather than just the creation of it. This was primarily due to the change in the medium itself, which encouraged critics and scholars to hear the score as "symphonic." It is the fluid and effective interaction of the music and image that may be the reason why this score also was perceived as more leitmotivic and borrowed than his previous scores.

RECEPTION

The reception was generally positive, and much of it revealed significant attention to the Soviet nature of the film and its score. Most reviewers regarded the film as a success, while claiming that aspects of film style and the plot were still "underdeveloped" and "primitive."[73] Reviews from *Komsomol'skaya pravda*, *Vechernyaya Moskva*, *Izvestiya*, and *Kino* declared *Golden Mountains* a "victory" for socialist film, "unarguably one of the best of our sound films, which appears with the guarantee of further victories already in the near future," a "serious attempt to deepen reality," and praised it for its "harsh and 'stingy' realism."[74] Of these reviews, one critic emphasized Peter's path to socialism as the correct "path of the millions," evoking the catchphrase that was used to describe films that complied with current politics—"intelligible to millions."

This intelligibility was also an underlying factor for the score's reception. Much of it considered the sound the most successful and realistic element of the film. Many reviewers focused on the score's *symphonism*, which was often construed both as unity and continuity, and as borrowing from the concert music tradition. In 1950, Shostakovich looked back on his work, and considered the year that he had written the scores for *Golden Mountains* and *Counterplan* to be a turning point in his career, a politically savvy move since many had publicly stated that these scores were such turning points.

Even considering his political motivations, his work on *Golden Mountains* was significant, since he had to negotiate between true speech, music, and sound effects. Because of the reflexive nature of his essay, he also emphasized how the two scores were noteworthy in their perceived "Soviet" quality as well as their ability to go beyond mere illustration. As he stated in reference to both films,

> They were already real Soviet sound films. I stress "Soviet" bearing in mind the thematic and ideal tendencies, and I therefore consider this work on these films important. I was lucky. At that time, many people still regarded music as an "illustration," an accompaniment to the images, but the directors of these two films, F. Ermler and S. Yutkevich, proved to be musical, and sensitively understanding of the role that music should play in sound cinema.[75]

Even with the gratuitous emphasis on things Soviet, he was clearly demonstrating how important it was for him that music be integral to cinema, and that these films be recognized as successful experiments as full sound films. The "people" who regarded music as "illustration" were real—such was the buzzword for film music since the late 1920s.[76] In perhaps subtle ways, Shostakovich still emphasized the importance of musical continuity in film scoring, and music's important narrative role in film.[77]

The general cinema press regarded the sound and the music of *Golden Mountains* to be a notable accomplishment, often stressing how the music engaged the images. Critics from major newspapers considered Shostakovich's music to be "interesting, fresh, corresponding to the action of the film," "clever, talented and inventive," and "expressive and organic," to such a point that the music "not [just] amplifies the film, but subordinates it, controlling the hall."[78] Other film critics, however, solely focused on Shostakovich's music, recognizing his vital importance to the development of role of the composer in sound film and his position as the one of the main composers of Soviet film music. One wrote:

> It is necessary to particularly note the musical composition of the film. The music of the young composer D. Shostakovich has risen to a high symphonic level. The exceptional expressivity of the musical phrase, the harmonic unity of the musical form with plasticity, [and the] emotionally saturated musical episodes *place Shostakovich among the distinguished composers of Soviet sound film.* The Soviet cinematography beats the best examples of musical formulation in foreign sound films as represented by Shostakovich. The musical public opinion is obliged to analyze in detail the creative path of this talented composer.[79]

The general press of the time bolstered Shostakovich and his reputation, setting him up for his next success: the score to *Counterplan*. The generally positive reception of this film and of his following score became the "turning point" that Shostakovich would cite almost twenty years later, in echo of certain supporters, and during the height of Stalinism.

Contrary to the general press, the majority of the critical evaluations of Shostakovich's film score came from specialists in film music who praised the synthesis of the music and image, or commented on the score's organization and unity. Cheryomukhin considered the "counterpoint" of the images and the music to be effective, interconnecting the various characters and their role in the film through leitmotifs.[80] Ioffe also begrudgingly praised the music/image relationship, stating that

> In *Golden Mountains* Shostakovich supplements not only dramatic visual shots, suggesting the relationship to the characters and the action, but also predicts the movement and content of the shots, preparing their appearances.[81]

Ioffe provided two examples of synthesis of the music-image: a description of Shostakovich's opening galop in the film that foreshadows the strike, and the parallelism of the underscoring to the action in the alleyway before the attack on Vasily. In the overall scope of the film, however, Ioffe complained that the score was fragmented because of speech, but unified by certain elements, writing that

> Instead of continuous development under the silent frames, the music is interrupted, often giving way to dialogue. But the composer struggles against the disparate episodes, [and] aspires to the dramaturgical unity of all of the musical material. The means of this unity becomes a leitmotif which passes through the film, which appears together with its characters and changes together with them.[82]

Ioffe was evidently uneasy with a different symphonic approach to film, where dialogue and music shared space. Even with the use of the leitmotif (or code) as a unifying element in this kind of scoring for the speaking film, he still thought that this system failed in connecting a fragmented score. He considered the lack of unity to be the result of the use of closed musical forms such as the fugue. Contrary to Egorova's use of the word, Ioffe chastised Shostakovich's use of such forms as "symphonic" in a singular sense of the term, and considered them useless for film music. Ioffe therefore received Shostakovich's score as unsuccessful because of its implied connection to Western art forms such as the symphony or fugue, a contradiction to Arnshtam's praise.

The methods of "leitmotifs" and counterpoint were also received as positive elements of the score. In a 1939 paper about cinema music, the conductor Nikolay Rabinovich found that

> Principally, in respect to *Golden Mountains*: this was the most interesting film in the use of music. In [the film], there already were fairly exact uses of the principle of sound, leitmotivism, [and] attempts [at] original counterpoint between the image and sound.[83]

Rabinovich had always been supportive of Shostakovich's music, dating from the time when he conducted the score for *Alone*. It is with this film that Rabinovich mentioned "leitmotivism" and praised the "counterpoint between the image and sound," two issues that concerned Ioffe and Cheryomukhin, and their perceptions of *symphonism* in the score. The leitmotif label, generally misunderstood by critics, evidently indicated praise of the score's unity rather than an emphasis on the adherence to Wagnerian principles.

In contrast to Rabinovich, musicologist Pavina Rïbakova found the songs that were used as leitmotifs to be an attempt at realism, a significant change from what she deemed the "refined, warped-psychological lines of *Nose* and foxtrotting rhythms of *Golden Age*."[84] She condemned the way in which Shostakovich used the leitmotifs, however, stating that his treatment of the motifs and their application to groups of characters in the film (the waltz for the factory owners and the "Golden Mountains" song for the workers) was "superficial" and "simplified."[85] She considered the score to be unsuccessful, and asked the composer to "overcome [his] mistakes and incorrectness," continuing similar rhetoric that many had used to describe Shostakovich's previous film scores.[86]

Rïbakova's comments were echoed by other critics as well, who declared the score formalist; they used the fugue as their primary target (see Example 4.4). Published in the suite form of the score and released in the first version of the film, but removed from the 1936 release, the fugue invited critics to condemn Shostakovich. The film's creators, notably Yutkevich (in his declarations to the studio) and Arnshtam, however, defended the choice of the fugue. In an earlier essay on *Counterplan* from 1935, Arnshtam described the fugue from *Golden Mountains*:

> The enormous fugue by Shostakovich for organ and the symphonic orchestra connected our complicated and studied counterpoint with the strike of the Baku and Petersburg proletariat, perceived by the spectator as a natural phenomenon, and not demanding explanations—this was the true sign of our success.[87]

Example 4.4: From the beginning of the fugue, which corresponds to the images of the strike of the Baku and Petersburg workers.
Excerpted from Manashir Yakubov, *"Muzïka k kinofil'mam, partitura"* (Moscow: Muzïka, 1987), 145, measures 7–11.

In a later essay, "Golden Mountains" (1977), Arnshtam still considered the fugue a success, as part of the idea that "great symphonic forms" were successfully used in the film score:[88]

> But Shostakovich was not afraid to bring into the cinema the most complex musical forms! And perhaps, principally, I consider his most significant success a fugue that he wrote for organ and large symphony orchestra.
>
> Two parallel episodes developed in the film—a strike in Baku and a strike in Petersburg. [There were] about sixty diverse montage pieces. [It moved] from static, extremely slowed down internal-frame movement to impetuous pieces of simultaneous execution of workers' demonstrations in Baku and Petrograd. [There was] refined parallel montage and rare unity in this fugue of Shostakovich![89]

For Ioffe, however, the fugue was too literal. He considered the theme of the fugue to be too "abstract" and "ready-made," a complaint related to his previously cited discussion about the lack of unity and "organic synthesis" in the score. Instead, he suggested that a revolutionary tune should have been used. He considered the scene to be "constructivist" (read: modernist) because Shostakovich created a "formal analogy" between the fugue and the development of the strike. He argued:

> Shostakovich tries to adapt for cinema ready musical forms, to interpret them [with] the shots. In the shots which [show] the strike expanding, including all the new masses and new convoys, he provides an organ fugue, the theme of which passes to all new voices, spreading and growing, shows the development of the strike; the theme of a fugue does not use a revolutionary song, but [instead has a] dramatic abstract manner. To use a fugue in this case reveals the constructivist decision of the task of connecting the music with the plot, so as to have gone according to the line of formal analogy.[90]

Cheryomukhin also complained of the fugue as unsuccessful:

> The fugue in film-music is encountered rarely. It is because it is difficult to execute. Truly, D. Shostakovich has written a wonderful fugue for the film *Golden Mountains*, [but] it is not entirely used well in the film.[91]

In the suite version of the fugue, the instrumentation consists of organ and full orchestra. The organ begins the fugal statement, followed by answers from the orchestra.[92] This also corresponds to the manuscripts, where the fugue begins with two lines in the organ, growing into five lines of music with the addition of the orchestra.[93] The organ and the orchestra had been understood by Arnshtam and critics to represent the unification of each group of workers (in Baku or Petersburg) building into an analogous interwoven musical texture. In this sense, the musical texture of the fugue acts as a cinematic signifier, specifically of the two groups coming together.[94] Although the concept of the fugue may reflect the idea of the proletariat, its "academicism" as an icon of Western concert music and its potential to be more "audible" than other forms of music and more "difficult to execute" as Cheryomukhin pointed out, goes against the proletarian idea and resulted in the negative reaction of critics such as Ioffe.[95] This approach is contrary to the kind of visual/aural polyphony of the hut scene in *Alone*, where the shaman's music, the hurdy-gurdy, and various sound effects are interwoven to evoke the character's state of mind. This modernist layering used in *Alone* is eschewed in *Golden Mountains* and replaced by a conventional polyphonic form nonetheless unacceptably Western and ultimately inappropriate for socialist ideals. This parallel between musical lines/instruments/textures and the quick paced parallel montage of the images was, therefore, the hallmark of the film, yet proved to be a negative focal point for film critics.

Even after contemporaneous reviews, the use of a "symphonic" form such as the fugue was still considered to be a "formalist" mistake in the film's score. In a 1936 article published just weeks after *Pravda*'s well-known article "Muddle Instead of Music," Sergey Bugoslavsky claimed that the fugue was a "formalist" mistake in a long line of Shostakovich's "errors" in film music.[96] In an article from 1950 on music and the history of cinema, Tikhon Khrennikov listed *Golden Mountains* as one of Shostakovich's early "constructivist, formalist" film scores, together with *New Babylon* and *Alone*. He went onto say, "In the films of this period we met the eclectic laugh of the grotesque, machine-like noises, the bourgeois, thieves' intonations."[97] Khrennikov then continued to address Shostakovich's success listing *Counterplan* as his recovery from his earlier films. It is possible that despite the cleverness of the metaphor of the fugue/strike, it was eventually removed from the re-release of the film in 1936 as a result of its generally poor reception by cultural critics. By 1950, the film was firmly established as a failure in comparison to his next film score, *Counterplan*.

The initial relative success of *Golden Mountains* was attributed to its creators' attempt at realism, which was the result of how critics perceived this as a synchronous sound film with seamless editing and symphonic scoring. Shostakovich's integrative underscoring, and the use of popular songs as codes that were closely fitted to the rhythm with the images and speech of the film, led some critics to an initial positive reception of his score. These factors enhanced a socialist topic, one that emphasized conversion of the individual and construction of the state, which was consistent with the changing political trends in filmmaking of the early thirties. The nod to modernist montage techniques from the twenties, and Shostakovich's use of Western "formalist" forms of music, however, led the film to eventual condemnation as a "formalist" excursion, especially after the enthusiastic reception of model socialist realist films such as *Counterplan* and *Chapayev* (dirs. Georgy and Sergey Vasil'yev, 1934).[98] *Golden Mountains* was, therefore, a short-lived and overshadowed example of the burgeoning socialist realist film and score. It was the first time Shostakovich's *symphonism* was employed in a sound-on-film work, which was variably defined by his colleagues and by critics. Although his music was celebrated and heard as powerful, the score was ultimately overpowered by the song-score of Shostakovich's most famous film music from the thirties, *Counterplan*.

CHAPTER 5

༄

Counterplan (1932)
and the Socialist Realist Film

Counterplan (1932, dirs. Fridrikh Ermler and Sergey Yutkevich) was the first successful socialist realist film under the new aesthetic, and embodied the state's directives for the arts from the mid-1930s forward. The thesis of the film, building a counterplan to the five-year plan, drove the content and structure of the narrative, encouraging a fragmented approach to the score that proved to be successful in a political climate that prized intelligibility. This approach resulted in a song score, a type that would prevail in Soviet films of the thirties. This song score was episodic in formal structure, with songs and occasional orchestral underscoring operating in closed form throughout. Various motifs and songs were codes that represented the thesis of the film and its supporting characters.

Throughout the film these codes acted as sub-theses for the overall objective. The songs operate as the primary codes throughout, representing a variety of popular and folk traditions, many of which were used to depict the Soviet folk for mass consumption. Contrary to the songs-as-codes, the orchestral underscoring utilizes common codes at play in early Golden-Era Hollywood film, demonstrating a connection to American filmmaking, a connection that was regarded as favorable at the time. Regardless of its American connections, the central song of the film was an enforced Soviet success, thanks to unprecedented media pressure and the use of Shostakovich's reputation by the state studio system.

Of the codes in the film, the "Song of the Counterplan" became the central thesis, and is an example of the transferability of musical ideas.

In 1943, the song was rewritten in the United States and used as a symbol of UN power, peace, and positive Soviet-American relations, if only
temporarily. Moving between nationalisms and ideologies, the context for
the song set the groundwork for this new musical-political relationship,
demonstrating the transferability and political power of a code designed
to sound "epic" and "triumphant." Over the course of almost fifty years,
the composer and the directors were celebrated as having created the first
true Soviet film—one that saw extraordinary support from the state and
its studios. Such reception for this film continued into the 1980s, when it
was still upheld as a classic in the twilight years of the Soviet Union.

"LET'S HAVE A COUNTERPLAN!"

Counterplan was conceived and completed within seven months from
January to November 1932.[1] This production aligned with the highly
propagandized rebuilding of industry and economy, culminating in the
catchphrase "Let's have a Counterplan" to the five-year plan.[2] In the context of this film, this meant that a new plan must be developed to finish
the equivalent of five years work in four years. The story of the film was
based on a real-life event, where workers at a Leningrad "Karl Marx" turbine factory succeeded in completing their work in a shorter time than
needed—their counterplan—from 1929–1931.[3] The subsequent development of the theme for the film followed, influenced by the reorganization of various groups such as RAPP and RAPM into state-controlled
Unions on 23 April 1932.[4] During its production and after its release, the
film was lavished with attention from the Party, local factories, and the
film studio, particularly since it was the only film commissioned for the
fifteenth anniversary of the October Revolution. It was adopted by every
organization and community in Leningrad, not just as an ordinary film
project but also as representative of the building of a new socialist society
through art. In a speech about the film, Sergey M. Kirov stated, "the film
Counterplan is the same Party and Soviet business as any economic-politi-
cal work."[5]

   The film's story operates using a circle of developed characters, which
acts as a new kind of socialist typage, thereby providing a sampling of an
ideal factory population in the late twenties and early thirties. The central focus is the change and growth of the older factory "master" Semyon
Ivanovich Babchenko from a drunken non-Soviet character to his acceptance and successful execution of the counterplan that eventually saves
the factory. Subsidiary but complementary to Babchenko's story is the

relationship between the strongly developed supporting characters Vasya, the Party secretary; and Katya and Pavel, who are a somewhat "bourgeois" young couple that eventually act as the "young guard," ultimately executing and representing the Party's goals. These characters also contribute to the film's sub-plot, a love story that softens the "industrial" side of the film.[6] Other supporting characters, such as the engineer Lazarev, are more neutral, but eventually convert to the cause. In keeping with the storyline trend of the early thirties that becomes the model plot for socialist realism, the character of the "wrecker" appears, depicted in the bourgeois engineer Skortsev. By the end of the film, a clear boundary is established between good and evil (Soviet versus bourgeois). When the wrecker attempts to foil the counterplan, the good work of the other characters wins out, which results in the expected happy socialist ending.

In this particular film, authorship over certain sections of music in the fragmentary score is somewhat contested, and shared. Beginning his work on the film score in the late summer of 1932 and finishing by October of that year, Shostakovich can be specifically credited with at least three sections of the score, and assumed to have participated in other sections not deemed immediately as music.[7] Shostakovich was, however, considerably involved on the set, watching the film in its early stages in order to understand how to score for it.[8] This was particularly important since he, like the other film workers, had little time to create his part of the film. Khentova explains his process, in part based on information from some members of the film collective:

> The method of the composer's work in the film was dictated by the short terms of its production that demanded simultaneous shock [udarnyi] efforts of the entire film-making collective. Shostakovich observed during the shootings as they were going on or watched a scene straight through, immediately composing music underneath—in these cases there was usually illustrative music ... But more often music was written in parallel with the filming, according to the script; and based on this, the composer followed his own visual, psychological representations, creating generalized sound pictures with independent semantic function.[9]

Yutkevich confirmed some of Khentova's statements about Shostakovich's approach to underscoring in an interview published in 1995. He stated, "We calculated time for music in film, according to the second, and he composed as much as was needed, absolutely exactly."[10] According to these witnesses, Shostakovich attempted to understand the film, and worked meticulously to match his music to the images, as he had with his previous scores.

It is always a question as to how much a composer works with sound operators on a film project, particularly since information on such relationships is rarely available. With this film, however, there is more information on the processes of creating music and sound outside of Shostakovich's direct compositional contribution; notes on manuscripts, and other documents offer additional information from which his involvement can be gleaned.[11] In some instances, Shostakovich wrote notes across his (extant) orchestral numbers as to how to proceed with ideas about instrumentation and the like, demonstrating a collaborative process.[12] In other instances, there are more explicit descriptions of the sound designers' teamwork. According to Yutkevich and Arnshtam, three people—Arnshtam, the sound designer; Ilya Volk, the sound operator; and Shostakovich, the composer—worked together to fabricate ambient factory sounds out of orchestral instruments to create the soundscape of a metallurgy factory.[13] Taking most of the credit, Arnshtam discussed the approach to the film's sound design:

> I had a very interesting experience with making the sounds of a factory in *Counterplan*. I am in principle opposed to any naturalistic "film-noise," which usually physiologically tires the listener with its disorganization and intolerable roar. This "film-noise" is usually intended for musically half-deaf directors and for deaf spectators.
>
> I used my own thought up "factory" in *Counterplan*. I had an original orchestra working for me, which consisted of several bassoons, clarinets, several violins, four contrabasses, a trumpet, and a flute. I had this orchestra at my disposal on all shoots and used their improvisation, and never went the way of the imitation of a factory's natural noise.
>
> I used the musical instruments only as timbral color, distributed on the elementary rhythmic design. In these timbres, it was necessary to enter the buzz of the lighting devices, which worked in all force of the 16 thousand of ampere. I tried to use the original orchestra with loudness not greater than mezzo forte on Hawaiian guitar. I think that the listener is grateful for it.[14]

Arnshtam's orchestral factory soundscape is completely opposed to the found-sound or modernistic "film noise" in the films of directors such as Dziga Vertov, who he indirectly references in his description.[15] He was interested instead in creating realism in sound through "timbral color," such as the high range of the flute as "metallic" sounds of the factory or the low, grumbling ranges of instruments such as string bass and bassoon, all kept at a low volume ("not greater than a mezzo-forte on Hawaiian guitar").[16] The improved technology—particularly the different recorders, condenser microphones, and the shooting of the film on the studio pavilions—allowed for this greater nuance, increased sensitivity, and quality of timbre. Speech and quieter sounds were easier to record, and the result was greater aural realism. As Volk related, the "sound of the water poured in a glass, quiet conversation, the song of Red Army men sounding in a distance, and so forth" were within the realm of possibility.[17] This technology gave Arnshtam the opportunity to accommodate the buzzing of the lighting devices (and possibly the cameras that Volk described) into the general soundscape as well.[18] The result is effectively realistic—there is a trace of factory-like sounds throughout the film that blend into the imagined sound of a factory.

In his essay about *Counterplan*, Arnshtam was suspiciously silent in his discussion of Shostakovich's music or music/sound involvement in the film. Avoiding Shostakovich's contribution altogether, he tended to speak of his own work on sound design in *Counterplan*, or on *Golden Mountains* (1931). He pointed out his contributions clearly:

> Cinematographers and film critics usually think that music in the "factory" is composed by Shostakovich. Some reviews of Shostakovich even praised him for this music. To me it is flattering that my pure cinematographic craft and technical work has been accepted as music by such a remarkable composer as Shostakovich. Shostakovich does not take offense, and for that thank you![19]

It is notable that Arnshtam denied Shostakovich any credit, especially since he appeared to be at ease praising Shostakovich in most of his writings about *Golden Mountains* and *Counterplan* when Shostakovich was responsible for the music. As Yutkevich had claimed, this particular "orchestral" approach to the creation of factory sound, however, would probably have required Shostakovich's assistance. Although the authorship is unclear, this detailed description shows a concern for realism specifically required for this film by the studio, using a technical approach that hearkened back to earlier modernist film experiments. Such a soundscape goes beyond codes, and demonstrates an interest in blending modernist techniques with socialist aesthetics, a common approach in some of Shostakovich's scores in the 1930s.[20] This collaborative and modernist approach to sound also highlights the fragmentary nature of the score, and the piece-meal approach to its creation.

Shostakovich had experience in the past with directors, such as Kozintsev, who had clear ideas about overall formal design, and Kozintsev had commented on Shostakovich's work as complementary to that form.[21] These sorts of commentaries are also seen in the writings of other sound designers/

directors. Arnshtam wrote about the scoring to *Counterplan*, although without Kozintsev's penchant for descriptive elaboration, and discussed how this score was exceptional in comparison to the symphonic-continuous design found in Shostakovich's earlier scores. Instead, Arnshtam described *Counterplan* as song-oriented, and expressed that the "symphonic" experience gained from working on *Golden Mountains* was not applied

> for the dramaturgic form *Counterplan* did not demand any sort of careful study from us. We have only constructed the symphonic [quality] in whole [closed] sections. This is all clear in the "white nights" [scene].[22]

Describing "whole" sections, that is, closed sections that act as moveable blocks that may or may not be repeated, goes against the kind of form that Shostakovich deemed symphonic in his other scores such as *New Babylon* and *Golden Mountains*. The scene that Arnshtam cites is the only moment of clear orchestral scoring in the film, and is itself a closed section that fails to participate in an overall symphonic (in his words, "dramaturgic") form. Instead the film consists of songs, and occasional and separate sections placed in the film as needed, often forming codes within the film. The episodic, independent fragments that make up the whole of the film lend the designation of "song-score" to *Counterplan*—a style of filmmaking and scoring that was prevalent in the thirties.

Underscored sections of music and songs act as codes and lend structure to the score, often fully contained within specific scenes and associated with the representation of characters that eventually serve the film's thesis. Underscoring, therefore, specifically Shostakovich's parallelism and anempathy, or in his own words the "principle of the shot" and the "principle of contrast," were also a means for musical characterization.[23] There are several scenes with underscored original music—the scenes of the evaluations of the turbine with recurrent music, the "white nights" scene, which interweaves with orchestral statements of the central song, and two scenes centering on Babchenko. Each of these is separate, different, and serves varied purposes and characterizations at certain moments in the film. These underscored scenes are also self-contained and closed, acting apart from the other musical moments in the film.

Since Babchenko is the central character who undergoes transformation in the film, certain codes are used to signify his position at a given moment in the story. Shostakovich's music appears twice for his characterization, once for his lunch and another for his public shaming, signifying his connection to older non-Soviet ways, and his path to reformation. Babchenko's lunch scene consists of a self-contained episode of music that

Example 5.1: Babchenko's lunch scene from the film (first five measures in piano reduction). For the entirety of this scene's music that is shown only in part here, I label the form as "Introduction (measures 1–8)—A (measures 9–16)—B (measures 17–36)"; the measures correspond to the published music.

See Manashir Yakubov, *Dmitry Shostakovich, Sobraniye Sochineniy v soroka dvukh tomakh, tom 41, "Muzïka k kinofil'ma, partitura"* [The Collected Works in Forty-Two Volumes, vol. 41, "Music to the Film Scores, Orchestral Score"] (Moscow: Muzïka, 1987), 475.

is highly repetitive and militaristic largely due to the brass and wind instrumentation and angular rhythms (see Example 5.1).[24] The main rhythmic idea is similar to that of the watch scene in *Golden Mountains*—a dotted quarter note followed by triplet sixteenth notes.[25] The music to this scene is through-composed with one section of repetition.

The selection of brass instruments was a conscious choice for Shostakovich, who noted this instrumentation, consisting mostly of brass, winds, and timpani, in an early draft of the scene in piano score.[26] Typically, a militaristic rhythm with brass immediately conjures images of war or revolution, as this kind of *intonatsia* is typically coded; yet here, Babchenko is enjoying his lunch, followed by a bottle of vodka (a symbol within the film of anti-Soviet behavior), dissimilar to the other workers. The next appearance of this music, however, solidifies a different meaning. The music appears as the workers and Babchenko are troubleshooting the turbine's problems, working overtime to solve them.[27] At this point in the film, it has been demonstrated that Babchenko's heavy drinking was directly interfering with the success of the turbines, and that overcoming his drinking problem would lead to the overall success of the factory. This code of abstract brass-military music, therefore, is codified by its second appearance. Initially it operates as ironic and later sincere, similar to the use of the song "How Good Life Will Be" in *Alone*.[28] Such use of a code, which usually signifies the militaristic, was interpreted as modernist and ironic by some contemporaneous critics. One reviewer, Emilya Frid, considered the music to this scene to be parodic, mischievous, and didactic. She read the music and image together as an ironic commentary that connects Babchenko's binge drinking with the first failure of the turbine, thus explaining why the music appears so grotesque and vigorous for a common, everyday scene.[29] Shostakovich made a habit of restating music for scenes that build in meaning in order to develop a character, as in *Alone* and *Youth of Maxim* (1934–35). This contemporaneous reception illustrates a continuing disagreement with how Shostakovich's music supports the development of Babchenko and the primary thesis of the film.

Another military-inspired code, a march, accompanies Babchenko when he carries a banner of shame (*pozor*) after having failed the other workers in the initial test of the turbine. This march, which only appears for a few moments before a large workers' meeting, is fully orchestral. Various reviewers regarded this scene, with the code of the march, as inhumane and lacking in realism—therefore failing to comply with the main aesthetic of this film. Ieremiya Ioffe complained that the composer lacked the ability to illustrate individual human characteristics, that is, realism, while Frid argued that the scene lacked humanity, and emphasized that Shostakovich represented the scene with a "wild and grotesque march."[30] This grotesquerie was apparently effective, since she also described the scene as "memorable."[31] Khentova, however, refused to employ such terminology, and attempted to explain Shostakovich's process through the eyes and ears of the actor who played Babchenko, Vladimir R. Gardin.[32]

"Procession with a Banner" subsequently sounded the very good music of the composer D. D. Shostakovich. But I have heard this music after the episode with a banner was played, and the composer saw the episode on the screen after music had been written to it. . . If I knew this music before I had started to shoot, undoubtedly, I would have performed "Procession with a Banner" a little differently. I think, that if D. D. Shostakovich had seen the episode on the screen before he began to write music, possibly, he would write it a little differently, too.[33]

Khentova explained that Shostakovich needed to compose an "abstract" musical representation of the scene because of its short production time and the usual demands of composing for film.[34] Although implying an unsuccessful music-image pairing, the march was still received as appropriately grotesque for a scene where Babchenko shames himself. Such a grotesque march, regardless of reception, aligns with Shostakovich's penchant for using idiomatic styles such as marches, galops, and dances to

Example 5.2a: The beginning of the White Nights episode, with the entry of the bicyclists on the embankment (upper winds only). The horn and strings, which include harp, play supportive harmonies, ending in D major at the end of this excerpt from the film.
Modified from the film and edition of Yakubov, *The Collected Works in Forty-Two Volumes*, vol. 41, Music to the Film Scores, Orchestral Score, 193, measures 1–8.

characterize the grotesque in his earlier works.[35] Although it failed to be realist in the way the actor or critics may have desired, it was still particular to Shostakovich's usual way of evoking the grotesque.

Another set of codes appear in the scene with two of the "young guard" characters, Vasya and Katya, as they stroll around Leningrad during its white nights. Started and finished with the "Song of the Counterplan" and in various instrumentation, this is the first scene that moves between diegetic background and non-diegetic underscored music that is closely anchored to the images. The Song is heard diegetically, and shortly thereafter, the music shifts to an underscored galop just as Vasya and Katya are nearly run over by a group of bicyclists (see Example 5.2a and Video 5.1). ⏵

Timed to the exact second, this scene's first instance of underscoring initiates a new section that mimics the activity of the bicyclists.[36] As Yutkevich related,

> He [Shostakovich] loved to watch pieces of film and suggest something. For example, in *Counterplan* bicyclists rode along the embankment. He watched and asked: "In which second do they ride by?"[37]

In this segment, Shostakovich is sensitive to adjusting the tempi, volumes, texture, and instrumentation to the minute shifts in the scene, much as Max Steiner's music "fit like a glove," and, therefore, closely mimicking speech and action in his scores.[38] To accompany a montage of images of steamrollers and of Leningrad awakening in early morning, Shostakovich varied the texture and instrumentation to "mickey mouse" the images—the music shifts to a full orchestral texture with full strings (over images of steamrollers), then to a quasi-grotesque section for solo xylophone (over images of workers), as shown in Examples 5.2b and 5.2c.

Example 5.2b: From the "White Nights" episode. The strings enter indicating a shift in texture and initiating the montage of Leningrad.

From the film and modified from Fragment Number 1 in Yakubov, *The Collected Works in Forty-Two Volumes*, vol. 41, "Music to the Film Scores, Orchestral Score," 194, measures 29–34.

With cuts back to the couple and their conversation, Shostakovich reduced the instrumentation to winds (mostly clarinets and flutes) and strings, [39] and the volume is lowered to accommodate a quiet solo in the violin that accompanies their conversation about love (see Example 5.2d).[40] This is precisely scored so that the music may coexist with the speech; Shostakovich was careful to lower the volume or finish the music altogether before a character speaks, as he had done in previous scores.[41]

Example 5.2c: From the "White Nights" episode, where the xylophones enter, accompanying the images of the workers.

Modified from the film and Yakubov, *The Collected Works in Forty-Two Volumes*, vol. 41, "Music to the Film Scores, Orchestral Score," 196, measures 61–63.

Example 5.2d: The shift to the violin solo (first five measures), corresponding with the couple's conversation about love.

Modified from the film and from the beginning of Fragment Number 2 in Yakubov, *The Collected Works in Forty-Two Volumes*, vol. 41, "Music to the Film Scores, Orchestral Score," 206, measure 1–30.

Example 5.2e: Moving away from the violin solo, a low volume wind introduction segues into a delicate wind and harp version of the "Song of the Counterplan."
Modified from the film and Yakubov, *The Collected Works in Forty-Two Volumes*, vol. 41, "Music to the Film Scores, Orchestral Score," Fragment Number 3, rehearsal 4, 208.

As a siren interrupts Vasya's speech, the music swells and the violin solo slows its tempo and changes its volume to accompany it. After the siren disappears, the music continues along a moderate tempo and changes to a new instrumental color (horns) before returning to strings. This texture provides a slow segue into the "Song of the Counterplan," which accompanies Vasya's cheerful acceptance of Katya's love for Pavel (see Example 5.2e).[42]

The use of a full orchestra to emulate the city at large, xylophones for steamrollers, and violins for love demonstrate that Shostakovich applied instrument-specific codes to typify the nuanced moments in this scene; that is, he used timbre to index a history of these codes to add a layer of meaning to the images as he did in his score to *Alone,* and in other early scores. Violins as cues for love, and strings for romance, for example, are common tropes of this time, ones that Shostakovich reuses in *Girlfriends* (1935–36) years later. He is also sensitive to tempi and volume, and sounds in the overall design, molding the music around the siren and speech; just as Yutkevich related, he was attentive to timing during his screenings of the scenes. This attentiveness was also echoed in his manuscripts, where he would often record the music's duration per scene in minutes and seconds. Instrumentation, volume, and tempo all work together to minutely shift with the changing contexts of this episodic scene, using instrumental timbres as codes that permeate the scene and act as primary cues that run parallel to the meaning of each shot.

Borrowed songs also operate as codes throughout the score. Each of these signifies character-building moments that frequently borrow from the folk, popular, and chamber repertories. Similar to how Shostakovich approached his scores to *Alone, New Babylon,* and *Golden Mountains,* such borrowings create a dichotomy of urban versus folk and worker versus bourgeoisie. To develop the wrecker character, Skortsev, the directors and composer chose the romance "Mne grustno" ("I Am Sad," 1848) by Aleksandr Dargomïzhsky to appear, foregrounded, in the diegesis. It first appears during the scene when Skortsev and his mother sing while she plays the romance on the piano. At this point in the film, this song, as does his nineteenth-century-styled apartment, establishes his social class as "bourgeois" and anti-Soviet. The words, audible in the diegesis, reinforce Skortsev's character and presage his future actions ("I am sad because you are happy . . ."). The final lines of song, from Mikhail Lermontov's poem of the same name, "I am sad because you are happy," summarize the singer-poet's sadness in knowing that the object of his affections will eventually be punished by Fate for her fleeting happiness. Adding to the code of these bourgeois tendencies, these lyrics in their initial appearance hold the potential to relay Skortsev's unhappiness with the factory's success and his confidence that the factory might fail in their plans. When the romance appears a second time, this unhappiness is confirmed: the numbers for the turbine are positive, signaling the end of Skortsev's wrecking. As he hears the numbers from his helper, Chutochkin, he ignores them and dreamily sings the bourgeois romance as an escape to a pre-revolutionary past from the momentary socialist environment. The final appearance of this bourgeois code thusly solidifies the meaning of the tune and its connection to the character's role in the film.

Such a reading of these lyrics was lost on critics; instead, the aesthetic of the song was criticized. Although she noted that the song was intended as a commentary of the character's state of mind, Frid wrote that this appropriation was ineffective precisely because the composer failed to see the "emotional and aesthetic essence" of the original music; its "parodic-satirical" manner failed to overshadow the context of the song itself. The application of a pre-revolutionary song was, according to Frid, inappropriate despite its intended meaning in the film's context.[43] Similar to Shostakovich's quotation of Tchaikovsky's "Old French Song" in *New Babylon* during the scene where the Commune burns to the ground, this presentation of the song as pre-revolutionary code, and the play on words is precisely what the composer intended for the impact on this scene—a kind of retreat to a past deemed in current politics as inappropriate but useful for creating accepted dichotomies of Soviet versus pre-Soviet.[44] This function of a pre-revolutionary song indicated a musical code specific to Shostakovich that he had been using since *New Babylon*, and one that had been largely present in the visual codes of avant-grade films of the twenties.[45]

Two other borrowed songs narrate Babchenko's drinking scenes, which illustrate his pre-Soviet mentality and set up his eventual conversion to the Soviet mindset. In one scene, Babchenko gets drunk alone in his apartment, while a record of a "gypsy romance" plays on the record player next to him.[46] This tune diegetically accompanies the various shots of Babchenko, his bottle, and later, his cat. The music in this scene acts as a reinforcement, or parallelism, to the images of Babchenko's indulgence of self-pity, and illustrates his pre-Soviet ways. Songs designated as "gypsy" (*tsyganshchina*) had specific meanings in Soviet Russia. Such a song, especially a romance, would have been considered a nineteenth-century genre, and cast to be heard as lascivious, indulgent, foreign, dark, and ethnically Other from Soviet culture.[47] This stereotyped use of a gypsy romance was designed to portray something ideologically foreign to socialist music (read: "Song of the Counterplan") and, therefore, to act as a reinforcement of the idea that Babchenko is not a Party worker, but a worker who is still tied to the old bourgeois ways.

A second song that accompanies Babchenko's drinking appropriates a Russian folk source, yet still codifies the characterization of Babchenko pre-transformation. Disappointed because of the failure of the first turbine, Babchenko sits and takes out a bottle of vodka, while a melody somewhat resembling the song "Ural'skaya Ryabinushka" (Ural Rowan Tree)

Example 5.3: "Ural'skaya Ryabinushka" (Ural Rowan Tree, oboe only).
Transcription from the film by the author and Christian Anderson.

plays in the underscoring on solo oboe with orchestral accompaniment (see Example 5.3).

This folk song has the usual markers of an urban version of a village tune, a kind of folk readily accepted as a symbolic representation of the working class in the Soviet teens, twenties, and beyond.[48] This song acts as a code that signifies the urban folk, but with an additional twist. Although this melody only momentarily resembles the folk tune, Frid identified this tune as "Ural'skaya Ryabinushka" upon viewing the film and argued that it has a counterpart in the image. She states that when Babchenko sits and looks at his bottle, a close-up shows the viewer/listener its label—"Ryabinovka" (rowanberry-flavored vodka), a term that has the same root-word as the folk song (Ryabin-).[49] Tying image and song in this fashion was a common technique applied by silent film accompanists and by Shostakovich, as seen in *Alone* with "Marsh budyonnongo" (March of Budyonnï) and *New Babylon*.[50] Such a technique drew criticism from Frid, where she disapproved of Shostakovich's inappropriate reference to an outdated, "intellectual," and silent film appropriate aural reference of a visual object (a triple play on word-image-sound), claiming that the scene lacks any emotional impact.[51] What Frid neglected to mention was that this song quotation appears a second time, when the turbine is yet again rejected. The exact same appearance of this code therefore builds, much like "How Good Life Will Be," and "I Am Sad," to indicate his repeated failure as a result of the bourgeois preference for excessive drinking.

Notably, however, this "folk" song acts as a negative, anti-Soviet signifier. The "folk" here fails to align with socialist realist ideas, whereas revolutionary songs like "Marsh budyonnogo" in *Alone*, or "Partisan's Song" in a later scene in this film would. By 1932, village "folk" music had come to signify something dangerous and "anti-Soviet."[52] This song is, therefore, a code for the anti-Soviet nature of a character who began the film as an example of a pre-Soviet personality.

The code of the revolutionary song, commonly employed in films to evoke Soviet ideals, supports the positive message of the film at critical

Example 5.4: "Partizanskaya" (Partisan's Song).
Transcription from the film by the author and Christian Anderson.

junctures. At the end of the housewarming scene, where a conversation between Pavel and Vasya turns to serious discussions about the factory's counterplan, Pavel walks over to a table staring thoughtfully as the revolutionary song "Partizanskaya" (Partisan's Song) slowly fades into the underscoring. This song was known to listeners of the time, and has famously endured, still being performed by the Red Army choir as a standard revolutionary work.[53] Mikhail Druskin noted that this song has a history of multiple rewritings of the text that eventually came to be known as the "Partisan's Song." The text first appeared 1920 and was popularized by the Red Army Choir in the 1930s. Little is known about the melody's origins, but some have described the tune as a "folk" melody, with common octave leaps and contour found in some village music.[54] In the context of this scene, the song repeats on a loop a total of three times. It continues until the end of scene where it builds into a crescendo and then fades in a decrescendo, fading out with the image of Pavel in contemplation about devising a counterplan. The most prominently heard part of the phrase is the second half of the song, as seen and heard in Example 5.4 and Video 5.2, underscoring Pavel's thoughts. ▶

This song certainly symbolizes the state, yet it also indexes the gendered power of a masculine Soviet state by using a male choir. The aural heft of the choir acts as a soundscape to a young male character who would devise the counterplan for a factory; at this point in the scene, the only female character in it, Katya, had been cut from the shot. The combination of this moment with a known revolutionary song—one that had been accepted as a symbol of the state and of urban folk song—confirms this song as a code of state power and masculinity. The signifiers of pro-Soviet and revolutionary stand in stark contrast to the Dargomïzhsky romance and other borrowed songs, where characters like Skortsev were portrayed as weak or foppish. The "Partisan's Song" was therefore an appropriate code that narrates the closing of a scene where gender and revolution are elided into the plot point where the characters devise a counterplan.

SONG OF THE COUNTERPLAN

Shostakovich's original song, "Song of the Counterplan," was the first song in Soviet Russian film music history to fly off the screen and into the daily soundscape of life in the Soviet Union and abroad.[55] It functions as the most prominent code throughout the film, appearing almost ten times in full chorus and orchestra or simply as orchestral variation. This code develops and builds in meaning throughout the film, and even decades later in other films and recomposed versions.

Composing the song as the centerpiece of the film was a significant challenge for the composer. As Shostakovich commented in a public setting,

> I settled in detail upon this song because it organically goes through all of the music in the film. It is perceived in the overture to the film, in the finale and in the choral parts. Its theme is felt everywhere. In this was the complexity of the work.
>
> I would like music to a film to play an independent role in order that it not bear traces of an accompanying character, [and] it not appear [as] an additional effect to this or that shot. Moreover, I would like the music in a film to be completely realistic and fulfill its ancillary function.[56]

Shostakovich has shown that he continued to regard his musical scoring for film as something other than merely accompanimental, a goal he discussed when writing for his first film score for *New Babylon*. He instead wanted his music to play an "independent role" and considered "Song of the Counterplan" to be organic and "felt everywhere." He also emphasized the idea of realism and the need to fulfill an "official function," hinting at the socialist realist function of his music in this film as per the studio's directive, and as realized in "Song of the Counterplan." These statements, therefore, reveal how, in retrospect, Shostakovich continued to perpetuate his principles from his earlier films and while keeping in line with accepted aesthetics for film music under socialist realism.[57]

The Song's multiple appearances and its flexibility allow it to act as a sophisticated and multivalent code, part of which is the result of this song's designation as the primary musical idea in the film. Others have noted the song's prominence since the film's premiere: Tatiana Egorova refers to it as a kind of "thesis" for the main theme of the film, while Khentova also claimed that the song was not intended to be "attached" to a specific character of the film, but to represent the "message" of the film.[58] The contemporaneous critic Mikhail Cheryomukhin also wrote,

> Not being associated with any concrete image or character from the film
> *Counterplan*, it ["Song of the Counterplan"] perfectly answered the general idea
> of its contents—energy, youth, vivacity.[59]

As Shostakovich described it, "Song of the Counterplan" first appears as a "general idea" at the beginning of the film over the credits in full chorus with orchestral accompaniment. It continues past the credits and into the film creating musical continuity or segue—a kind of overture that was similar to those in Hollywood films.[60] Using the song as an overture over the credits connects the film's thesis to music. This first appearance of the song as overture was noticed by scholars such as Khentova, Ioffe, and Egorova, who discussed Shostakovich's choice of an overture as a departure from the musical introductions of previous films and as a reference to operatic organizational structure.[61] This overture, which foreshadows both the musical and cinematic thesis of the film, becomes "organic," as Shostakovich suggested, just as an opera overture, or a contemporaneous Hollywood film introduces and connects the main musical and dramaturgical themes of a work.[62]

The next appearances of the Song are in the diegesis, sung by the one central female character in the film. In the first scene of the film, Katya sings the Song *a cappella*, finishing her rendition before she pokes at her husband to get out of bed. She sings the first verse and the refrain, repeating the last two lines of the refrain that refers to the glory of the country at the beginning of the day ("Vstayot strana so slavuyu/Na vstrechu dnya"). This is the second time that all of the words of the first stanza and refrain are heard; in this instance, however, it is clearer and in the diegetic foreground instead of the disembodied chorus of its first appearance in the overture. The Song appears a third time at the housewarming scene, where Katya sings the song three different times and in different ways. Sitting on the sofa, she sings the fourth verse of the song in minor mode and slowly, mirroring her melancholic state. Instead of singing in the standard duple meter version of the song heard in the score thus far, she sings in triple meter and plays a rhythm commonly used in the melodic line of a contemporaneous guitar/vocal piece—a waltz-like quarter note–dotted quarter–eighth note—before she fades out, leaving the verse unfinished. This kind of rhythm would be considered bourgeois for a song that is associated with socialism because it resembles the urban romance—a genre that was generally understood to be formalist by 1932. As Vasya walks over to a table, Katya picks up the guitar nearby and continues with the sixth verse of the song in minor mode with accompaniment (see Figure 5.1).

Her singing style resembles vocal/guitar salon music that uses the aforementioned rhythm in the melodic line, accompanied by strummed chords in the guitar on beats one and two. "Song of the Counterplan" thusly has transformed into a chamber piece that reflects the mood of the characters, in this case, the boredom of Katya and Vasya as they wait for Pavel. Just after Pavel finally arrives, Katya bounces around the apartment singing the song again, this time without lyrics, *a cappella*, and in its usual major mode and moderate tempo. After the three characters settle down, Katya begins to play the guitar and sing the sixth verse of song in major mode and with a more active left-hand articulation, before she is hushed by Vasya (see Video 5.3). ⏵ In this scene overall, Shostakovich demonstrates how he successfully varied the song depending on the mood of the characters and their situations, even within a short time frame, to become an "organic" part of the film. This scene also accentuates femininity—the song is associated with a female character (for the first and only time), a domestic setting, and an instrument known for its use at home and with possible bourgeois connotations. This domestic use of the song contrasts with the

Figure 5.1: Katya singing "Song of the Counterplan."

masculine ending of the scene, where the male choir singing "Partisan's Song" sounds beneath Pavel's determination for a counterplan.

Notably, Katya is the only character in the film that knows this song and sings it diegetically. It is strongly associated with her, and it changes according to her mood and the mood of the scene. She is the sole musically talented person in the film, and often serves as the sensitive (read: feminine) character who enthusiastically supports the men of the factory. Instead of using an ironic song to comment on a scene, as with "How Good Life Will Be" in *Alone*, Shostakovich used a sensitive, musical female character as his diegetic musical voice, a stark contrast to other borrowed songs such as "Partisan's Song" and "I Am Sad." This may be the kind of organicism and realism about which he wrote when referring to "Song of the Counterplan"—it becomes a song that anyone can use. The directors, Arnshtam, and Shostakovich gave Katya the power to voice the film's primary theme—she is the one diegetic entity to reflect and "realistically" musicalize the idea of the film from the composer's perspective, and (perhaps paradoxically) echo the masculine Soviet ideal associated with power and revolution at that point in filmmaking. Similar to Caryl Flinn's analysis of the female voice in Hollywood cinema, placing this song in Katya's voice could be read as a strengthening of the socialist realist meaning of the song and its potential for the Soviet every(wo)man.[63] This subtle choice of using a female character to voice a revolutionary song is continued in Shostakovich's later scores—notably in his score to *Girlfriends*.[64]

The Song makes its next appearance as a frame to the "White Nights" scene, initiating and completing the sequence. Moving between diegetic and non-diegetic space, the scene is initiated by a siren, which segues into "Song of the Counterplan" sung informally by people, with guitar accompaniment, in a passing boat on the Neva River. After the song is heard diegetically and fades when the boat floats out of the shot, the music shifts to the aforementioned underscored segment of music over a montage of images. At the end of this segment, the siren returns then disappears, and music of this segment continues along a normal tempo and changes to a new instrumental color (horns) before segueing into strings again; and lastly, a slow segue into "Song of the Counterplan," which accompanies Vasya's cheerful acceptance of Katya's love for Pavel (see Example 5.2e). The Song therefore acts as a frame for the "White Nights" scene, always murmuring in the background. It supports the main thesis of the film, as does the romantic sub-plot.

The Song as a code, in orchestral underscoring, acts as a sound bridge at the end of one sequence and into the next: Katya leaves Vasya alone on the embankment, while the music swells over the intertitles and over the fade and cut to the next scene where Babchenko and Lazarev work.[65] The orchestral version of the song ends with a firm cadence, as opposed to fading out, closing the form of the Song. The song comes to a cadence just before Lazarev speaks ("good work"), carefully timed to the exact second, contributing to the sense of a closed form. This form is similar to *Golden Mountains* and Hollywood films of this time; the song variation, which began at the end of the "White Nights" scene, has a closed form containing symmetrical and clear variations of the song phrases with closed cadences, fitting like a glove.[66] The "White Nights" scene and following scenes formally represent the film as a whole in its exactness of the timing between the music and image, and the episodic nature of the score.

The Song makes its last appearance at the end of the film, after the engineers find that the turbine is in working order. The moment that Babchenko's kopek balanced on the turbine stands on its own, the blast of the trumpet segues into another orchestral version of the sixth verse of the Song. This version, similar to earlier orchestral versions, continues over a montage of images of happy workers, Babchenko giving kittens to Vasya and Katya, and into the next scene where Babchenko stands at a dinner table while he prepares a toast.[67] The meaning of song-as-code completes in a rounded fashion; it is appropriate to use the last stanza of the song to end the film, just as the first stanza was used in the overture of the film and in Katya's singing of the song in the first scene. The song here not only celebrates the conclusion of the film, but it also operates as musical continuity; it links the scenes as they cut from one locale to another, as it also connects the entire film from beginning to end. In some of the orchestral parts for the film's recording, it is clear that Shostakovich linked the beginning and end through instrumentation—some of the parts included instruments associated with a folk orchestra, including *domra* and *balalaika*.[68] In the overture and in the "White Nights" scene, the song also acts as a kind of glue, playing over cuts (fades in and out) between different locales or ideas in the film. The Song's flexibility as a general "thesis" of the film, as opposed to a semantically fixed leitmotif, allows it to be exploited as a tool for musical continuity by the composer. Shostakovich ultimately managed to achieve some continuity in a fragmentary song score.

Compared to codes in Shostakovich's earlier film scores, "Song of the Counterplan" is more prominent than the episodes of general underscoring. Its careful placement throughout the film contributes to the "organic" quality that Shostakovich described, and led to the commonly held notion that the film's score was song-based.[69] As with *Golden Mountains*, this code unifies the film and what would normally be perceived as fragmented episodes. The song-code appears at moments to punctuate the action and often serves a link between disparate locales. The Song generally stands for the main theme of the film, but its transformations, particularly in the housewarming scene, show that it can relate more personally to the characters and their moods, ideas, and actions. Each time the code emerges it takes on another meaning. It builds into a representation of the general idea of the counterplan by the end of the film, narrating a parallel to the growth and enthusiasm of the workers. The Song's catchiness also lends itself to being remembered easily, thus reinforcing the code system that Shostakovich devised for the film.

Some scholars have theorized that "Song of the Counterplan" was successful because it emulated certain song styles or borrowed from past music, leading to charges of plagiarism. In her analysis, Egorova claimed that the tune is a combination of proletarian/post-revolutionary song and lyric song and uses the golden mean.[70] She also wrote that its symmetry, the rising fourths, and melodic structure allow this song to be an amalgamation of the above song styles that would speak to a contemporaneous listener. Citing L. Mazel, Khentova related that the song's "singability" in terms of intervallic construction, meter, and its clear melodic construction contributes to the song's popularity and effectiveness in the film.[71] Khentova related that scholars believed that Shostakovich's song resembled some melodies from Nikolay Rimsky-Korsakov's operas and popular songs by Aleksandr Chernyavsky and Aleksandr Vertinsky that might have led to the few charges of plagiarism that were leveled against him.[72] All of these descriptions are vague and interpretative. No one, including the composer, has written about the intended style of this song. Regardless of any possible influences, there is no evidence to suggest that Shostakovich plagiarized the song.

Undoubtedly, this song was the most popular aspect of the score. As a result, many people have tried to claim it as their own. Yutkevich claimed that the song resulted from his "initiative." [73] Khentova states that Ermler thought of it and Arnshtam helped in revising the song.[74] After Khentova's publication and Yutkevich's interview, Egorova also wrote that Ermler suggested the song.[75] The existing sketches of the song do suggest that Shostakovich went through many different variations and revisions, probably in consultation with the lyricist before it was finished.[76]

It has been commonly related that "Song of the Counterplan" underwent several transformations before it was completed.[77] Shostakovich commented, "I worked a lot on it [Song of the Counterplan], making ten variants, and only the eleventh satisfied me."[78] In her analysis of the song, Khentova shows nine variants of the song, from the beginning of the process to the final product. Her discussion highlighted how Shostakovich started with a small idea that was worked and reworked until finished.

Her observations came from fragments that were held in both the Glinka Museum of Musical Culture (VMOMK) and RGALI (via Arnshtam) as related at the time of her book's publication.[79] Some sketches from the archive of the Glinka Museum of Musical Culture, which are the ones with which Khentova also worked, show that Shostakovich did edit the song considerably.[80] Shostakovich moved between the keys of E-flat major, C major, and F major, eventually settling on F major. He also experimented with the contour of the melody, mostly trying to decide whether to begin with an ascent or descent. Some of sketches, probably the middle part of his process, showed Shostakovich trying to fit the syllables of the certain stanzas of the lyrics to the pitches.[81] Overall, the process shows that Shostakovich began working with the melody, eventually including the lyrics as part of his final sketching of the song.

The finished song has rising fourths and symmetry, and is in the key of F major, the key upon which Shostakovich decided for the final version of the song (see Figure 5.2).[82] The song was simply written, with clear antecedent-consequent phrases. The predominant interval is a fourth, found often at the beginnings and endings of the phrases. Another prominent and powerful trait is the octave leap in the last half of the second phrase, in some ways referencing the urban song tradition and lyrical Russian village music that Egorova mentions. The overall contour of the line—stepwise descent followed by a stepwise ascent that fills out the octave, with leaps of a fourth at either end of the phrase—in some ways does correspond to various song traditions, including urban song. The duple meter and the strong emphasis on the first beat of every measure also lend it a march-like quality reminiscent of revolutionary song.[83] The claim that the tune was built on previous song traditions, and the song's success and positive reception, may be explained by its clear harmonic and melodic structure and its allusions to contemporaneous song traditions.

Although a mix of borrowed and original songs and symphonic underscoring, the score to *Counterplan* is reliant on songs to unify the film. The variation of "Song of the Counterplan," within and outside the diegesis, unified the work at strategic dramaturgical points throughout the film. Other borrowed music, such as the Dargomïzhsky romance, the on-screen recorded gypsy romance, the "Partisan's Song," and the allusion to "Ryabinushka" all show how the composer used codes to simultaneously comment upon the overall theme of the film and the pro- or anti-Soviet nature of individual characters. The underscored music, including the repeated music from the turbine check scenes, the flag scene, and the music to the "White Nights" episode developed differently than "Song of the Counterplan." They were closed musical forms, often through-composed;

ВСТАЕТ СТРАНА СО СЛАВОЮ

Песня из фильма «Встречный»,
музыка Д. Шостаковича.

1.
Нас утро встречает прохладой,
Нас ветром встречает река.
Кудрявая, что ж ты не рада
Веселому пенью гудка?

ПРИПЕВ:
Не спи, вставай, кудрявая,
В цехах звеня,
Встает страна со славою
На встречу дня.

2.
И радость поет не скончая,
И песня навстречу идет,
И люди смеются, встречая,
И встречное солнце встает.

ПРИПЕВ:
Горячее и бравое,
Бодрит меня,
Страна встает со славою
На встречу дня.

3.
Бригада нас встретит работой,
И ты улыбнешься друзьям,
С которыми труд и заботы,
И встречный, и жизнь пополам.

ПРИПЕВ:
За Нарвскою заставою,
В громах, в огнях,
Страна встает со славою
На встречу дня.

4.
И с ней до победного края
Ты, молодость наша, пройдешь,
Покуда не выйдет вторая
Навстречу тебе молодежь.

ПРИПЕВ:
И в жизнь вбежав правою,
Отцов сменя,
Страна встает со славою
На встречу дня.

5.
И радость никак не запрятать,
Когда барабанщики бьют:
Навстречу идут октябрята,
Картавые песни поют.

ПРИПЕВ:
Отважные, картавые
Слова звенят,
Страна встает со славою
На встречу дня.

6.
Такою прекрасною речью
О правде своей заяви.
Мы жизни выходим навстречу,
Навстречу труду и любви!

ПРИПЕВ:
Любить грешно ль, кудрявая,
Когда, звеня,
Встает страна со славою
На встречу дня?

Figure 5.2: The "Song of the Counterplan" as it appears in the newspaper *Komsomol'skaya pravda*, 11 November 1932.

From *Komsomol'skaya pravda*, "Vstayet strana so slavoyu," 11 November 1932. The song appears here in the same key and meter as it does in the manuscripts and in the published excerpt in the older *Collected Works* (Yakubov, *Sobraniye Sochineniy v soroka dvukh tomakh, tom 41*, 477).

or if they recurred, the music remained the same as the context changed. The variety of the quoted songs, the strong and well-articulated presence of the film's main song-code, and the concise and economic use of a small amount of underscoring (compared to *New Babylon*) contributed to the characterization that *Counterplan* was the first true non-symphonic "song score" that would become the standard for many Soviet films in the thirties.

RECEPTION

According to many reviewers in the press, *Counterplan* was an overwhelming success. Almost every review of the film began with a statement about how it was a contribution to the "construction of socialist art," and foreshadowed what would become the common rhetoric of Stalinist socialist realism. One critic from *Komsomol'skaya pravda* considered the film to be of "Soviet quality," while another from *Sovetskoye iskusstvo* considered *Counterplan* to be a true "mass film." Two years prior to the official establishment of socialist realism, this same critic from *Sovetskoye iskusstvo* related that lately "we have talked a lot about socialist realism in art," and continued to proclaim that *Counterplan* was built on "cinematographic realism." The critic claimed,

> We see as this realism principle the rich combining of the elements of healthy romanticism, happy comedy, light grotesque irony, spelled out in the practice of Soviet cinematography. Not only [should there be] arguments about the creative method, but also the practical one. And we see how this principle is used to ensure the correctness and lucidity of the film.[84]

The realism, or socialist realism, described here includes elements such as "grotesque irony" as part of this burgeoning realist aesthetic. Notably, these elements were received as having a realist purpose as opposed to a formalist one, as was also attempted, but badly received, in Shostakovich's previous scores to films such as *Alone*. Other reviews of the film similarly regarded it as entirely socialist and intelligible, or flatly rejected the possibility that any of its elements were formalist. P. A. Blyakhin, the current deputy chairman of Glavrepetkom, commented that the "director-communists"

> refuse to have elements or vestiges of intelligent aesthetics and formalism, which were still visible in *Golden Mountains* (Yutkevich) and in *Fragment of an Empire* (the last work of Ermler).[85]

Critics from *Kino* also alluded to the film's lack of formalism by stating that
the film was not "experimental," but instead "emotional" and "victorious,"[86]
while those from *Pravda*, considered the input of real-life workers as a key
to the film's authenticity, realism, and ultimately its success.[87] Words such
as "lyricism," "organicism," and "authenticity" also alluded to the film's successful application of realism.[88] Still other critics focused on the film's lack
of stereotypes as an example of its realism, while others considered the
film generally successful in its balancing of socialism and entertainment.
Alternatively, film and literary professionals such as Grigory Kozintsev,
Bela Balázs, and Viktor Shklovsky—and party officials and known critics such as Boris Shumyatsky and Mikhail Bleiman—entered into heated
debates about the film's narrative, plot, and representation of the characters, and argued that the film lacked clarity and the character development.
Although most viewers appeared to celebrate the film and its successful
realism, the elements of an intelligible and well-crafted film were still hotly
debated among its specialists.

As with *Golden Mountains*, Shostakovich considered *Counterplan* to be
a turning point in his film music career likely because it was one of his
first full-sound film scores and among the first to be considered successful.[89] Unlike *Golden Mountains*, however, *Counterplan* was an enormous
success, particularly in terms of sound design. The film's reviews were
suspiciously hyped to be excessively positive, having almost no critical
commentary except from specialists; and the reviews praised the Soviet
ideology in tandem with the film's sophisticated sound design and quality.
Although the focus of several reviews was on the idea of the counterplan
and on art imitating life or its intelligibility, there were some reviews of the
sound and music. Outside of the hyped Song, the timing, volume, nuance,
speech, and other quirkier aspects of the sounds design were praised, placing Shostakovich alongside the sound designers Volk and Arnshtam. The
Song, however, was the most enduring musical aspect of the score, becoming reused, recomposed, and re-signified decades later. Its popularity and
relative sophistication in sound design made *Counterplan* the greatest success of Soviet sound film in its time.

The press mostly agreed that *Counterplan* was the best socialist film in
terms of sound and dramaturgical construction, especially compared to
earlier films such as *Golden Mountains* and *Men and Jobs* (dir. Aleksandr
Macheret, 1932).[90] Although rarely providing detail as to what was particularly good about the soundtrack, other newspapers agreed that the
speech, music, and sound effects were integrally well connected with
the images in the film. At times, aspects of the sound design were considered as equally important as Shostakovich's music.[91] One critic from

Kino specifically mentioned and praised Arnshtam and Volk along with Shostakovich for the high quality of the sound:

> The famous composer D[mitry] Shostakovich wrote interesting music. Especially successful were the moments of powerful dramaturgical sound and soft lyrics, which permeate some scenes (the morning [scene], white nights [scene]). The quality of the sound in this film exceeds all that has been achieved in this respect to Soviet cinematography. And here one needs to give credit to the magnificent work of the sound designer L[eo] Arnshtam and sound designer [Ilya] Volk.[92]

Shostakovich's music was still well noted, despite the sometimes equal attention granted to all aspects of the sound design. The critic for *Izvestiya*, who wrote that "it is impossible not to note the good music of Shostakovich and the splendid quality of the sound," agreed with the assessment of *Counterplan* as a better model for sound film in regard to its score and dialogue.[93] *Vechernyaya Moskva* briefly described Shostakovich's music and the sounds of the factory as effective and of "great artistic taste."[94] *Sovetskoye iskusstvo* went as far as to suggest that Shostakovich's music was an "organic" part of the film, a comment that echoed Shostakovich's earlier writings about scoring:

> The music of Shostakovich is organically integrated into the general artistic system and construction of the film. Its role is not only to escort or accompany. The music in *Counterplan* not only talentedly [*talantlivo*] accentuates the situation—it is, together with the other forms of art, united in sound film to help in revealing these situations; it analyzes the separate episodes and imparts the appropriate ideological-semantic sound sequence of events. The wonderful sound of this film should be noted in the exemplary film theater "Udarnik."[95]

This reviewer considered Shostakovich's music to be not only integral to the sound design but also ideologically appropriate, that is, effectively socialist realist. Significantly, there is no mentioning of any formalism or shortcomings in any aspect of the overall sound design, including Shostakovich's music.

Even the often critical film music scholar Ioffe found Shostakovich's music to be effective, focusing on how the score provided the appropriate expression needed for the images. He related,

> In *Counterplan* Shostakovich enriches the graphic means of the music with a musical processing of noise and sounds, transforming the latter into emotional-expressive musical elements. There is the clatter and the din of the factory which

is carrying out a counter plan, [and] the noise and clatter of a factory on break. Here Shostakovich not only provides a sound life of a factory which is not present in *Golden Mountains*, but also saturates the music of a machine emotionally, making it express the experiences of the people working at the factory. It is the same way in the episode of the "White Night[s]," [where] the clatter of masons turns into the cheerful playing of xylophones... He has moved notably from technologism and grotesque music to human [and] social experiences.[96]

Typically, Ioffe negatively reviewed Shostakovich's early film scores.[97] Here, however, he praised *Counterplan* through comparison to the failed endeavor of *Golden Mountains*, implying that *Counterplan* was in line with current ideological beliefs, that is, it was appropriately intelligible. Instead of hearing the "cheerful playing of the xylophones" as grotesque, which could be one probable interpretation, he congratulated Shostakovich on being more "human" in his musical expression, a positive socialist realist quality that was preferable to any modernist, that is, grotesque, experimentation with sound, especially by 1932. Depicting Shostakovich as more humane and less grotesque reveals the intensity of the hype created around this film and its release, and a desire to portray him as appropriately socialist realist.

Even with the praise of other aspects of the score, Shostakovich's scoring and his "Song of the Counterplan" were the best received parts of the soundtrack. Many newspapers, scholars, and film music history texts gushed about the full Soviet grandeur of the song and its timely and effective representation of socialist ideals. *Vecherniy Leningrad* wrote in praise of "Song of the Counterplan" and quotes some of its text, while *Komsomol'skaya pravda* provided the text from the song and a full reproduction of the music in the column to the right of an article (see Figure 5.2).[98] Every history text over the course of the past fifty years, including those of Egorova, Frid, the *Composers of Soviet Cinema*, to mention a few, all discussed *Counterplan* as having had a major impact because of its "Song of the Counterplan."[99] In 1935, only three years after the premiere, Arnshtam commented,

> Truly, in *Counterplan* there was greater success. This success was the little song, which is sung now by millions of workers in the Soviet Union.[100]

The song "flew" off the screen, as reviewers have noted, and was used in festivals, demonstrations, and played on the Moscow radio, becoming familiar to millions of people.[101] In his description of the success of the song, Shostakovich prided himself and boasted that it even became a wedding song in Switzerland.[102] It also became popular in various countries for at least ten years after its release.[103]

Writing in 1950, Shostakovich remarked with satisfaction on how successful this song had become, and how it had outlived the film and became a separate entity. Shostakovich made a point of reusing the Song in *Moscow, Cheryomushki* in 1959, and he wrote several letters to Stalin reminding him of the Song's success in order to negotiate his position and fame.[104] This Song was celebrated abroad, and was taken as a symbol of Soviet-American alliance during the Second World War. Harold Rome, an American song composer for film and theater, arranged and wrote new English lyrics to the song in 1942 and published it in the United States as the "United Nation's March."[105] This song was used shortly thereafter in an American film in 1943 called *Thousands Cheer* (dir. George Sidney). This film was a megamusical production, with numerous Hollywood stars such as Gene Kelly and Judy Garland, featuring the MGM orchestra with Jose Iturbi conducting. "Song of the Counterplan," disguised as the "United Nations March," appears at the end of the film as a climax, with the UN Chorus singing the new lyrics such as "the hope of humanity singing; song rising strong from the earth." (See Figure 5.3.)

This film was designed to be a patriotic pick-me-up for the American viewers during the Second World War. Since the United States and the

Figure 5.3: The UN Chorus at the end of *Thousands Cheer.*

Soviet Union were allies for a brief time, it was no surprise that a *New York Times* reviewer noted that in addition to tons of Hollywood stars, there was

> All this, we might say, and Shostakovitch, [*sic*] too, for the Soviet composer's "United Nations Salute" is performed under Mr. Iturbi's baton as the thundering climax.[106]

The reviewer clearly recognized Shostakovich as a Soviet composer, in this case, one who unwittingly contributed to the Allied cause implied by this musical film. The musical markers of this song that make up a narrative complex (that is, the duple march, singable melody, etc.), therefore, appear to have resonated with Rome, and with the producers of *Thousands Cheer*, to signify patriotism, unity, and utopic optimism. Although *Counterplan* was concerned with a specifically pro-Soviet agenda and *Thousands Cheer* a collection of musical skits, the sentiment was similar enough between them for this song to act as a thesis for both films.[107]

Counterplan, indeed, was a turning point in Shostakovich's "film life." The film was remarkably and unpredictably successful for its time, partly because of its famed "Song of the Counterplan," the strength of the sound design in a truly full-sound score, and importantly the strongly enforced Soviet ideology, that is, "intelligibility," espoused by the studio. As with other film scores, codes were developed throughout, but the primary difference with this score was its intense popularity in a watershed year for Soviet history. The underscoring was planned and executed well, sounding as "seamless" as Hollywood films of the thirties.[108] Largely due to improvements in sound technology and Shostakovich's increased sensitivity to scoring-under voices and sounds, the underscoring became almost "imperceptible."[109] Those writing about the music at the time, including scholars such as Ioffe, were supportive of the score and eschewed any criticism or claims of grotesquerie or inappropriate use of the music and images. Significantly, "Song of the Counterplan" represented the film and its thesis, complementing current strategies employed for Soviet propaganda.

The overwhelmingly positive reception and the lack of recognized formalist problems in *Counterplan* reveals the beginning of the potential for state-controlled reception that continued under Stalinism. Even at the All-Union Conference on Thematic Planning in 1933, *Counterplan* was deemed "the leading model for entertainment film."[110] The theme of the film and its adherence to what was considered realism at the time (the "authentic" input of the factory workers, the mythology of the counterplan in life and art) foreshadowed what would later be deemed "socialist realist."[111] The music, particularly "Song of the Counterplan," resonated with the imaginations of some film critics and film music scholars of the time and throughout the twentieth century. This may have been because the song's style seemed inexplicably familiar to listeners, and the film was supported by the state and resonated well with state politics, especially after the reorganization of 23 April 1932. The ideology that this film encapsulated, and the ability for "Song of the Counterplan" to live beyond the film's premiere allowed *Counterplan* to become the model for many Soviet films of the thirties. It firmly and successfully established Shostakovich's career as a film composer in the eyes of the state and of the public.

The song-score of *Counterplan* essentially freed Shostakovich from his past "failures" (as viewed from 1932 and forward) and became canonized as Shostakovich's first major film score success. It also became the approach to scoring that he used in his following film scores, including the *Maxim Trilogy*. Because *Counterplan* was a song-based score with separate and episodic yet strategically placed independent fragments, it became the norm for the thirties, when scores became less "symphonic" in Arnshtam's sense of the term. This may have resulted from the influence of *Counterplan* and also from the collective experience that other new film composers may have learned from their work with realist film. It may be, therefore, that underscored music in realist film, as it was in Hollywood in the thirties, was fated to be "imperceptible" because music that was too complex and therefore too easily heard would be considered inappropriate, or in the language of Soviet times, "formalist." Shostakovich's score, resulting from his experience with modernism, and his growth into a film composer who was able to adapt to the socialist realist aesthetic (along with directors Kozintsev, Trauberg, Ermler, Yutkevich, and Arnshtam) became the foundation for Soviet film scoring in the thirties. Despite the need to create film music that would be "intelligible to millions," Shostakovich still managed to maintain the imprint of his personal musical style, such as the creative thematic transformation of "Song of the Counterplan," without being regarded as "grotesque" or "inhuman"—characterizations that the total code of the Song carefully avoided.

Two films—*Golden Mountains* and *Counterplan*—were created during two years that saw significant changes in the role of film and film music that called for topics of socialist reconstruction and growth. Each of these films fulfilled that requirement. *Counterplan*, however, was far more successful because of its politics, its realism, and its omnipresent Song. In 1936, on the heels of the *Pravda* attack on *Lady Macbeth of Mtsensk District*, Sergey Bugoslavsky listed *Counterplan* as the first instance in which Shostakovich "forgot" how to be "intricate and original," and his true talent shined through. [112] In 1950, Tikhon Khrennikov's assessment of Shostakovich also agrees with Bugoslavsky's declaration fourteen years earlier, where he listed Shostakovich's *New Babylon, Alone,* and *Golden Mountains* as formalist excursions, while praising his "Song of the Counterplan" as a brilliant and appropriately Soviet example of his work.[113] Such political hype continued to build in more meanings for the code of the film's representative Song, being both a model for Soviet filmmaking for decades afterward and a classic of Soviet cinema. In press from the Soviet 1980s such language surfaced, though tempered somewhat, praising *Counterplan* as exemplary and notable because of its multivalent song-as-code; even fifty years after the premiere, and almost forty years after its recomposition in the United States.[114] "Song of the Counterplan" and the film's score thus became one of Shostakovich's greatest political and musical successes.

CHAPTER 6

∽

Youth of Maxim (1934–1935) and the Minimal Score

Of all of Shostakovich's early film scores, his work for *Yunost' Maksima* (*Youth of Maxim*, dirs. Grigory Kozintsev and Leonid Trauberg, 1934–35), and the following films in the trilogy, was the most successful although exceptionally minimal. *Youth of Maxim* was received well, rivaling the popularity of another recent hit, *Chapayev* (dirs. Georgy and Sergey Vasil'yev, 1934). Although he would go on to write significantly more original music for *Vozvrashcheniye Maksima* (*Return of Maxim*, 1937) and *Viborgskaya storona* (*Vyborg Side*, 1939), *Youth of Maxim* was an unusual experiment with diegetic sound and speech, and near lack of original underscoring. Shostakovich contributed music to the Prologue of the film, a segment that represented an extension of his previous work with the directors Kozintsev and Trauberg. The remaining music and sound consisted primarily of songs, and was musically edited with some support from the composer. Shostakovich's involvement was minimal and often indirect in this film; his thoughts on image and sound that began to take form in the late 1920s, particularly in collaboration with Kozintsev and Trauberg, were evident in its sound design. The manner in which the directors used musical sound was also an extension of their work with the composer over the course of almost six years. This certain use of diegetic song suggests that Shostakovich's theories about sound and image persisted through the directors' choices despite his relatively minimal involvement in this score. Shostakovich's influence therefore peers through, blurring the line between director and composer, and emphasizing the collaborative approach that would persist into some of Shostakovich's final scores.[1] As such, it is imperative to consider the sound design as a whole, as with his earlier film scores; the musical choices made by the directors and the composer, and Shostakovich's direct contribution in the form of the Prologue are integral to film, and demonstrate that scoring is frequently a process informed by multiple authors.

THE IDEA OF THE (MALE) HERO

During the 1920s, the notion of the war/historical film centering on a single hero gained popularity and became a common type in 1930s cinema. In the mid-1930s, such films as *Chapayev, Youth of Maxim, Girlfriends* (1935–36), and others established the idea of the male hero (or three heroines) rising from a peasant upbringing and maturing into an urban revolutionary.[2] The directors, Kozintsev and Trauberg, spent years formulating *Youth of Maxim* as a story of an apathetic factory worker who is encouraged to become a leading revolutionary because of several life-changing events, including the death of his friends and exposure to underground Bolsheviks. The film was immensely successful; and due to its success, the directors wrote extensively on the process of finding the hero trope and developing Maxim as a sympathetic, attractive, and winsome Russian character, initially akin to a revolutionary *Till Eulenspiegel*.[3] The idea of a trilogy—the addition of *Return of Maxim* and *Vyborg Side*—came about gradually, and by 1932 they had decided they would have a three-part account of the hero's life.[4] According to Kozintsev's accounts, they began developing the idea of the hero at the time they were also completing *Alone*, from 1929–30.[5] The first film was finished in 1934 and released to the general public in January 1935, several years after its initial conception.[6] Their work on the two separate films of *Alone* and *Youth of Maxim* overlapped, and shared some characteristics of the lone individual's development as part of the socialist plan. *Youth of Maxim*, however, appeared to be more special to the directors in formulating the perfect happy-go-lucky, Soviet-appropriate hero. Much of Kozintsev's and Trauberg's writings focus on this conception and development, moving between the discussions of the pre-revolutionary era, the notion of a figure appropriate for depicting the past as well as current 1930s trends of the Soviet hero, and the musical formulations of an epoch.[7]

With this film overlapping with *Alone*, the directors decidedly divided the role of sound in each film differently—*Alone* would be musical while speech would be favored over scoring in *Youth of Maxim*. In justifying the lack of original underscoring, Kozintsev and Trauberg both wrote that speech would be favored over non-diegetic music for several reasons. Trauberg related that *Alone* would have little dialogue, so "continuous, varied, and brilliant" music would be written by Shostakovich instead; whereas *Youth of Maxim* would favor dialogue, with the exception of Shostakovich's contribution to the Prologue.[8] Trauberg's statement implies the difficulty that they had with recording speech in *Alone*, where they realized too late in the process that continuous dialogue would be impossible.[9] *Youth of Maxim*, then, became an opportunity to explore the possibilities of a design that was dominated by dialogue and source sound.

Despite the minimal original scoring, Kozintsev related that music played a dominant role in the conception of the film and development of its hero. Citing how several of the film's diegetic songs came to him, the director mapped how each song functioned as narrative in the story of the film; the importance of music was clear in the directors' handwritten notes and scenarios.[10] Only partially a result of technological necessity, Kozintsev considered diegetic song more real, that is, closer to the hero's story, which justified his preference of source sound over original scoring.[11] Throughout the film, each song, whether sung by characters or played on *bayan*, is carefully timed within and aligned with specific scenes. [12] The intentional use of ambient sound, including that of factories or trains, also reveals how the directors were playing with sound. The careful use of sound bridges, timings, and sound montages aptly demonstrate that they were continuing some of the same sound/music experiments of their previous works, while integrating the design into a laboriously crafted story.[13]

SONG

The directors were specific in their choices of songs, their narrative function, and type of ensemble, and how these factors would create a sense of time and space. These songs are all diegetic, emanating from the world of the characters, and designed to illustrate the scene as much as costume, lighting, or *mise-en-scène*. Only one song runs throughout *Youth of Maxim*, and the remaining films of the trilogy; the others are more localized and structurally support particular scenes. Some are for voice and *bayan* or guitar, while others are for *a cappella* solo or chorus. Song serves a direct purpose, and acts as code—to illustrate the world of the characters, their class divisions, their struggles, and the overall theme of revolution and the ideal hero.

The most recognizable song from the film, "Krutitsya, vertitsya shar goluboy . . ." (Whirling, twirling blue ball . . .), functions as the only leitmotif in the film.[14] (See Example 6.1.) The film begins with Maxim singing it as he

Example 6.1: "Krutitsya vertitsya shar goluboy . . . ," (Whirling, twirling blue ball. . .) from the beginning of the film.
Transcription by the author and Christian Anderson.

walks into the frame; reappears when the three friends meet before work at the factory; and returns at the end. It is sometimes accompanied by off-screen *bayan*.

Typically, in revolutionary films with male protagonists, *a cappella* folk song represents the working-class attributes of the hero and his connection to the revolution.[15] Kozintsev struggled with the choice of this song, writing that they had long been considering which song would best suit the character of Maxim and the environment in which his heroism would be born. After listening to Boris Chirkov, the actor who played Maxim, sing some village songs, Kozintsev related, "We began to look for songs that would be a different color [*kolorit*], not a village [color], and at the same time not be of operetta or *chantant*."[16] When Kozintsev heard "Whirling, twirling . . ." on the street played by an accordionist, he decided that it would be the song for Maxim, saying that it brought to his imagination images of an "ugly life" and within it, a sudden appearance of a "great, lyrical song."[17] The directors set the song to clearly represent Maxim and his happy-go-lucky sensibility within a drab urban context—he is an embodiment of the song at every point. He sings it solo at two points in the film—during the credits and at the end—and sings it as part of an ensemble when making merry with his friends on their way to the factory at the start of the film proper. ⏵ (See Figure 6.1 and Video 6.1.) Only once does the song manifest in the *bayan*, an instrument that follows him and other characters in the diegesis. In the last shots of the film, Maxim walks away from the camera as the *bayan* takes up the song that he started in the previous scene with Natasha, forming a sound bridge between locales (from inside to the countryside), and acting as a kind of underscoring to Maxim's departure.[18] The song appears only at times of gleeful happiness, showing a facet of Maxim's character that disappears in more serious moments in the film. Nonetheless, it traveled into the

Scene/context	Song/style/genre
Opening of film, before credits	"Krutitsya, vertitsya shar goluboy..." a cappella, solo
(Prologue) Beginning party scene (after the sledding)	"Oira Polka" on *bayan*
(Prologue) Party of the Elite	Waltz on piano
Maxim, Dyoma, and Andrey meet before work	"Krutitsya, vertitsya shar goluboy..." a cappella, trio
Maxim on street; political meeting; mourning Andrey's death	Waltz on *bayan* (three times); additional flourish after the *bayan* player sits with Maxim
Death of another co-worker; carrying of the body; street protest	"Vy zhertvoyu pali," a cappella, chorus
Maxim and Polivanov, in prison	"Varshyanka," a cappella, chorus
Maxim at the lake and outdoor meeting	"Lyublyu Ya letom s udochkoi..." guitar and voice
Saying goodbye to Natasha; cut to him walking away in the countryside	"Krutitsya, vertitsya shar goluboy..." a cappella, solo then *bayan*

Figure 6.1: List of songs and their appearances in *Youth of Maxim.*

last two films of the trilogy as his leitmotif, and became the most recognizable song of the film series.

Unlike the trilogy's leitmotif, other instances of song—for *bayan*, piano, or voices—appear in the narrative locally. Some songs are contained within a few moments in a scene, while others act as bridges across episodes. The first time the *bayan* player appears alone is after the opening of the Prologue. The player continues one of the songs that Shostakovich quotes, "Oira Polka," as he walks with New Year's revelers. The *bayan* player acts as a kind of folk character (he is listed in the opening credits), observing and commenting on the action through music, similar to the holy fool (*yurodivyi*) in *King Lear*, a later collaboration with Kozintsev and Shostakovich.[19] Each song that he performs is localized in the sense that it continues a musical thought (as with "Oira Polka"), or runs as a thread through a set of scenes. In his second appearance, he plays a waltz as he meets Maxim on the street and wanders through the frame, almost as a kind of diegetic musical commentary. When he next appears, he is still playing, and musically continues from the point where he exited as he makes his way to a political meeting. He lastly appears, yet again offscreen at first, when Maxim is mourning.

The only time he speaks in the film is when he approaches Maxim to comfort him, after which he performs a brief flourish (see Figure 6.2). This idea of making music itself a diegetic character, particularly that of a *bayan* player, achieves what Kozintsev claimed the directors wanted—to represent the epoch through contemporaneous music.[20]

The music associated with the partying aristocracy in the Prologue of the film narrates differently than the *bayan* songs. Although the *bayan* player firstly emerges with the partying bourgeoisie, his later associations with Maxim and the workers clearly establish him as a sympathetic revolutionary character. A waltz on piano, followed by an accompanied song in the apartment of aristocratic revelers takes a different tone. Just as the *bayan* narrates the workers, an offscreen waltz on piano narrates the scene in the apartment where Polivanov encounters an old colleague who insists that the revolutionary spirit is dead. His speech clearly supports a bourgeois inclination, with music supporting him. In opposition, Polivanov eventually leaves, only to be nearly run down by the party exploding in the foyer into a parade of people, with a token euphonium player and makeshift

Figure 6.2: The *bayan* player.

percussion. Music serves an illustrative purpose, according to Kozintsev—
to show the pre-revolutionary epoch in its "stupidity" and "pathos."[21]

In contrast to the songs of the character of the *bayan* and "Whirling,
twirling . . . ," the song "Lyublyu Ya letom s udochkoi" (I Love Summer
with a Fishing Pole) operates subversively in the hands of Maxim. At the
denouement of the film, where the workers have organized an outdoor
meeting in the country, Maxim serves as a gatekeeper by singing "I Love
Summer . . ." self-accompanied on guitar. Taking on the air of a loung-
ing, indifferent peasant, he directs inquiring people to the next gatekeeper, who pretends to be fishing, before making their way to the hidden
meeting (see Figure 6.3).

This song, with lyrics about a carefree summer life fishing at the creek, is
based on the pattern of a popular song waltz with triple meter and chords
on two and three.[22] (See Figure 6.4.) Its style is consistent with Kozintsev's
desire for songs of the epoch; this style of song was popular at the end of
the nineteenth century, and continued to be popular into the twentieth
century.[23] This song continues to be recognized today; at the time of the
film's release and shortly thereafter, Chirkov's ability to sing and play led
some to believe that Maxim was a real person, while others still associate
this song with the character Maxim, neglecting any other history of it.[24]

Figure 6.3: Maxim with guitar singing "Lyublyu Ya letom s udochkoi" (I Love Summer with
a Fishing Pole).

Lyrics to "Lyublyu Ya letom s udochkoi," first stanza	
Люблю я летом с удочкой	I love summer with a fishing pole
Над речкою сидеть,	Along the creek I sit,
Бутылку водки с рюмочкой	A bottle of vodka and a glass
В запас с собой иметь.	From my own reserve.
Бутылку водки с рюмочкой	A bottle of vodka and a glass
В запас с собой иметь.	From my own reserve.

Figure 6.4: First stanza from "Lyublyu Ya letom s udochkoi" (I Love Summer with a Fishing Pole) from *Youth of Maxim*.

This song was clearly effective for audiences, and blurred the line between reality and fiction—a common goal of Soviet film in persuading audiences to believe in the socialist cause.

Ensemble is another factor that emphasizes song as representative of solidarity and power. Most of the songs in the film, of the *bayan* player or sung by Maxim and his crew, are for solo or small group, acting as commentary in the case of *bayan*, or as the representation of a character. Two songs, "Varshavyanka" (Warsaw Song) and "Vy zhertvoyu pali" (You Fell Victim), are performed as large ensemble numbers within the diegesis, both in moments that signify revolution.[25] "You Fell Victim" emanates only from the characters, after a second worker is killed in the factory. The men gather around the body, and start singing as they pick up and carry the body into the streets. The singing group of men continues over several cuts, following them as they stop in the street. Even the *bayan* player, who emerges from the bar with Dyoma playing "Whirling, twirling . . .," immediately halts and starts playing the same song as the workers—a clear illustration of his position as worker/sympathetic observer and commentator. Facing the police, they revolt; at which point, Maxim reveals his revolutionary leanings. This song, a kind of funeral march, was famous and strongly associated with the revolution and with death by the 1930s.[26] The associations are clearly understood and reinforced here: the song is the narration of their collective breaking point and revolt. There is no indication that Shostakovich necessarily chose this song to narrate this scene; the directors could have been as familiar with it as the composer. The song does appear later, however, in Shostakovich's Symphony No.11 (1957) and his film score to the *Great Citizen* (1937–39).

The other revolutionary song, "Warsaw Song," similarly expresses the solidarity of the workers. While in prison, Polivanov tells Maxim to sing with him.[27] In an act of defiance, he begins, and Maxim takes his cue as they work through the stanzas of the song. The other imprisoned workers hear their song and pick up one by one creating a chorus divided by the prison walls. Similar to "You Fell Victim," this tune has roots in revolution, and initially was a Polish revolutionary song.[28] It was frequently played during the time of the revolution and the Civil War, building associations with that period.[29] Just as with the previous song, "Warsaw Song" plays on nostalgia, demonstrates solidarity of the workers, and reinforces the narrative. Choosing two obvious and recognizable revolutionary songs to be diegetically sung by a choral ensemble was a sure bet—Kozintsev kept to the intention to illustrate the era, and audiences immediately identified with the associations.

Other diegetic sounds, from footsteps to factory whistles, were illustrative of the era, the diegesis, and of the theme of revolutionary struggle. Several moments in the film have added, overdubbed sound—such as Polivanov's footsteps as he climbs to his upstairs apartment before he encounters the police—this overdubbing allowed for a sweetened effect. Such moments as these were carefully chosen; plenty of others could have had synced sound, but were silenced instead, such as the sound of the train over the speech of the engineer near the end of the film. Still other moments were "mickey-moused"—the moment the owner of the factory raises his hand to silence the crowd, a machine sound accompanies his action, comically satirizing his speech. More obvious segments of machine-as-soundscape are created to underscore the cemetery scene and Maxim's escape. The arrangement of overdubbed factory whistles act as a kind of underscoring to Maxim as he stands in the cemetery during Andrey's funeral. This kind of sound collage is reminiscent of experiments of the 1920s with urban sounds in the concert hall—a modernist way of engaging discourses about the masses and urban soundscapes.

Similarly experimental is the music that is heard diegetically during Maxim's escape from the police, who invade the secret meeting at the end of the film. After Maxim spots (and is spotted by) the bourgeois family enjoying their picnic, complete with phonograph playing a song, he runs away while being accompanied by that song offscreen—an effective sound bridge, and demonstration of aural dominance of the very people chasing him.

Weaving together diegetically presented urban sounds as a form of narrative was familiar to the directors. They experimented similarly in *Alone* with the hut scene and the use of the hurdy-gurdy; and other scores by Shostakovich including *Golden Mountains* also played with the concept of machine-as-orchestra.[30] As with *Alone*, trends in sound design of the 1920s still persisted into the 1930s under the pretenses of something more realist—such modernist experiments found an inconspicuous place to finally function as real.

SHOSTAKOVICH'S PROLOGUE

Although it is his only direct contribution to the score, Shostakovich's music to the Prologue also continues many of the experiments of his past collaborations with the directors. Kozintsev and Trauberg agreed to have Shostakovich write only for the opening of the film because of their intent to experiment with diegetic song that was representative of the era, and because overdubbing sound was prohibitively difficult.[31] Concentrating on era-specific songs was important to Kozintsev in particular, who wrote that music of the turn of the century would properly evoke pre-revolutionary Russia, focusing specifically on "Oira Polka" as an example of the "pathos" and "stupidity" of the time.[32] Kozintsev wanted to have several kinds of music that were characteristic of 1910—"the 'Oira,' a gypsy choir, the singing of some sort of cabaret singer, [and] maybe the Krakowiak."[33] Shostakovich obliged by introducing a version of these styles/tunes in layers for his minute and half of music for the opening.[34] This segment is clearly demarcated into smaller sections, with a total of six segments that repeat. Within each segment, there are mostly symmetrical statements of the respective borrowed songs of 1910. The divisions of segments and layering of tunes are visible at-a-glance in Figure 6.5.

The first four segments (A–D) contain the borrowed songs: "a+b" is the "Oira Polka"; "c+c" is the Krakowiak; and "d" is "Ochi chyorny" (Dark Eyes).[35] Each musical idea is introduced every sixteen measures, layered atop another, eventually make way for the transition to the solo soprano section (Section F, segment e). As with his previous experiments in layering quoted material in *New Babylon* and *Alone*, Shostakovich positions different choirs of instruments against each other. The "Oira" is nervously set for winds, the Krakowiak in the brass, and "Ochi chyorny" in the strings. ▶ (See Video 6.2.) Each instrument group also takes on the characteristics common to their song's practice—the winds have faster hectic rhythms that mimic the ornamental variations common to polkas, the trumpets play a lead strident melody over the ensemble typical for polka bands, and the strings (with support from tuba and trombones) repeat the sequences common to orchestrations of the song. The long-held associations of winds and brass with polka bands, and strings with romance and so-called "gypsy songs" such as "Ochi chyorny" contribute to the clashing of these ideas and associations, acting as codes and achieving what Kozintsev called "the

A	B	C	D	E	F	E	A (cut)	B	C′ (cut)	D′ (cut)	E′
Intro+a+b	a+b	a+b	a+b′	e	e′	Repeat	Repeat	Repeat	Different voicing (strings)	Different voicing (strings)	Same rhythm
	c+c	c+c		unison	solo soprano						
		d	d								

Figure 6.5: Graph of segments in Shostakovich's music for the Prologue. Segments A, C′, D′ were cut in the previously cited commercial version of the film, but are written out in the published score. See also Yakubov, *Collected Works*, vol. 41.

я футболистка, в футбол играю	I am a footballer, I play football
свои ворота я защищаю.	My goal I defend.
напрасно	In vain
я ножки сжала	I gripped my legs
мяч проскочил	The ball slipped
я проиграла!	I lost!

Figure 6.6: Lyrics from Shostakovich's contribution to the Prologue, as heard in the film.

monstrous cacophony of 1910."[36] His last goal, "the singing of some sort of cabaret singer," was provided by Shostakovich in the form of a brief soprano solo in the center of the segment (Figure 6.5, Section F). Based on the rhythms of the polka, the singer imitates the orchestral line of the segment, with the lyrics shown in Figure 6.6.

The style of singing is spoken and excited, common to the stage, or contemporaneous *estrada*, and is synced closely with the images of giddy people celebrating New Year's Eve during a sleigh ride. The following segments repeat the music that was already heard, with some modification, over the same set of busy images of people and their sounds; drafted scenarios indicate that there was "music and whistling in the background."[37] The music effectively satisfied Kozintsev's ambition for songs of the era, and accommodates the busy nature and editing of the images of the partying bourgeoisie. The contrast for the other diegetic songs, associated with the workers, was created; yet the song codes quoted by Shostakovich were nearly imperceptible because they functioned as underscoring. Newspaper critics, scholars, and audiences were surprisingly silent in regard to Shostakovich's underscored Prologue; only a few mentioned that there was little underscored music.[38]

RECEPTION

To date, *Youth of Maxim* is one of the most popular of Kozintsev's and Trauberg's films. The enormous amount of press released during the initial and public screenings of the film reveal this popularity, and set its reputation for the remainder of the century. The majority of the press centered on the film's potential to be a cult classic, how it compared to the directors' previous works, and significantly, the music. Several articles in major papers made direct comparisons to the past modernist works of the directors. Some interpreted the previous films and their "eccentrism" as antithetical to *Youth of Maxim*, while others created a teleology of their development from the FEKs workshop towards an accepted socialist realist ideal.[39] To be sure, elements of their past film style persisted into their most current film; but the general and sudden celebration of past films that were once considered mild successes or failures indicated a new turn in their careers as directors. Elements of the film, and especially its main character, certainly created an overwhelming popularity for it which smoothly paved the way for the rest of the trilogy.

The film was easily dubbed the newest classic, and was directly compared to another recent cult hit, *Chapayev*, in the press. Some even exclaimed, *"Youth of Maxim is only comparable with Chapayev."*[40] Although *Chapayev* was considered a successful "historical" film based on a real person, *Youth of Maxim* was regarded as truer to the idea of the model Soviet man, regardless of its fictional base.[41] Audiences could relate to this handsome *Till Eulenspiegel* with a revolutionary backbone—he could sing, be a good friend, and fight in the revolution—all aspects of ever-changing Soviet masculinity.[42] Kozintsev and Trauberg related that when they screened the film, local workers shouted along and laughed with it, as if Maxim was a real person that they already knew.[43] Other newspapers, unsurprisingly ones such as *Komsomol'skaya pravda*, boasted that 500,000 viewers were being led to the film's openings, and people exited the theater singing songs from the film.[44] *Komsomol'skaya pravda* also argued that *Youth of Maxim* was "realistic" for the youth of the 1930s, and provided a proper Soviet model.[45] The actor Chirkov noted several decades later that Maxim was a kind of beacon for young people at the time; he related that he received multiple letters about how people enthusiastically "love and understand" Maxim, and named their children after him.[46]

The reception of *Youth of Maxim* clearly engaged music, but remarkably differently than previous films. It was already a trend in 1930s film reception to focus on song in the historical/war film, as seen in the press for *Chapayev* and *Counterplan*. *Youth of Maxim* was no different; critics focused on several songs of the film, almost never mentioning Shostakovich's involvement in the sound design. Four of the songs, all sung in the diegesis, were mentioned—"Warsaw Song," "You Fell Victim," "I Love Summer...," and "Whirling, twirling ..."—of them, the last two were strongly associated with Maxim. "Whirling, twirling ..." became such a hit (it was that song that the critics observed workers singing in the street), that any possible previous history of the song is virtually unknown today. Since the actor, Chirkov, was a decent singer, some audiences were led to believe that this song functioned as a form of reality. Combined with Chirkov's charm and the directors' savvy choice of song, "Whirling, twirling ..." became the perfect realist film song; music such as this was integrated in the narrative almost seamlessly in a satisfyingly popular and socialist way.[47] *Youth of Maxim*, in terms of image and sound, finally had achieved the intelligibility to the millions that the industry had once proclaimed necessary for Soviet cinema.[48]

The usual critics were unusually silent about the composer's direct contribution. Very few press articles mentioned elements of Shostakovich's scoring, such as the "Oira," while others simply stated that there was extremely little underscoring or other music.[49] Mikhail Cheryomukhin and Ieremiya Ioffe, frequent commentators on Shostakovich's early career in film scoring, hardly mentioned *Youth of Maxim*. Cheryomukhin briefly cited "Whirling, twirling . . ." as an example of a folk song that became popular because of its use in a song-score film genre and as an example of how songs can develop with characters within a film.[50] He fails to mention anything about Shostakovich's underscoring specific to this film. Ioffe, however, does mention the underscoring, and was less historically considerate in his analysis. He wrote,

> In *Youth of Maxim*, the composer does not create new methods, nor does he seek new paths. Here he writes music only for the Prologue, which demonstrates no dramatic positive experiences of the underground-revolutionaries, but [instead] the negative characterization of the bourgeoisie's vulgarity in its entertainment, weaving in the polyphonic movement of the Oira and Krakowiak.[51]

This brief and only statement by Ioffe about *Youth of Maxim* is typical of previous condemnations of the composer's use of "bourgeois" or "formalist" style markers and musical codes to vilify a particular group, in this case the pre-revolutionary bourgeoisie. Ioffe clearly chastised Shostakovich for his only direct contribution to the sound design in a manner reminiscent of earlier critiques: anything potentially representative of the pre-Soviet past was automatically inappropriate, even when employed to represent that past. Together with the suspicious silence in the press in regard to Shostakovich's Prologue, this statement suggests that Shostakovich's underscoring perhaps was strategically ignored.

AFTER *YOUTH OF MAXIM*

After the success of *Youth of Maxim*, it was clear that the directors would have an easier time selling the rest of the trilogy to the public. In *Return of Maxim* (1937) and *Vyborg Side* (1939), Shostakovich was finally invited to contribute further to the sound design.[52] Since technological capacity for overdubbing and recording was steadily, though slowly improving, such involvement would prove easier; but more importantly, the experimental divide of speech versus underscoring appeared to be exhausted. Shostakovich's involvement in the following films would be greater, and credit would finally be given to him.[53] His music would still be episodic, but greater than the minute and a half contribution of the Prologue to *Youth of Maxim*. To be sure, *Youth of Maxim* was an interesting experiment in sound design, with a desired focus on the power of speech over other sound. Nonetheless, the directors continued their older, modernist ideas about sound and image, creating a sound design that appeared seamless, effective, and realist. Although almost exclusive of Shostakovich's direct involvement, music was integral to the film in a new way, betraying the effectiveness of diegetic song, and the directors'—and implicitly, Shostakovich's—persistent experiments with layered underscoring and sound bridging found in the composer's earlier scores. *Youth of Maxim* was the film to make the directors' career, and it veered them toward a path of future work with Shostakovich.

CHAPTER 7

༄

Girlfriends (1935–1936)
and the "Girls of the Future"

A midst another significant shift in cultural politics from 1935–1936, the film *Girlfriends* (*Podrugi*, 1935–36, dir. Leo Arnshtam) premiered with Shostakovich's score. At this point, Shostakovich had several successful film scores, including *Counterplan* (1932) and *Youth of Maxim* (1935). He also had written scores for films that used women as protagonists, such as *New Babylon* (Louise) and *Alone* (Kuz'mina). In both of the latter films, which were created during a waning period of radical feminism, the central female characters were based on historical personages or recent events, and were accompanied by other male characters, either as antagonists or complements. These women were at the center, but were not the point of the overtly Soviet narrative; instead, these heroines were integrated into the story.[1] The scores were similarly constructed; they were less supportive of the gender of the character than the specifically Soviet narrative of the film.[2] It was with *Girlfriends* that a conscious construction of femininity in cinema initiated a new beginning in the work of Shostakovich and the film's director Leo Arnshtam. *Girlfriends* resembles, in terms of story and discourse, the classic Soviet film about the positive male hero, except with three feminized heroines; and these heroines were created with the intent of reaching a female audience. The music, both original scoring by Shostakovich and borrowed song, participates in the creation of this narrative of a feminine "Soviet Woman" by using various codes to cue the proletarian past, the new Soviet youth, and the girl/woman. Audiences and critics, as seen in press and archival documents, received this film as a representation of women; it jibed with Soviet historical films of the time in the way that it narrated a history of women's involvement in the revolution to serve a Soviet agenda. The film's score was composed during changes in musical politics and, interestingly, was received well despite the attacks that began in January 1936 on the opera *Lady Macbeth of Mtsensk District*, a work that also foregrounded a female character. Examining these cinematic and musical codes within such a context offers a perspective on Shostakovich's scoring for the Soviet heroine, and how this score is situated in his overall output.[3]

The story of the film revolves around three young girls from factory-worker families—Natasha, Zoya, and Asya—who live in the outskirts of St. Petersburg in 1914. After a factory incident where Asya's mother dies, Asya seeks out the comfort of her friends, thusly establishing the girls' solidarity. With a sudden need for financial support, they decide to sing for income at a local inn (*traktir*) named "The Keys to Happiness." After failing to interest the all-male audience, the girls are thrown out of the *traktir*, and are confronted by an older man, Silych, and his friend Andrey, who mentors them and teaches them a new song, "Zamuchen tyazheloy nevoley" (Tormented by Heavy Bondage). In the next scene, the girls appear again at the *traktir* with their new song. It goes over so well that it attracts the attention of the police, resulting in a tsarist police raid that attempts to control the all-male crowd of workers who are roused by the girls' song. This event ends the introduction of the film and signals the girls' transformation into young socially conscious citizens.

With a wipe, the girls are then shown five years later in 1919 as nurses on the Civil War front, picking up just before they volunteer to become nurses for the war. Dressed in military garb, the girls enter a recruitment event and encounter Andrey, who has been promoted to and acts as a high-ranking officer and rouser; they also see their young childhood friend Sen'ka, who leaves for the front. After this reunion, followed by a discovery that Zoya and Sen'ka are intimately involved, one of the girls' grandmothers delivers an inspiring speech about duty to the state and their duty as women to the crowd of girls before they depart for the front. As the film progresses, the girls have several adventures, with each girl representing a set of Soviet female types. Asya, regarded as the childish one, remains a central character throughout the film, and dies heroically at the end after a shootout between the girls and the enemy. Natasha is quieter but thoughtful, while Zoya acts as the aggressive, take-charge character. The design of Asya's character, and her interactions with Zoya and Natasha, demonstrate how each of these characters dealt with war, friendship, and romance. In the final scene, where Asya dies after being shot by an enemy soldier, Andrey gives a soliloquy to the camera prompting the female viewers of the film to remember their forebears and fight for women in the socialist cause, making the presumably progressive objective of the film clear and direct.

The film's plot and character development, constructed by Arnshtam and based in part on the autobiography of Raisa Vasil'eva, are in some ways typical of Soviet war films or historical films with male protagonists.[4] The formula of the Soviet novel, as described by Katerina Clark, or the representation of masculinity often canonized as popularly Soviet in these historical/war films resonates with the narrative features of *Girlfriends*.[5] Some of these features include a focus on an historical topic that is seen as a teleological movement towards the socialist ideal, generally adhering to burgeoning tenets of early socialist realism, while others focus on the youth and masculinity of the heroes.[6] Films such as *Chapayev* (dirs. Georgy and Sergey Vasil'yev, 1934) and *Youth of Maxim* particularly idolize young males through a historical lens that supports contemporaneous Soviet ideology.[7] They have central male characters that fight during a war or revolution; exhibit growth and change; become part of a war or war-like denouement; and sometimes experience a death unto life, where the changed man walks into a field signifying the bright future as a new Bolshevik (as in *Youth of Maxim*) or is sacrificed for the cause (as in *Chapayev*).[8] Together with advances in sound technology and growing state support for filmmaking, the characters of these films symbolized a new heroic male and became a formula for Soviet film of the 1930s. These films were regarded as momentous historical and "educational" films, and were fresh in the minds of viewers/listeners just as *Girlfriends* was released.[9] Some of the characters' traits and plot of *Girlfriends* resonated with these male heroic films. Instead of one male figure, a kind of female solidarity was affirmed by the three girls confronting the war together, necessitating the film's inclusion into the emerging historical/war film canon as a definitive woman's war film.

With its focus on the growth of three young girls as *Komsomol* (Communist Youth League) youth fighting in the revolution, the fashioning of the war/historical narrative of *Girlfriends* indicated a sea change in the portrayal of female leads. In the previous films of Kozintsev and Trauberg, for example, women were strong lead characters (Louise in *New Babylon* and Kuz'mina in *Alone*), but they were portrayed as parts of a whole.[10] Certainly, they can be analyzed from a feminist perspective, especially in light of the radical feminist movement in Soviet Russia in the 1910s and 1920s, but they were not films about Soviet women so much as films attempting to satisfy new Soviet directives in cinema.[11] Partly in response to Hollywood cinema, films from the mid-1930s that were billed as comedies or as dramas had celebrated actresses such as Lyubov Orlova, in films such as *Tsirk* (*Circus*, dir. Grigory Aleksandrov, 1936); or Yanina Zheimo (who plays Asya in *Girlfriends*) in films such as *Razbudite Lenochku* (*Wake up Lenochka*, dir. Antonina Kudryavtseva, 1934) and *Lenochka i vinograd* (*Lenochka and the Grapes*, dir. Kudryavtseva, 1936). Although sometimes popular, none of these films with the new blond superstar occupied the same category of Soviet war/historical film.[12] *Girlfriends*, as a female war film or as a Soviet revisionist historical film, was therefore a sort of rarity in 1936: it was a film attempting to fulfill what was becoming a formula for the Soviet film, similar to what Clark outlined as a formula for the Soviet novel.[13] As such, it was a clear first example of a Soviet woman's war/historical film that responded to trends of socialist realism and masculine film heroes, acting as a potential complement and perhaps a response to films with similar topics with male protagonists.

Specific tropes and the storyline reflect some of the current trends in war/historical filmmaking, while including commentary on women's social roles. The film thusly was designed to model femininity for audiences, particularly younger females. In some ways, the narrative of the film can be read as male "phantasy," as Laura Mulvey has famously argued, where male spectators (and in this case, possibly creators) identify with male characters, and whose gaze control the female subject(s). Such control renders the female unimportant or individual, according to Mulvey.[14] A reversal can be seen here, however, if such a formula were assumed for Soviet film (which did regard Hollywood as a model at times): the intended audience is female (and less importantly, male); the women of the audience are asked to identify with the three girls; and more specifically, to see themselves as a continuance of a Soviet history that functions beyond the film. In other words, there is a presumed female gaze of the spectator; a gaze that was created by both men and women to persuade females that they are a part of a proletarian/socialist tradition by representing *Girlfriends* as something new and Soviet, but nonetheless as real and historical. As Denise Youngblood has noted, "Yes, they [the girls] are hardworking and courageous, but they are also pretty and charming, very feminine."[15] This film represents a new femininity in war/historical films, something beyond the usual historicism of such films by/for male spectators that are designed to celebrate a new socialist future.

The way in which the male gaze is constructed in the diegesis affirms the girls' positions in the film and supports the idea of this being a woman's film. The men in the film—that is, Andrey, Silych, and Sen'ka—are represented by celebrated actors, as gazed upon by female viewers, rendered important insofar as they serve the three girls.[16] The men's roles were not passive, as Mulvey argues in Hollywood film, but active.[17] They prod the girls to action, albeit in a visible patriarchal construct, initiating them into a man's world via the *Komsomol* youth system. The depiction of these men is seemingly passive, possibly confusing the idea of a male gaze; they act only to serve the girls in this film. Simultaneously, however, their power within the system is implicit, and their goal (and that of the film) is to initiate these girls into that power system. Thus, the gaze may be constructed for a female spectator, but the implied dominance of a larger, masculinized power structure may remain patriarchal. As such, it does not guarantee that a female audience may have identified with this film as a representation of their current lives.

As Tania Modleski argues, women may have more agency than is assumed in Mulvey's analysis—agency created by filmmakers and by viewers.[18] Such nuance helps to explain how individuals may work within a power structure, however patriarchal, to find identity and agency. Whether female audiences and reviewers identified as was intended by the studio is another story.[19] Unfortunately, it is difficult to know whether or not women genuinely believed in this film as a representation of their positions in society. The press sometimes identified with the male characters first and often suggested that the girls were submissive to a larger, patriarchal system. Much of the press talked about its success as a woman's film, and used language to indicate that this film represented a kind of initiation into a male system; but no official press appeared to speak from a female perspective even in a formal public forum. Occasionally an article would directly praise the film as the first Soviet film with heroines,[20] while others focused more on the spirit of the revolution and how "girls" are part of that history.[21] Both of these perspectives perpetuated previous feminist ideas that began a decade or two earlier. Critics also used feminine language to describe the female characters and plot—some wrote that the girls were "softly" constructed but not too "sentimental."[22] Some critics used language evocative of fables. One writer from *Iskusstvo kino* noted that the film and its characters were "enchanting," and unusual for revolutionary films.[23] These descriptions were often used together with statements about how *Girlfriends* was a female version of *Chapayev* (and sometimes lacking by comparison), thereby affirming the socialist importance of the film and targeting its desired audience.

Other aspects such as costuming, character behavior, and film style also create a position for these girls as powerful, but within a patriarchal construct. As Mulvey argues,

> going far beyond highlighting a woman's to-be-looked-at-ness, cinema builds the way she is to be looked at into the spectacle itself. Playing on the tension between film as controlling the dimension of time (editing, narrative) and film as controlling the dimension of space (changes in distance, editing), cinematic codes create a gaze, a world, and an object, thereby producing an illusion cut to the measure of desire.[24]

How these three girls behave, are costumed, and how film style portrays them are the cinematic codes that create gaze, in this case, a gaze to instruct women on how to model a Soviet, *Komsomol* lifestyle and create a female mythology similar to that created by male revolutionary films. Speech and language throughout the film reinforce the centrality of the heroines, and how they are young women consciously folded into a revolution and connected to the *Komsomol*. Yet the positioning of the girls and their behavior places them in subservient and passive constructs. Andrey is the leader of the unit, and acts as a friend and brother-figure; Silych is their father figure, an old "underground" Bolshevik; Sen'ka is their childhood friend and Zoya's love interest; and finally a grandmother, played by the celebrated actress of theater and of cinema Mariya Blyumental'-Tamarina, encourages them to serve in the revolution and emphasizes their duty to the state before their duty to being mothers and wives. Their positioning in this diegetic microcosm of an idealistic Soviet society sets up their behaviors as naïve and subservient, and allows such behavior to be permissible.

As David Hoffman and Wendy Goldman have shown, women's roles, notions of difference, and feminism changed dramatically in the mid-1930s. As Hoffman has noted, "Whereas posters and films of the First Five-Year Plan [late 1920s and early 1930s] presented a neutered female image— stern, broad-shouldered, plainly dressed women workers—those of the mid-1930s depicted women as flirtatious, sensual and dressed to accentuate their femininity."[25] This observation jibes with women's representation in *Girlfriends*. Civil War costuming combined with heavy makeup, girls' talk of domestic life beyond war, and camera angles and shooting such as close-ups with soft focus calls attention to their femininity and reinforces the centrality of these heroines. Their actual positions in the army, too, emphasize this point—they are nurses not commanders, and are ill fitted for combat. With the exception of the feminine Zoya, they are outfitted in men's uniforms, hiding their feminine shapes and emphasizing their position in a patriarchal construct. To further illustrate the girls' out-of-place-ness, Zheimo, a known comedic actress, makes a point of characterizing Asya as comedic through gesture—she assists Zoya when she steps out of her masculine over-sized shoes, tripping over herself, physically demonstrating her small stature and "cuteness"—a point well observed by the press.[26] Zheimo intentionally portrayed Asya as "cute as a button" (as she is called in the film, and repeated in the press)—she cited her work in the circus (read: FEKs) and American film as her inspiration for this style of acting.[27] Notably, film style compounds this representation. The camera angles often look straight ahead or down on the girls, not up as one might see in films like *Chapayev* or *Youth of Maxim*; and soft focus is clearly used in romantic or tragic moments (Zoya's rendezvous and Asya's death). Together with the girls' positioning in the film, and ultimately within Soviet society, such behavior, costuming, and some details of film style could be read as an illustration of how the girls operate within a patriarchal construct. As other scholars such as Hoffman and Emma Widdis have noted, such visual cues that permeated society endeared women to a "woman's" story in attempts to persuade them to desire a similar Soviet life.[28]

Some of the features of the film's style are consistent within the film, suggesting a unique directorial style that indexes with some traits that appear peculiarly feminine. The editing throughout is consistent, fades are often used to move between scenes, there is a mix of shots (LS, CU, etc.); and in parts, the film has some of the features of a Hollywood-styled feature film. As a whole, however, it is unique to Arnshtam (and if one believes Yutkevich, a part of the Leningrad school of filmmaking).[29] There are few medium shots and they are often of war scenes; the takes are short, the editing fast, there are multiple close-ups, and a privileging of speech that contribute to the narrative. The main difference is the use of soft-focus in close-ups of the girls' faces during tragic or romantic moments, and the angle of the camera's gaze when positioned between male characters that suggest a departure from the usual style of a contemporaneous war/historical film.

These small divergences appear to act as the "cinematic codes" that Mulvey notes in Hollywood films; these codes create a different Master Plot, a female version within a male construct.[30] Certainly, sound is one of these cinematic codes, and it has its own set of conventions. Sound and music play a similar role within the film; editing and/or shooting that resembles a Hollywood melodrama is reinforced when music often associated with melodrama is combined with the image. Some of the music/sound codes in *Girlfriends* could be easily read as neutral or male outside the film. With image, and sometimes without image, some of the sounds arguably can be read to demarcate the feminine.

SOUND DESIGN

Sound design in *Girlfriends* can be summarized as consisting of speech, borrowed song, or newly composed underscoring. Similar to many sound films of the mid-1930s, it privileges speech. Music, however defined, moves between the foreground and background spaces.[31] Borrowed song permeates the film, and plays an obvious role in representing the development of the girls and situating them in the time of the revolution. The underscoring, the only part of the sound design that was clearly Shostakovich's contribution, operates differently. Underscoring eases transitions between scenes, or operates dominantly, if only momentarily. Unlike scores to earlier films such as *New Babylon*, both the songs and Shostakovich's underscoring work to create a modest sound design, with a total of twenty-three musical cues, which selectively operate in tandem with image (see Figure 7.1). A likely product of sound films of the time, the selective amount of music nonetheless acts as or contributes to the narrative, and to the building of cinematic codes of the feminine.

Cue	Event	Type/instrumentation	Action
1	(Opening credits)	String quartet	Opening
2	Year 1914, Workers' residence	String quartet	Overview; accompanies the neighborhood bustling, children running around, etc.
3	Girls wait for parents	SQ, trumpet, piano	Girls sitting around the apartment, waiting
4	Men at the *traktir*	SQ, trumpet, piano	Images of men drinking, in misery, speaking of revolution
5	Children's song	Four children's voices	Children first time singing at *traktir*
6	"Zamuchen..."	Four children's voices	Children at the river with Silych
7	Call (Silych's begins story)	Trumpet solo	Silych's tells story of the his son's death on the Potemkin
8	Silych's story	SQ, trumpet, piano, harp	""
9	"Zamuchen..."	Song, four voices, chorus	Girls sing at the tavern
10	Year 1919, Girls walking	Organ, trumpets (3-6)	They walk with a wipe from girls to women
11	"Internationale"	Banda	Plays in the background as the meeting happens, girls are sent off to war
12	Girls tend wounded soldiers	Timpani, harp, organ	Girls on the field tending to soldiers
13	Enemy in nearby town	Banda	Indicates the proximity of the enemy
14	"Internationale"	Solo theremin	Silych and the girls fight off the enemy while on the train

Figure 7.1: Table of musical cues with instrumentation.

Cue	Event	Type/instrumentation	Action
15	Zoya in the forest	String trio	Zoya walks to meet her lover
16	Zoya and Sen'ka in forester's hut	String quartet, piano	Romantic rendezvous
17	Fanfare (Sen'ka's arrival)	Trumpets, drum	Sen'ka arrives to meet the gang
18	Fanfare (Andrey's arrival)	Trumpets	Andrey arrives
19	(Girls and the chicken)		Girls chase the chicken
20	"Gdye eti. . ."	Song, 2 voices	Nostalgic talk of life and life after war
21	Asya and Zoya rescued	Orchestra	The calvary comes, Asya is shot
22	Fanfare (Asya's death)	Trumpets	Asya's final words and death
23	Andrey's soliloquy	Orchestra	"Girls of the future. . ."

Figure 7.1: Continued

The few times that it has been mentioned or momentarily discussed, the score to *Girlfriends* has been branded as a "symphonic" score.[32] There are several ways in which the term "symphonic" may be applied to film scoring at this time. What could make this score seem symphonic would be either continuously running music, or some connection between musical segments that favor orchestral instrumentation. This score, in comparison to Shostakovich's previous works, would therefore be less "symphonic" by this definition. The ten musical fragments, or *preludi* (preludes) as others have called them, which Shostakovich wrote for small ensemble, are frequent, brief, and contain no recurring ideas or leitmotifs. This is a departure from the song scores or fragmentary scoring of *Alone, Counterplan,* or *Youth of Maxim.*[33] More frequently, this score appears to use *leittimbre* and references musical codes/tropes—several trumpet calls/fanfares repeat to signify war, and string ensembles with varying and unusual instrumental additions (organ, harp, etc.) narrate romance or act as general underscoring. Strings, trumpet, organ, and harp are the recurring instruments throughout; their respective timbres suggest musical associations as they build meaning within the film. The recurrence of these timbral associations and the codes they invoke are the closest thing to "symphonic dramaturgy" as Egorova labels it. Fellow composers and critics, however, heard these musical segments as more fragmented, that is, less symphonic and less connected.[34] The score overall has unity, and operates as narrative, but it lacks the "symphonism" of Shostakovich's previous scores. The score nonetheless is unified through several kinds of sound—diegetic song, ensemble underscoring, and musical codes—along with speech and sound effects.

SONG

There are a total of four borrowed songs within the film that advance the plot or illustrate a scene, most of which are diegetic and/or sung by the central characters. Two of the songs appear in the first half of the film and are associated with the girls. Unlike previous film scores they are restricted to the first part of the film, and are sung by the girls and Sen'ka in the *traktir* full of drinking men. The first is a song about poppies, a children's song that they practice on their own and then take to the busy *traktir* to sing. No one listens, and the group is thrown out into the mud. This failure sets up their first meeting with Silych, the old "underground" Bolshevik, who teaches them a new "folk" song while telling them the story of his son's death on the *Potemkin*.[35] After learning this song from Silych, known as "Zamuchen tyazheloy nevoley" (Tormented by Heavy Bondage) they perform it at the local *traktir* with great success, but only after Andrey and Silych have quieted the crowd to force them to listen, and have encouraged the children to restart. The young group of singers eventually rouses the audience to their feet singing, and after they finish, the police enter the *traktir*. Silych distracts the police, and Andrey, and presumably the children who are not shown at this point, are ushered out. The men of the *traktir* revolt after the police figure out the distraction, and the scene fades to the next.

This performance at the *traktir* revolves around the song "Tormented by Heavy Bondage" and the girls' success, representing their presumed and eventual conversion to the Soviet cause via the two men and a song. The film was edited to clearly show how the song stitched together disparate communities—three girls, a boy, and a room of drinking men. "Tormented by Heavy Bondage," therefore, is a narrative turning point, representing a kind of initiation into both a man's world (indicated by the *traktir*) and what would become the Soviet future (as indicated in the remainder of the film). This heavy-handed intent was clear to those sharing a similar agenda—critics at newspapers such as *Pravda* went as far as to quote the song, and analyze it as the central point of the film; others even described the film in musical terminology, emphasizing how the film itself was a kind of song, and that the girls "sing" their way through it.[36]

This song certainly has its roots in revolution, and was clearly known prior to the film's making. "Zamuchen tyazheloy nevoley," loosely translated as "Tormented by Heavy Bondage," dates from the late nineteenth century and describes misery resulting from oppression.[37] With lines that describe death, vengeance, and heroism of the masses, the song has resonated with audiences, fittingly is associated with the Russian revolution, and was canonized during the existence of the Soviet Union (see Figure 7.2).[38]

The setting of the song in the film is certainly dramatic—the girls begin the first few stanzas, and the men in the audience one by one pick up the rest, building in harmony as they sing and thusly expressing solidarity. This kind of harmony-building is common to Russian oral tradition and singing folksongs, either in urban tradition or in village practice; certainly orally transmitted song with harmonization also can be found in many other world traditions.[39] It brings to question how the composition of this scene came about. There is no extant score or manuscript for this song, suggesting multiple possibilities, among them the possibility that Shostakovich emulated folk tradition in his writing, as he had done with *Alone*,[40] or that Arnshtam and Shostakovich both may have asked the actors on the set to sing in a tradition commonly known to all.[41]

Although this song is borrowed, and possibly chosen by Arnshtam rather than Shostakovich, it does appear in connection with Shostakovich several years later. His String Quartet No.8, a frequently analyzed work from Shostakovich's output, employs this tune. Many musicians and scholars have noted the possible use of this song as material in the quartet, and have drawn connections between it and Shostakovich's emotional state; very few to almost no one has traced his first exposure to this song back

Наш враг над тобой не глумился	Our enemy is not mocking you
Кругом тебя были свои	We were all around you
Мы сами, родимый, закрыли	We ourselves, my dear, have closed
Орлиные очи твои.	Your eagle eyes.
Не горе нам душу давило,	Our souls were not weighed down with woe
Не слезы блистали в очах,	Nor did tears shine in our eyes
Когда мы, прощаясь с тобою,	When we said farewell to you
Землей засыпали твой прах.	And your ashes were engulfed by the earth

Figure 7.2: The first few stanzas from "Zamuchen tyazheloy nevoley" as heard in the film (after the children restart).

to this film score.[42] The other quotations from this quartet have been discussed; identifying the source of this song brings up questions about meaning, and the connections between Shostakovich's film experience and his concert music.[43] Because of the lack of material evidence about this scene from *Girlfriends*, it is unknown in what detail Shostakovich and Arnshtam talked about this song, if at all. All that is currently known is that it materializes in the film as a part of the sound design. Arnshtam was a particularly discerning sound designer, and he claimed to have composed some music attributed to Shostakovich; it is just as possible that he chose this song as a pivot point in the plot.[44] Regardless, Shostakovich knew this song at this time. Within the context of the film, the song appears only this once, acting as the turning point common to the development of a hero (or heroines) in historical films, thereby exhausting its narrative potential. Within Shostakovich's output, it opens up the possibility for an intertextual reading—one that suggests that the String Quartet No.8 looked back to this film moment of the girls' eventual conversion to a Soviet cause.

"Internationale" is another song that creates a strong impression in the film. It is heard twice and in association with war. The tune is first heard in the second section of music in the second half of the film, where the girls are shown as young adults in a group of *Komsomol* women preparing to leave for war.[45] The tune is heard as non-diegetic dialogue underscoring (a kind of *banda*), but its placement in the background and context of the scene suggest the implication of an offscreen, diegetic band.[46] It accompanies the entire scene: when the girls listen to Andrey, when Zoya accidentally meets Sen'ka before he heads off to war, and when the girls eventually leave for the front. A brass and percussion band, therefore, sets the scene to establish a military context. No one indicates that they hear the music, which implies that this music is non-diegetic underscoring that is becoming common to sound films at the time; or it implies a nod to Italian opera tradition and the *banda sul palco*.[47] Shostakovich's familiarity with opera and his previous experience in cinema allow multiple readings, but a certain effect is achieved—a military context is set, and the music nevertheless functions as a kind of underscoring, diegetic or not.

The second appearance of "Internationale" is foregrounded, and oddly scored. Written solely for theremin, the song functions as non-diegetic underscoring that accompanies Silych and the girls commanding the train and fighting off enemies (see Video 7.1). ▶ As with all of the other songs in this film, there is no extant manuscript for this setting of "Internationale"—Shostakovich or the musically inclined Arnshtam could have chosen the instrumentation for this scene. The choice of theremin, however, was familiar to Shostakovich—he had used it once before in the lost sixth reel of his previous film score to *Alone* in order to evoke a turbulent storm.[48] For Shostakovich, the theremin was already associated with agitation; in this scene, it is the sole instrument, and chosen to create tension in the retreat from the enemy. This musical choice predated any consistent use of this relatively new instrument of the time, which disallows any sort of timbral associations that would be common to other instrumental music of the past. This favored use of the theremin does suggest, however, that it was readily available to him and was a choice over the alternative possibilities of a brass band—the usual instrumentation throughout the film for military scenes. Coincidentally, Shorinofone (*shorinofon*), Tagefone (*tagefon*), and later the Variophone, an apparatus that recorded sound onto film in an ornamental manner, were available at Lenfil'm Studios and to Shostakovich beginning with his work on *Alone*.[49] The newest technology, like the Variophone and the theremin were available at Lenfil'm Studios from the late 1920s forward.[50] Given Shostakovich's penchant for new music and technology, it is plausible that he was exposed to this new instrument and chose to integrate it into his film scores beginning in 1929. Choosing a theremin for a version of "Internationale" was, therefore, a modernist twist on a Soviet tune. Experimental in the late 1920s and early 1930s, though becoming less so by the time of *Girlfriends*, such a timbral choice doubtless resulted from the availability of resources and Shostakovich's experimental inclinations.[51]

The last complete song of the film, "Gdye eti tyopli nochi" (Where are those warm nights?), is sung by the girls entirely in the diegesis after they catch a roaming chicken and start to prepare it for dinner. The song is cut short, interrupted by an enemy who discovers their dinner; but the two verses of lyrics that are finished are nostalgic, and address a lover—a fitting song after their discussion of what they plan to do after they leave the front (see Figure 7.3).

где эти тёплые ночи	Where are those warm nights
где так пел соловей	Where the nightingale sang so
где эти карие очи	Where are those brown eyes
кто их ласкает теперь	Who is caressing them now?
в вечер осенней порою	Sometimes on an autumn evening
выйду я в сад погулять	I go out for a walk in the garden
ночка ещё не настала	The night has not yet come
буду я милого ждать.	I will wait for my love.

Figure 7.3: Text for "Gdye eti tyopli nochi" as heard in the film.

The singing together bonds them as friends, similar to moments in *Chapayev*, a contemporaneous film that contained several folk songs sung between men. *Girlfriends* was often compared to *Chapayev* in terms of content, even by Joseph Stalin; it is unsurprising that songs are used in this genre of film, and in moments like these between characters. The performance practice is similar; Zoya begins the song and Natasha joins, breaking away to harmonize, a technique similar to folksong practice. The primary difference between this moment between girls and the ones in *Chapayev*, however, lies in the topic of the song. Instead of implying battle or having references to war and masculinity, these girls sing of romance and love, and a return to a domestic life beyond the front. This kind of romantic song is uncommon for a historical film of this time, but it is appropriate if viewed as a "woman's film" where women are temporarily integrated into a male system of war. This song sets them apart as different, and it is interrupted by an enemy soldier, a reminder of their place.

TRUMPET CALLS AND SOURCE SOUND

Another aspect of the score, in which Shostakovich presumably participated, is the strategic placing of trumpet fanfares and calls.[52] Trumpet calls/fanfares appear five times throughout the film, and are associated with the usual images of war. The first instance appears in a way similar to the first use of "Internationale"—it occupies that "fantastical gap," a space between the diegetic and non-diegetic, while it accompanies Silych's storytelling of his son's death on the famed *Potemkin*.[53] The tune is brief, approximately thirty seconds, and is limited in range and variety of pitch. Its brevity suggests the formula of a bugle call, though it was likely played on trumpet (see Example 7.1).

As Silych is speaking, the quiet trumpet call is momentarily the only foregrounded music as it pierces through during a crucial moment of his story, provoking him to look to a ship on the Neva River (and prompting the girls to do so as well). It is an offscreen diegetic sound source—Silych indicates this by saying "the Reveille plays" (*zorya igrayet*)—though the call simultaneously references the character's past as if it beckons from the *Potemkin's* ghosts, and ends as he continues his story. This is a unique use of the trumpet call; it is different from the fanfares in the rest of the film, being diegetic and using the formula of a call. Its layering under speech demonstrates the capacity of sound film of the time. The call also embodies a common trumpet trope, in this case more specifically the bugle, signifying the militaristic and inviting the listener to sympathize with Silych's story and ultimately the Soviet cause.

Example 7.1: The trumpet call from Silych's story.
Transcription by the author and Christian Anderson.

The four other instances in which the trumpet fanfares appear operate differently in the narrative, but still signify the usual trope of military/war. The next fanfare is part of an ensemble, with four trumpets and organ.[54] This scene as a whole has a design of moving between diegetic and non-diegetic and from past to future, representing the girls' growth. After the *traktir* raid, the girls run to their grandmother. As the church bells toll in the diegetic background, the grandmother bids them to "go, go," at which point they turn and walk together, and a single bell toll rings non-diegetically, but in the foreground. After a wipe and an intertitle showing them five years later, an elaborate and chromatic trumpet fanfare begins and continues for another thirty seconds until the organ enters. A musical exchange between organ and trumpet continues over the girls walking, until we see them enter a building to dress and attend a last meeting before leaving for the front. The timbral choice of trumpet, and the elaborate fanfare coupled with organ, assists in illustrating this metaphorical march into the future (of the Soviet Union). This choice also provides a militaristic meaning consistent with the previous trumpet call and with historical trumpet/brass tropes.[55] This is the only instance of the film where a trumpet trope is associated with the three girls specifically, suggesting a broader meaning within the film; at the same time, it signifies their transition into this male world of war, positioning them with the Soviet cause. Read alone in the film yet historically associated with the military, the trumpet trope builds from the meaning of revolt (Silych's son on the *Potemkin*) to the girls' joining of the revolution, situating them firmly as heroines in a war/historical film context.

The remaining three instances of trumpet fanfares are mostly associated with the male characters, particularly Andrey and/or Sen'ka, and ultimately Asya. The first two are grouped together and they accompany Andrey as he brings news from the front, discusses strategies with the girls and Silych, and exits. This group of two are separate fanfares: the first is a

Examples 7.2a and 7.2b: The two fanfares announcing Andrey's exit, in two parts.
Transcription by the author and Christian Anderson.

variation on rhythms and ideas Shostakovich already used in the previous
fanfare; and the second is a nearly exact repeat of a section of the fanfare
that accompanied the girls, with the exception of a small coda that repeats
the formula also used elsewhere in the film. Both of these trumpet fanfares
can be heard as codes that make them more than a usual bugle call, given
their length and complexity. Shostakovich uses the same stereophonic
effect from earlier, and uses a triplet rhythm followed by a minor third,
reminiscent of similar motives commonly heard in trumpet fanfares, and
late nineteenth- and early twentieth-century music.[56] These two fanfares,
stacked back to back, were recorded at separate times as indicated by a significant change in timbre from one to the next (see Example 7.2).

Examples 7.2a and 7.2b: (Continued)

The final fanfare, only forty seconds, accompanies Asya's death. This fanfare is exactly the same as the previous one, with the exception of a small coda. Although it does coincide with Andrey's entry, associated with the army, and is used in a kind of transition/entry for a character, it begins with the moment that the characters realize Asya has passed. For the first time in the film, then, the trumpet call is associated primarily with a single female character, and it situates her in a line of martyred heroes. The consistent near repeat of these fanfares and their similarity to each other maintains a certain meaning consistent with the historical signifiers and within the film, which narrates the inclusion of the girls into this military tradition upon Asya's death. Ultimately, the trumpet calls/fanfares indicate the usual militaristic context; within this film and its overall genre, the trumpet trope is further refined to signify a male world of power and war into which the girls have been initiated.

Because of the better advancements in sound recording since *Alone*, and his experience as a sound designer, Arnshtam could layer sound in new ways. Throughout the film, when speeches are given, stories are told, or when parents call to their children, Shostakovich's scoring works in connection with speech in a way that becomes typical for sound film. There are moments, however, in which this layering is more complex. When the *traktir* is introduced, for example, the camera consciously scans the crowd showing vignettes of each of its inhabitants, many of which are singing songs or telling jokes. In films where speech was difficult to balance with other recorded sounds, speech took precedence; but here, Shostakovich's underscoring moves alongside the men's songs as a kind of contradiction and complement. It sets the mood and is established as non-diegetic underscoring by its placement in the sound design, but can be read to compete musically with the men's songs. This could be cacophonous, in the way that the hut scene in *Alone* appears to be; but with better recording technology, these two competing musics are heard in separate spaces, diegetic or non-diegetic. Such a possible division of space highlights the way in which Arnshtam and Shostakovich were thinking about film sound. The role of scoring and its positioning with the film's space was changing unsurprisingly in connection with newer technology.

SHOSTAKOVICH'S SCORING

Shostakovich's contribution, in terms of ensemble or orchestral scoring, consists of almost half of the total musical cues. Twelve separate cues, outside of the trumpet sections, are scattered throughout the score. Of these twelve, one section of music was borrowed and added to the introductory credits after the film's initial 1930s release; this music comes straight from his First String Quartet (1938).[57] This addition was made in the 1960s rerelease of the film, the only version that appears to be available today.[58] Another musical section was written for the film but never used; it accompanies the girls' chase of the chicken that they eventually cook for dinner.[59]

The other ten sections of music are presumably original to the first release of the film; of them we have eight known manuscript fragments.[60] All of these sections of music function non-diegetically in the film, either in the foreground or background, and/or as dialogue underscoring. These sections share instrumental similarities as well as functional ones; almost all build on a string ensemble core with added instruments, or consist of militaristic-inspired ensembles (drum, etc.). The texture of each section is often thin, with the exception of the orchestral sections at the end of the film. Generally, Shostakovich's contributions are considerably varied, but can be easily grouped according to texture, instrumentation, and function. Each of these aspects interact with musical codes that, when combined with image, establish this film's genre as a Soviet woman's war/historical film.

After the credits and the excerpt from String Quartet No.1, the images show a residential neighborhood and factory in the outskirts of St. Petersburg in 1914. The first section of music accompanies images of the Factory of the Russian-American Rubber Manufacturing Association, and the impoverished neighborhood showing children in rags and their mothers calling them inside. The second section shows the families waiting at home and the children hearing the news of an accident. The third moves location to the *traktir* named "The Keys to Happiness." Each of these musical sections sets the tone for the scene, and acts as background to speech and action.

The first section begins after shots and diegetic sounds from the neighborhood, beginning with the intertitles "Many in the factory's buildings . . .," and it shows children walking from their homes and towards the gates of their community. The instrumentation is for string quartet, with voicing and style common to Shostakovich's earlier work. After the gates are closed by an officer due to a strike, the music halts, only to pick up as the children run from the gates. Their running is accompanied by descriptively rushing downward figures in the quartet. ⓹ (See Video 7.2.) The music for these few minutes sets the scene and accompanies the image in a way similar to silent cinema; the music is general enough to let the intertitles speak, and the music to the children's running resembles that of "hurry" music of silent cinemas past.[61] Ieremiya Ioffe commented on the music to this and the following scene as effective in depicting the children generally, and as specifically "proletarian," against the background of serious poverty and destitution—a way of stating that the "intonations" that Shostakovich employed not only referenced the action of children playing and running, but also acted a complement to a pro-socialist message implied in the film's *mise-en-scene*.[62]

The following scene is lightly scored, as the children run to Zoya's home to wait for her mother after a day of striking. After only dialogue between the girls and the grandparents, a light texture of string quartet, piano, and trumpet pick up after Zoya's mother enters the home. A viola solo with accompanying drone, reminiscent of the opening of the second movement of the String Quartet No. 1, begins with intertitles and images of the family waiting. The texture shifts to active polyphony, and the addition of muted trumpet doubled with piano is heard as the mother enters, falling back to a thinner texture of melody plus drone. The music ends as the mother sits to eat; she begins her story about the day and the injury of Asya's mother. Used sparingly and closely tailored to the images, the sextet follows the movement of the characters, leading or aligning with the characters' movement and moods. This light arrangement is common to sound films, and bears a resemblance to music in Hollywood films; a kind of underscoring that is trying to be seamless and "unheard."[63] This scoring betrays the general aesthetic trend that was moving from constant symphonic underscoring to minimal and seamless lighter textures. The choice of string core plus one or two more instruments allows for this aesthetic to take shape, just as Shostakovich took the opportunity to experiment with a new genre.

The next scene fades to a *traktir*, where workers are drinking, singing, and telling stories. Shostakovich's scoring enters with the image of the *traktir*'s sign ("The Keys to Happiness"), and overlaps with the singing men, establishing different spaces.[64] There are two separate instances of underscoring. The first establishes the scene, with quiet dialogue underscoring in sextet (string quartet, piano, trumpet), with an octave-doubled theme that echoes folk practice traded between the violin and piano, with added interjections of triplet patterns in the trumpet. It uses a block form in antecedent-consequent eight- and four-measure phrases, and exchanges the main melodies between the three instrument groups: violin, trumpet, piano, and string quartet (see Example 7.3).

The melody is new, but the instrumentation is continued from the previous scene; and the triplet pattern in the trumpet, and the short-short-long pattern in the melody are echoed throughout the score particularly in the trumpet fanfares.[65] This music accompanies the men in the *traktir* as they talk about the misery in their lives, and it stops when the newspaper carrier enters. After Andrey reads the news, and begins to speak of injustices, a different section of music returns after the children have entered and sung their "poppy song," and the men start to riot. The music, now played by a larger ensemble and imitating "hurry" tropes, continues functioning as dialogue underscoring (in a conversation between Silych and Andrey) and accompanying the riot, reducing in volume to allow speech to dominate during conversation.[66]

Another instance of dialogue underscoring appears after Silych has befriended the girls, and has taught them a new song. As he begins to

Example 7.3: Opening of the *traktir* scene, first eight measures, with the primary melody.
Transcription by the author and Christian Anderson.

tell the story of his son's death on the *Potemkin*, the bugle call interrupts, and he looks toward the ship on the Neva. After the call, a men's chorus enters, scarcely heard, for approximately one minute before a final two- to three-second bugle finish. These two tropes—of using a reveille to mark the time of day and relate to Silych's story of his sailor son, and using a male chorus when speaking of revolt—establish Silych's character as an underground revolutionary and his reasons for becoming one.[67] The chorus ends just as Silych finishes the story; and Andrey floats up to the bank in a boat, upon which Shostakovich's underscoring enters with a melody in the violin accompanied by the rest of the quartet, consisting of harp, trumpet, and piano. A change in instrumentation, predominantly a thin texture with violin line over pizzicato strings and a change in mode (from minor mode choral underscoring to major mode septet), indicates a shift in mood accompanying Andrey's entry. The entry/exit of music throughout this scene, from bugle call to septet is carefully scored to stay under speech, and establish the men as important to the girls' future. Overall, the underscoring of the first half of the film mimics that of Hollywood dialogue underscoring and uses carefully chosen tropes to establish the characters' positions for the rest of the film.

MUSIC AND MILITARY

Aside from the fanfares and appearances of the "Internationale," the second half of the film has two other moments of military music that situate the girls in this war/historical film. Fading from the scene at the meeting and into images with the girls in the midst of battle tending to the wounded, sound effects (of bombing) and speech make up the sound design. After approximately one minute of establishing the context, underscoring enters, consisting of an undulating line between organ, harp, and timpani. This line slowly moves between a whole step and a fourth, creating an eerie effect particularly when it doubles the harp's line. This is a similar effect to what Shostakovich used in *Alone*, but for a different function—instead of indicating the sound of an instrument as with the *dombra* player in the Altai, here the unusual ensemble creates a backdrop for war. As with other musical sections, this segment is brief, closing with a cadence in the organ before Asya climbs onto the railroad tracks to look for the train.

The next segment of music is an offscreen *banda*, similar to the previous presentation of "Internationale," signaling the enemy. This quick musical bit signals the enemy's approach by operating spatially, which creates tension as the girls await the train to pick up the wounded. Lasting barely one minute, the *banda* ends just before the train approaches, leaving room for speech, and a reunion between Silych and the girls. Generally, these two instances confirm the context for the film, either as unsettling underscoring to narrate the girls' anticipation, or as *banda* ensemble that signifies the enemy and builds upon the previous *banda* appearance as an established trope of war. Each approach to musical narration situates the girls as an integral part of the war effort.

MUSIC AND ROMANCE

A set of romantic, wintery love scenes, heightened by Shostakovich's underscoring, highlights *Girlfriends* as a woman's war film. These scenes begin after the girls' retreat by train and are shown tending to wounded soldiers in a field hospital. In the middle of performing her duties as a nurse, Zoya receives a message to meet someone at a cabin in the forest; thereafter two related sections of underscoring accompany her on her journey. The first section is a montage, with fades in and out, of Zoya walking through the forest ending with her arrival in the cabin. Approximately one and a half minutes of music follow her, consisting of string trio. It begins with violin solo over pizzicato accompaniment and ends with slow moving lines between all three instruments, finally concluding with three solo pizzicato notes. This is the thinnest string texture so far in the film—similar moments, with sparse writing for solo and accompaniment appeared in the first half of the film—but this texture mimics Zoya's solo walk through the forest. Again functioning as background underscoring, Shostakovich uses texture and instrumentation to evoke Zoya's journey.

The following scene is central for musical representation of femininity, and marks it as a woman's war film, while also connecting it to contemporaneous film music. After Zoya enters the cabin, the underscoring picks up when Sen'ka surprises her, initiating the second of the pair of musical instances in this episode (see Figure 7.4).

Shostakovich changes his underscoring dramatically, and the melody/harmony, instrumentation, voicing, and texture recall nineteenth-century romantic traditions and contemporaneous film scoring in Hollywood romance films.[68] This underscoring is associated with many images, and it appears in two parts within this scene complex—Zoya and Sen'ka embracing, resting, chatting, and then followed by a montage of the forest and the girls eventually finding them both in the cabin—therefore allowing some potential variety of musical code or ideas. Instead, in this unique moment Shostakovich varied the music within a romantic style to maintain continuity. After the couple initially meets, the texture thickens and begins with an ascending solo violin line emerging from a shimmery tremolo of slowly moving chords in the string quartet accompaniment. (See Video 7.3.) ▶ This music simmers beneath the dialogue as the couple flirts (a kind of dialogue underscoring), moving through minor mode suspensions with a

Figure 7.4: The first moment when Sen'ka and Zoya meet in the cabin.

Example 7.4: Romantic rendezvous cue, from the couple's first moment of meeting through their kiss.
Transcription by the author and Christian Anderson.

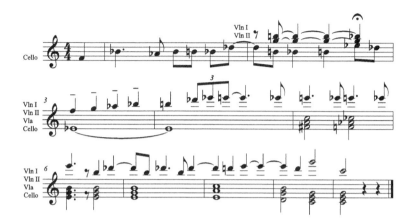

cadence on a major chord as they kiss, altogether strongly reminiscent of nineteenth-century romantic traditions and contemporaneous Hollywood scoring practices (see Example 7.4); in particular, certain elements of this underscoring are reminiscent of the opening Prelude and various arias with the same material throughout Richard Wagner's *Lohengrin*.[69]

In the unpublished extant manuscript of this scene, the voicing chosen by Shostakovich indicates the instruments' ranges (from cello to first violin).[70] (See Figure 7.5.) The clarity of the composer's hand, and timing, as indicated in the number of measures and closeness to the final soundtrack, also suggest that this manuscript was the final sketch before he started orchestrating for string quartet (and later in the scene, quintet). There are a few pitches that are present in the sketch that are absent in the transcription, and the key is a half step lower in the manuscript. These differences suggest minor revision between the sketch and final soundtrack; certain liberties taken by the studio performers (*legato* in the first violin and the fermata as seen in the transcription, for instance); and also the change in the film's speed from reel to digital media that would have raised the key a half step. Ultimately, the writing for this scene was clearly designed to sound romantic even before the finer elements of performance were added: the extremely high range of the violin written in the upper treble line and the sighing figure accentuated by held chords in the lower instruments shows that Shostakovich already had decided how the instruments would be voiced (see Figure 7.5).

Other codes also combine here to evoke romance: the solo violin with the wide vibrato, the intimacy of a string quartet, and the slow tempo to

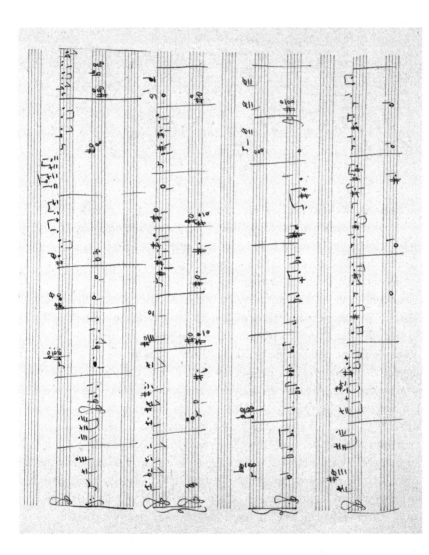

Figure 7.5: Excerpt from Shostakovich's unpublished sketch of the romance scene. Reproduced with permission from Irina Shostakovich, and the copy provided by VMOMK.

Source: VMOMK, f.32, No.2303, page 1.

name a few. After fading in and out of scenes of them kissing then resting (with the implication of sexual activity in between), the images of the forest are shown with another ascending chromatic melodic line in the first violin reminiscent of romantic song (with melodies still evocative of much nineteenth-century lyrical writing, including the opening of *Lohengrin*, and somewhat of *Des Knaben Wunderhorn*) with greater harmonic movement in the remainder of the quintet, now with piano adding chordal emphasis.[71] Figure 7.5, Shostakovich's sketch, shows the continuation of the violin line after the major chord where the couple kisses (measures 10 and 11), which aligns with the images of the forest and the couple. At this point, the texture thickens when music is placed in the foreground to be the only sound in the film, and the volume is raised, shifting the viewer from the internal world of the couple back to the external world of the front.[72] After visually and aurally fading back to the couple, who discuss their future after the war and a family, the ensemble thins and slowly fades out just before a hard cut to the other two girls standing in the cabin, who have arrived unheard.

The sound world embraces this couple, and contains codes that viewers would likely identify as romantic in style, texture, and instrumentation, notably the emphasis on string instruments and slow lyrical melodies. This sound was derived from earlier silent cinema practice, and of course from opera and melodrama. What is striking about this passage is how much it resembles certain composers known for lyrical writing (Wagner is one possibility; Musorgsky, Pyotr Tchaikovsky, Nikolay Rimsky-Korsakov are others), much in the way Hollywood practice draws upon the musical past for its material. There is a connection between the two practices that is perhaps unsurprising: both cinemas are deriving their musical codes from European musical traditions. Here, Shostakovich sounds deliberately feminine in his musical choices. The music narrates the couple's intimacy in a way similar to what one would find in Hollywood romance scenes and in past silent cinema practice. It seems that listeners heard a connection as well; as one American reviewer observed, the scene was "over-long and shows a bad Hollywood influence."[73] The musical codes exploited here reinforce this scene of romance, resonating with contemporaneous notions of femininity—as Hoffman has argued, romance and motherhood were celebrated traits of femininity at this time. In fact, women were encouraged by the state to occupy the dual role of mother and public worker.[74] This set of scenes in particular gives voice to Othered aspects of the female characters, and their roles differ from those of male heroes in similar films such as *Chapayev*—these girls are drawn to be more than warriors, that is, they look beyond the front to a domestic life instead of accepting death or heroics as their final end.

Ioffe also confirmed this particular view in his rather positive description of the film's score. At the end of a comparatively lengthy discussion of the score, he concluded with a few statements about Shostakovich's "pastoral and elegiac" themes that underscored this wintery love scene. Ioffe claimed that the "method" that Shostakovich used throughout the score, that is, using attentive underscoring to connect with the actions and emotions of the characters, supported the "central idea" of the film in several different "contexts." In his last sentence of this description Ioffe asserted, "Shostakovich saw the essence of these contexts as love."[75] The scoring throughout this winter love scene emphasizes this representation by cementing the codes associated with romance, love, and with the world of the feminine while maintaining the girls' position in a war context, and ultimately within a film where they function as the positive heroes.[76]

THE EPIC AND ORCHESTRAL

Texture and instrumentation are two aspects that change dramatically in the scoring of the last few scenes of the film. In these scenes, two new orchestral cues appear: 1) when the rest of the group, including Silych, goes to rescue the girls from two enemy soldiers; and 2) after Asya's death. Since the majority of the film was an experiment in small ensemble writing, it is curious that Shostakovich appreciably changed instrumentation, and cued another set of codes. The first orchestral cue begins as the enemy soldiers line up Asya and Zoya to shoot them, and continues over a montage of images of Silych and Natasha rushing to rescue them before the final shootout. The brief snippets of melody and full orchestral accompaniment are in the same tradition as silent cinema hurries and contemporaneous films with chase and/or scenes of struggle—the music is repetitive and sequences briefly, trading between instrumental groups, and follows the action closely (a kind of parallelism, as with Max Steiner's idea of fitting music "like a glove"), and changes when the girls are rescued and the shootout begins.[77] The music thins in texture and ends with the scene fade out.

The second orchestral cue appears when Andrey cradles Asya's head to his heart and begins a speech about the socialist cause and her death, playing throughout the remainder of the film. This orchestral cue is an *Adagio*, and has characteristics common to this kind of indication such as slow moving lines and minor mode. This cue underscores Andrey's soliloquy and his speech to the camera, that is, to the "girls of the future" (*podrugi budushcheye*). After he closes his speech the scoring bridges the fade into a final image of the remaining characters atop horses riding toward the camera. From the *Adagio*, the orchestral texture thickens with the addition of brass and full ensemble in a typical final fanfare one finds in cinema of the time. The orchestral segment here is far from unusual; in fact, it strongly resembles the same sorts of cues used in previous film finales in Soviet and other films. These two separate orchestral sections operate in the narrative as epic—evocative of battle, struggle, and heroism—inspired by the same tropes found in contemporaneous films.[78] In so doing, this aligns the film with its time and more importantly with other war dramas with heroes who similarly die in the end. As with other musical narrative moments in the film, these also situate the girls within the genre of a war/historical film.

MUSIC + GIRLS

Throughout this film, various forms of sound have articulated the position, emotional state, and overall character of the main female protagonists. As Caryl Flinn has argued in regard to Hollywood film, music can give voice to a female character, working as narrative to give her agency.[79] Music in *Girlfriends*, either diegetically or otherwise, clearly gave voice to these women, a voice embedded in the context of the usually male dominated war/historical film. Diegetically, songs like "Tormented by Heavy Bondage" and "Where are those ..." gave them direct voice and power—they received the attention they needed through "Tormented by Heavy Bondage," which initiated them into a different world that would increase their status, though governed by men; and through "Where are those ..." they built friendship and camaraderie. Occasionally, even the trumpet call and/or fanfare eventually aligned with their positioning as central characters, as with Asya, albeit folded into a man's world. Shostakovich's scoring in particular acted as their voice, and illustrated their desires both situated between a male world of war and a female space of implied domesticity, friendship, and romance; it placed them between a male war context and what is a constructed (and presumed by the film's makers) female subjectivity. Music in this film, therefore, narrates this previously unarticulated voice of women in war/historical film—the borrowed tropes of war associated with men's war films, and tropes of romantic opera/song are among the codes appropriated by Arnshtam and Shostakovich to situate women as part of Soviet history-as-film.

RECEPTION

The reception of *Girlfriends* differed from that of contemporaraneous films such as *Chapayev* and *Youth of Maxim*. It was received well, but it did not achieve the cult status of these other two films. Pre- and post-premiere reviews were generally positive, especially from *Komsomol'skaya pravda* and *Pravda*, but the number of reviews was fewer, and little was directly written about the music. For such a positive response to the film's topic, it being Arnshtam's first independent work, and generally positive remarks about the sound design, it is puzzling that the film was neglected in the early Soviet sound film canon, and overshadowed by similar films with male heroes.[80]

Much of the press about *Girlfriends*, either mentioned sound or discussed it at some length. Given the recent privileging of speech in the sound design of cinema, most reviews focused on speech, or the character's intonations. In praise of Zheimo's performance, for example, one reviewer mentioned her approach to speech intonation as an important aspect of her representation of Asya.[81] If any music was mentioned, critics focused first on diegetic song over Shostakovich's scoring. Some critics considered "Where are those. . ." important; *Pravda* went as far as to reprint the lyrics in the article.[82] In most other cases, the song "Tormented . . ." in particular was singled out as serving a narrative pivot point early in the film. A critic from *Vechernaya krasnaya gazeta* gleefully asserted that the girls sang their way through the film, even though they only sing two songs together. This critic quoted the lyrics of "Tormented by Heavy Bondage" in order to argue the song's importance to the film and its cause.[83] *Pravda* also published several small articles attempting to demonstrate multiple points of view in support of the film and its representation of the *Komsomol* establishment; it focused heavily on the importance of song in representing the children's growth. "Tormented by Heavy Bondage" was considered by critics to be a serious focal point in the plot, and one of the most significant moments in the film.

Shostakovich's underscoring, however, was either ignored, or if mentioned, simply reviewed as "good." Newspapers such as *Iskusstvo kino* and *Kino* in particular were more detailed in their praise, and tended to publish more about the film's music. Mikhail Cheryomukhin, a past critic of Shostakovich's cinema music, wrote favorably of the score as whole. In his article from a set published in *Kino*, Cheryomukhin extolled Shostakovich's scoring as "organic" and "dynamic."[84] He also took the time to state directly how Shostakovich's scoring "never sounds like folk-craft" (*remeslenno-prikladnoye*) and is "far from primitive illustration."[85] Such a conscious declaration of how the scoring is somehow distinguished from less sophisticated approaches is notable, particularly when Cheryomukhin borrowed language ("primitive illustration") that was used by Shostakovich when describing his approach to film music when scoring New Babylon.[86] Equal praise was given to Shostakovich's attention to the "dramatic structure of the music," again echoing some of Shostakovich's past language about how "integral" music is to image and film narrative.[87] Also noted by Cheryomukhin was what he called Shostakovich's "virtuosic command of orchestral texture, color, and timbre"—a nod to his choices in instrumentation, and how these aspects were favored in Shostakovich's score.[88]

He continued to praise specific sections of the film where he considered sound design to be effective. Discussing how music operated within a scene as a whole (and carefully noting the integration of various sounds, not just underscoring), Cheryomukhin identified the first *traktir* scene as most interesting for the use of music (of multiple people singing diegetically with non-diegetic underscoring), describing the scene as a "delicate mosaic of tunes" that was emotionally and structurally effective.[89] He criticized other sections for being weak—the "optimistic major" of certain scenes, particularly in the beginning—while also claiming that moments that use "minor" (assumingly referring to mode) were successful.[90] The scene when the girls hear the White Army in the distance indicated by the offscreen *banda* is another that Cheryomukhin cited as poor and ineffective. Although generally a strong review, Cheryomukhin ends by asking Shostakovich to abandon "episodic-fragmented use of music" in the film, vaguely referring to the brief sections of no more than three to four minutes for which the composer habitually and necessarily wrote throughout the film.[91]

Cheryomukhin's analysis reveals a certain taste for film music emerging at the time that appeared to be embracing an overall symphonic approach. Preferring the "mosaic" of musical layering of one scene, while chastising the composer for a lack of continuity and use of the "optimistic major," resonates closely with a Hollywood aesthetic. In such an aesthetic, scoring is continuous in some cases, and/or firmly based on tropes or codes already in use and codified in silent film practice or previous musical styles. Certainly this is no surprise, since Shostakovich was well versed in both cinema practice and the history of music styles; but Cheryomukhin's expectations show a shift from silent practice, perhaps as dictated by notions of socialist realism, and an embrace of some of the same approaches that Shostakovich first explored when writing for New Babylon.

In the months and years after premiere, Girlfriends continued to be well received, though overlooked and almost left out of the canon in comparison to other films such as Chapayev and Youth of Maxim. The film was shown abroad (France, United States) in the early months of 1936, while its domestic showing began as early as October 1935 and continued into the following year.[92] Stalin reviewed the film several times in late 1935, praising it alongside other similar films.[93] The Soviet press received the film mostly favorably, as noted above, while the reception of the screenings abroad was varied, but generally supportive.[94] A few years later, in 1938, the studio released a silent version of the film, demonstrating that many theaters across the Soviet Union were still unable to handle sound film.[95] In the late 1950s and early 1960s, a *Sovietskiy ekran* retrospective was formed to celebrate Civil War films from the 1930s. Among the films listed— *Chapayev, Dvadtsat'-shest' komissarov* (*Twenty-Six Commissars*, dir. Nikoloz Shengelaia, 1932), and *Mï iz Kronshtadta* (*We Are from Kronstadt*, dir. Yefim Dzigan,1936)—*Girlfriends* was the only film that specifically concerned women. Not completely forgotten, *Girlfriends* was mentioned, however inconsistently.[96] After the January 1936 attack on Shostakovich's *Lady Macbeth of Mtsensk District*, an article by Sergey Bugoslavsky continued the critical praise of *Girlfriends* with a brief overview of Shostakovich's film music achievements. Citing Shostakovich's failings, he argued that the use of organ was formalist in *Golden Mountains* and *Girlfriends*, while labeling the introductory toccata of the latter (omitted in the post-1936 version of the film) as abstract.[97] Only the "lyrical" moment between Zoya and Sen'ka was considered valid in his definition and discussion of socialist realism, a complement to Cheryomukhin's description of the same scene, and one received as reminiscient of Hollywood by an American reviewer.[98] With less detail and in a long list of Shostakovich's film scores, Khrennikov echoes this sentiment decades later, citing Shostakovich's first few film scores as formalist (*New Babylon, Alone*, and *Golden Mountains*), and the remainder thereafter to be appropriately socialist, citing *Counterplan* and *Girlfriends* as the turning points.[99] Within the context of Shostakovich's film music output, *Girlfriends* survived as Soviet enough, echoing a sharper divide between formalism and socialism that emerged decades later.

CONCLUSION

While there had been a steady increase of the presence of women in what was deemed Soviet film in the 1920s and 1930s, these female characters were part of the whole narrative, exemplifying how women's equality was a vital part of the overall Soviet cause. *Girlfriends* was the first film, however, that showcased women as central heroines *and* feminized them in an effort to attract a different form of audience attention. Several aspects of film style illustrate this difference—the characters' positioning within the film, their costumes and heavy makeup, editing, acting (and the star power of certain actors), and importantly, the music. Codes of war and romance solidified their position as pretty and charming "girls" on the front placing them in the value system prized under Stalin—a dual role of public work atop expected domestic duties.[100] Music most certainly cued this duality with references to war by using trumpet calls; timbre; revolutionary songs, diegetic and non-diegetic sound/music; and cues of romance akin to late nineteenth-century opera that simultaneously recalled contemporaneous Hollywood practice. In terms of Shostakovich's film music output at this time, the scoring is original but fragmented, with little in the way of recurring motif. Instrumentation, texture, and timbre were consistent, as critics/composers like Cheryomukhin noted, creating a *leittimbre* throughout—a new emphasis on a small string-based ensemble just prior to Shostakovich's publication of his first experiment in the genre of string quartet. Songs, too, played a strong role in narrative, and his unique orchestration of the "Internationale" equally demonstrated his distinctive sense of timbre. Although episodic in approach, the music to this film marked a new frontier for Shostakovich—new textures (that of a small string-based ensemble), unique approaches to timbre and timbral combinations, and the modest use of music all narrated a differently represented and potentially more feminine Soviet woman. The musical and visual representation of this new woman indexed some of the sociological changes in Soviet culture, Arnshtam's experiment with women-as-heroes and Hollywood-style filmmaking, and socialist aesthetics. As such, hearing these "girls of the future" would be fundamentally altered in Soviet war film produced during Stalinism and beyond.

CHAPTER 8

༄༅

Epilogue

"Shostakovich's orchestration is the language of Babel."

G. Kozintsev, "O D. D. Shostakoviche"

S hostakovich's early scores were situated within a changing political scene, one that placed new emphasis on the Soviet, and worked in tandem with new technologies and aesthetics for sound-on-film. Each score had its own politics: each director had great interest in or experience with sound aesthetics, and sought to create a film that was seen as a mainstream "intelligible" Soviet experiment. Shostakovich was the link between these diverse films, which allowed him a wide range of experience, and the opportunity to witness the social and artistic transition from silent to sound film. Each score built on musical codes of the past, *intonatsii* in Asafyev's words, creating a parallel narrative to the image, and ultimately referencing current politics and their connection to musical trends.

New Babylon (1928–29) was one of the last of the silent films in the Soviet Union, and one of the first original scores for which Lenfil'm studios hired a composer. Its history is complex, and reveals much about the studio's internal politics and perspectives on musical process. The concept of the film composer was under heavy debate at the studio and in the cinema community, and was a sore point for musicians already in the field of film music. Lenfil'm cautiously hired the young and internationally renowned Shostakovich in order to ensure the success of its experiment with the "film composer" in the twilight years of silent film. The score betrayed many trends of its time, and illuminated the early experiments and burgeoning film-music theories of the directors Grigory Kozintsev and Leonid Trauberg, and the composer. Attempting to find a style and language that would surpass previous forms of silent film illustration, Shostakovich wrote a continuous symphonic work to narrate the film. Using the continuity common to silent film accompaniment, yet attending to nuances in the editing, shooting, and character development, he organized familiar codes within the score to integrally synthesize with the images. The film and score both demonstrated a concern with current trends in filmmaking, the emerging original score and the Russian film composer, the role of sound and music within Soviet cinema, and the notion of intelligibility and creating homegrown Soviet film. Even with the good intentions of the studio, composer, and directors, the film received a difficult premiere, and has since been a debated work. A long history of rediscovery and re-editing of the score and film have followed, complicated by the cultural politics of the initial premiere, misunderstandings of its contexts, and the difficulty of representing silent film and its score today. Shostakovich clearly was a pioneer in early film scoring, and this first experience gave him the tools to continue developing his skills as one of Russia's first and preeminent film composers.

Shostakovich continued to develop his ideas in his score for *Alone* (1929–31), with the directors Kozintsev and Trauberg. *Alone* was a transitional film, both in terms of cultural politics and of the emergence of sound cinema. Intelligibility was still the watchword, and the scenario and score were closely evaluated by the studio to be appropriately Soviet and accessible. The extraordinary revision of the scenarios indicated a struggle with the Soviet presentation of the topic of a heroine and her transformation, and a turning point in the directors' approach to the representation of the ethnic Other during their experience with on-location shooting in the Altai. In retrospect, the directors claimed that *Alone* was a musical film, instead of a talkie. Yet, music and sound were evidently an integral part of even the earliest scenarios; and Shostakovich was clearly charged with creating nuanced musical representations of the characters. The composer sketched unused musical numbers for folk instruments for the Oirat villagers, or at least attempted to represent them, and he worked with the directors to create musical images of the voice of certain characters, such as the *bai*. Sound technology and the available recording equipment, however, was severely limited, forcing the directors to rely mostly on music to vocalize and narrate the characters and their actions, and produce very few moments of synchronized speech. Having continuous music was nearly impossible because of the instability of the technology, and was aesthetically less appealing for the emergent sound film; as a result, the music was written in a number approach and unified primarily by recurring motives, timbres, and other codes. Despite these restrictions, the score was creative and experimental, revealing the same theories and ideas that the director-composer trio employed in their approach to *New Babylon*. The layering of sound in the hut scene, for example, showed their interest in maximizing the potential of sound film by layering found sounds and underscoring to narrate the complexity of a scene's space and characters. Such creative maneuvering around the difficulties inherent to early sound film was nonetheless met with mixed reviews. Caught between shifting definitions of realism and lingering interest in squelching "formalism" in film music, the reception was both supportive and critical of the film's sound design. Intelligibility was still being defined, and the cinema community was still attempting to satisfy current demands for the acceptable Soviet film. Shostakovich was placed in a unique position to contend with the aesthetics of sound design, technological demands, and the cultural politics of the Soviet mainstream film that was frequently packaged as "intelligibility."

Similar to the politics and aesthetics of *Alone*, *Golden Mountains* (1931) was immersed in the debate over the ideal Soviet sound film. Still caught between the aesthetics of silent and sound film, and the discussions of intelligibility, Shostakovich agreed to work with two other known figures in film culture who were former FEKs members and sympathetic to modernism and music, director Sergey Yutkevich and sound designer Leo Arnshtam. These two artists had different ideas about the symphonic score than what Shostakovich had encountered earlier. The director, sound designer, and composer approached *symphonism* as the borrowing of genres from concert music, and the use of recurring motives and codes to unify the score. Shostakovich was encouraged by Yutkevich and Arnshtam to compose a fugue to musically narrate a strike, for example, which they believed was a realistic and evocative approach to scoring. Realism was central to the sound design, and the trio embraced musical representations that drew upon modernist techniques and folk songs, yet this approach was met with a difficult reception. Similar to *Alone* and *New Babylon*, musical representations of the characters were uncomplicated and attempted to satisfy critics who were continuing to enforce intelligibility as a necessary component of the true Soviet film. Although the songs, timbres, and underscoring were skillful and creative, even with continuing glitches in sound technology, Shostakovich's scoring and the film were received well enough, only to be overshadowed by *Counterplan*. *Golden Mountains* never became a canonical film; nonetheless, it was a significant work that exhibited how Yutkevich, Arnshtam, and Shostakovich collaborated to create a new kind of symphonic score, while coping with pervasive issues in sound technology and cultural politics.

Shostakovich worked with Yutkevich again in his next score to *Counterplan* (1932), co-directed by Fridrikh Ermler. With the assistance of considerable media promotion and the dominance of a single song in various permutations throughout, *Counterplan* was considered the first true film accomplishment of Soviet sound cinema. It epitomized the intelligibility that so many of its advocates wanted since the late 1920s. The film's theme was based on a real-life event; the characters were simple and straightforward; and the score revolved around a single, catchy song originally written for the film. Although the directors and composer still negotiated with the intricacies of the sound film, the cueing was rhythmically more precise, and synchronization was improved. "Song of the Counterplan" was the first prototype of the emerging socialist realist film song, and was the centerpiece of the score; Shostakovich spent considerable time fashioning the song. His underscoring was similar to previous fragmentary scores, such as *Alone*, where he wrote for scenes or in fragments that were closed in form. The score was, however, unified by the central song, resulting in a "song score." The Song appeared in assorted permutations, either as a song or woven into the underscoring, as did other codes that were localized and contained within a scene. Many of the Song's variations functioned similarly to contemporaneous Hollywood films, which suggests that the film's popularity was linked in part to the emulation of the appealing structure and musical approaches of Hollywood cinema—a kind of film style (but not content) that was popular in the Soviet Union since the 1920s. The success of the film, which was excessively promoted by the studio, press, and by state figures, paved a path for the directors and the composer. Shostakovich later used the popularity of the Song to his advantage; and the Song became a hit across the world, and was recomposed and re-signified. *Counterplan* was easily canonized as the classic Soviet song film, and its hit song was a solid example of coding the Soviet popular. The score was a watershed for Shostakovich, and was regarded by critics and interested parties as a turning point in his film music career.

Youth of Maxim (1935) was another successful version of the song score, the first of its kind for the directors Kozintsev and Trauberg. The directors chose the film's topic when they began work on *Alone*, and then decided to create one musical film and one speaking film. *Youth of Maxim* thusly was chosen to be the speaking film, with minimal original scoring. The score only contained a brief scene with Shostakovich's underscoring, with several preexisting songs recurring throughout the film. The central song, "Krutitsya, vertitsya shar goluboy," (Whirling, twirling blue ball) was Maxim's theme throughout the film, and the following two films of the trilogy. This song and several others were the guiding music for many of the characters throughout; their placement and usage, although unattributed to Shostakovich, betrayed the same techniques that the director-composer trio had employed in their previous films. Shostakovich's direct contribution, to the Prologue, also aligned with the directors' approach to representing the characters and the epoch. The film was a huge success, particularly in its depiction of the ideal Soviet male hero. The music, both the song and underscoring, was hardly discussed or was simply dismissed in the press. The critics' silence in regard to the original music suggests that it was strategically ignored because it failed to suit the musical norms for intelligibility in Soviet cinema.

Girlfriends (1935–36) continued a trend of women as heroines (since *New Babylon* and *Alone*), but with a specific relationship to the shifting politics of Soviet feminism of the mid-1930s. Similar to *Youth of Maxim*, this film emphasized the role of the new Soviet heroine in war/historical films. This was Arnshtam's directorial debut, and some of his future films, also with Shostakovich's scores, continued to spotlight the Soviet heroine. Shostakovich's score, however, contained more underscoring than the previous song scores that featured a male hero. It was symphonic, in Arnshtam's sense, in a way similar to the score for *Golden Mountains*—musical vignettes and songs permeated the score and reappeared as needed. It was also Shostakovich's first exploration of the chamber string ensemble in film. Heavily relying upon the strings, he coded the feminine through the original music, borrowing from Hollywood trends and the nineteenth-century musical past. The coupling of romance and war, and representing the new Soviet female were reflected in the score and the film as a whole. The film was modestly canonized compared to Shostakovich's previous work with *Counterplan* and *Youth of Maxim*, but did persist as an example of the woman's war film. Similar to *Youth of Maxim*, and to some degree *Chapayev* (dirs. Georgy and Sergey Vasil'yev, 1934), the borrowed songs were better received and discussed than Shostakovich's music. Audiences instead preferred to address songs in lieu of the composer's work, demonstrating that a lack of clarity still persisted in terms of intelligible underscoring. Songs in general continued to be favored, particularly in films of this genre.

Evidenced by this complex and pioneering early work in cinema, Shostakovich was one of the first and most prominent Russian film composers. He serendipitously began composing original scores for cinema at a time when the film composer as a concept was created, and gained exclusive experience with early sound film and the beginnings of its firm establishment in the Soviet Union. Along with the usual issues that composers around the world experienced with the transition from silent to sound film in the 1920s and 1930s, Shostakovich also contended with the politics of the Cultural Revolution and early Stalinism. He collaborated with people who would become some of the most celebrated directors in Soviet film, and continued work with many of them just as he worked with newer directors. Although his experiences were fraught, and his experiments were keenly watched and deeply criticized, his early scores demonstrate the complexity and disagreement in terms of cultural politics, aesthetic concerns, and ultimately the difficulty in defining the intelligible Soviet film and its score.

Although this study pauses at the years 1935–1936, Shostakovich continued to compose for the Soviet Russian cinema for much of his life, ending his film career with one of the directors with whom he began: Grigory Kozintsev.[1] Shostakovich continued to develop many of the same techniques, approaches, and even codes of his earlier work into his later film scores, and matured as he worked with directors and sound designers. His last scores for Kozintsev's films, for example, still exhibited stylistic and aesthetic traits found in their earlier collaborations.[2] Shostakovich wrote for different genres, including a brief foray into the Soviet cartoon, yet still wrote for genres as pervasive as the war/historical film.[3] Two of his last scores were for Shakespearean adaptations, and were directed by Kozintsev: *Gamlet* (*Hamlet*, 1964) and *Korol' Lir* (*King Lear*, 1971).

Since Shostakovich's death in 1975, audiovisual media has undeniably become more accessible and faster paced. Yet, Asafyev's notion of an encyclopedia for an era—in his words, the "intonational reserve"—still applies. Some musical codes persist, and are sometimes connected to an individual or his work, but are challenged by faster transactions that are happening in new media. The speed at which these codes circulate, and the ways that they are circulated may be the reason why musical codes in early film scores are interpreted similarly by audiences today as they were in the 1920s and 1930s.

In the case of Shostakovich's early music for cinema, he wrestled with establishing himself as a film composer and with scoring for Soviet films. In the case of his music broadly, audiences attached and still attach consistent meanings to his music often with visual accompaniment, just as he sought to musically narrate image in stage and film works. That listeners attach specific visual media to his music continues a common social-musical history (where audiences relate that they hear stories or see images in connection to concert music), as it also continues a common history of shared meaning between concert and film musics, which has been and still is mediated by codes, political contexts, his reputation/reception, and the genre/form/style transgressions in his own work as specifically evidenced in his film scores. In other words, audiences unconsciously mediate the slippage between the concert work, the stage work, and the moving image through music and sound, just as Shostakovich negotiated similar issues in scoring, and simultaneously employed in his film scores some of the same techniques, styles, forms, and codes (think: *symphonism*, the fugue, *leittimbre*) of the musical past and of his own concert and stage music. Ultimately, Shostakovich approached the film score as he would any other musical work, but with the intent to fully understand the medium of film through his musical perspective. As such, he brought similar musical ideas into the medium of film music, manifesting as *symphonism* (however received and defined), codes, style, forms, instrumentation, *leittimbre*, motif, and so forth. Audiences undoubtedly still hear across genres today; just as Shostakovich was "symphonic" at times in his film scores, audiences hear his symphonies as images.

Since film music was such a significant part of his musical career, a question remains as to how it indexes with Shostakovich's concert/stage music and his reception. It is now evident from these discussions about his early film music that Shostakovich regarded scoring as a worthy medium, and worked to incorporate his knowledge and skills as a concert and stage composer into original scoring and sound design for cinema. Yet it is curious as to how audiences generally hear Shostakovich's music, especially when they accompany their listening with images, imagined or manifested in media. About music post-Shostakovich, Peter Schmelz has asked, "What Was Shostakovich and What Came Next?," and answered with a discussion of how Shostakovich's reception unfolded in music communities in the later years of his life and after his death.[4] Prior to and following his article, others have examined Shostakovich's reception into the late twentieth and twenty-first centuries focusing on most genres of his output. In the spirit of complementing those discussions and directing them into the arena of audiovisual media, and as a point for reflection on what comes next after Shostakovich and his film music, I look at participatory multimedia in the particular form of YouTube. This is not to exclude other forms of reception, other internet sources or websites, or previous reception histories of his repertory outside of cinema. I single out YouTube as an object for study to briefly open up the question of how codes persist and how they index with the reception of Shostakovich's music. The discussion is necessarily selective. The point is to show how codes endure today, and how some ideas about Shostakovich's concert and stage music are articulated in media, and thusly illustrate how audiences are participating in an audiovisual discussion of coding, reception, transnational politics, and intelligibility in a post-Soviet sense of the word. Shostakovich's music thusly inspires audiences to participate with and powerfully respond to it; in a sense, Shostakovich as a concept and his music generally has become intelligible beyond the Soviet definition, that is, it has been and still is simply popular. Just as Shostakovich was trading in musical codes and modifying them for use in his scoring for early Soviet cinema, audiences today in various media forms including YouTube recreate and recycle those same codes, using Shostakovich as a subject.

THE DICTIONARY OF AN EPOCH

My examinations of Shostakovich's early scores incorporate what these codes may mean generally, pointing to Asafyev's ideas about *intonatstii*, and what they meant to listeners at the time, whether they were interested studio personnel, music/film critics, or average filmgoers. Music and sound in these films, as in others, were heard as narrative—much in the way that Asafyev explained, albeit in a broad and occasionally amorphous manner—how *intonatsii* were (are) embedded in one's time, a "dictionary of the epoch."[5] For many listeners, this "dictionary of the epoch" is integral to how we hear, as various subfields of semiotics and analysis have aptly demonstrated. In regard to Shostakovich specifically, however, listeners have been peculiarly fascinated with understanding these codes in myriad ways: through hearing stories, recreating histories, or inserting themselves into revised Cold War historical narratives. Scholarship has in some ways reflected and responded to these trends.[6]

The combination of Shostakovich's codes, approaches to form, and speed are part of what makes him an interstitial composer—to borrow Arved Ashby's phrase—one situated between late nineteenth-century visual/ musical traditions and burgeoning ideas about early twentieth-century music for cinema.[7] His approach to early film scoring suggested genre transgression and transferability of codes; and scoring for cinema necessarily required him to work within time constraints. Time and tempo—or rather, speed—was an integral part of working with a film team, as was the necessity to shift between scenes with originally scored musical fragments. This sort of cinematic thinking permeated his other work. His Piano Concerto No.1 (1933), for example, a concert piece composed in the same period as *Counterplan* and *Youth of Maxim*, exhibits some of the fragmentation and unity of his film scores, particularly in the finale. The leaping from idea to idea, the rapid shifting of musical focus creates a pastiche that resonates with contemporaneous cinematic montage.[8] It is specifically reminiscent of the scene from the fourth part in *New Babylon*, and the hut scene from *Alone*.[9] The frenetic pace coupled with the multiplicity of styles creates a polyvalent effect—much in the way the combination of image and sound create narrative meaning in cinema. The *intonatsii* in which Shostakovich traded have continued to permeate our cultures today; since twenty-first century listeners have yet to meet the appropriate "crisis" in the Asafyevan sense—that is, a significant shift in our shared musical dictionary that alienates us from past dictionaries—our ears are still tuned to Shostakovich's codes, forms, and tempi, among those of other composers of the previous century.

Sound and music in cinema arguably perpetuates and recycles this dictionary, and operates as part of a soundscape, of which Shostakovich was a part. As biographers relate, he was imagistic in his approach to music early in life, and his symphonies have been heard as dramatic in form.[10] He was exposed to varied musical trends in the 1920s, and was an active part of Leningrad experimental musical life.[11] He was musically diverse, and able to exercise this talent through playing as a *pianist-illustrator*, and eventually producing music for opera and film.[12] It was because of his opera *Nose*, and his relative fame, that directors and studios took note of his ability to musicalize image.[13] From *New Babylon* forward, he developed film music theories alongside directors of his time, becoming intertwined with their thinking about sound and music. Kozintsev, for example, repeatedly remarked on Shostakovich's talents and abilities to hear what Kozintsev's images would demand, and produce music exactly as he wanted.[14] The director, along with others such as Yutkevich, also admired Shostakovich's ability to write concisely, and for specific timings to a moment in a film—a talent sometimes seen as a failing. Kozintsev reiterated: "Art that is written to order is not at all bad art."[15] This conciseness, the diluting of an idea to an essence that was immediately communicable yet powerful was something composers had been doing (and would continue to do) for opera, theater, and film. Indicated by his writings from *New Babylon* and forward, Shostakovich was part of the early theorizing about how music should specifically engage image, and how original scoring was integral to cinema.[16] The film experience he gained through this interstitiality, having been situated at the cusp of a new musical genre with long roots, and seeing this genre through the better part of the twentieth century, was a part of his musical thinking and arguably part of the reception of his music overall.

RECEPTION AND MULTIMEDIA

The reception of Shostakovich's music has been a special one over the course of the twentieth century, complicated by Cold War politics, shifting politico-musical trends, and specifically Western perceptions of things

Russian and Soviet. His reception was complicated at home and abroad, and situated in times fraught with significant political changes.[17] A few years after his death, in 1975, his purported memoirs were published by Solomon Volkov, in a book that was shown to be a loosely corroborated biography instead of an interview-based autobiography.[18] After Laurel Fay's informed and researched response to the potential fraud of the book was published a year or so later, an argument rooted in nationalistic sentiment and Cold War politics erupted.[19] Throughout the 1980s, and culminating in tense debates in the late 1990s, the so-called "Shostakovich controversy" appeared as an unexpected debate that hinged on perceived dichotomies that were a result of these sentiments. Various scholars of Russian music, particularly in the West, responded to writers propelling the idea of Shostakovich as dissident or rebel and who were seeking answers to or support for monolithic stories created in response to Shostakovich's music.[20] The reading of biography, political pasts, nationalistic sympathies, and personal agendas was hotly debated and contested by scholars, creating a pull between perceived dichotomies of West and Other, of specialist and general listener.[21] After a provocative session on Shostakovich at the American Musicological Society in 1999, and the publication of books that were defensive of Volkov's stance on Shostakovich, debates hit a peak only to fizzle out thereafter. Malcolm Brown's *A Shostakovich Casebook* set many theories to rest and provided a thorough and balanced series of perspectives on the debates.[22] In the 2000s, the debates have simmered but remnants linger in general perceptions of the composer. This controversy placed in the foreground the complexity of the narrative reading of a composer's music and life in the twentieth century, and emphasized the role of world politics in art.

Naturally, much more exists of Shostakovich's reception and scholarship outside of this controversy, and scholarship on Shostakovich in the West has grown immensely over the past several decades.[23] The way in which visual media has been integrated into Shostakovich's reception is unique, and reflects some of the sentiments that began before and persisted since the controversy.[24] Shostakovich appears to be a kind of icon; and like many composers who are also treated as iconic (e.g., Beethoven), Shostakovich's current reception is complicated by newer forms of media, just as Shostakovich's involvement in newer forms of media (e.g., cinema) in his time had an impact on his work and perceptions of it.

Scholarship on sound and media of late has engaged the trope of sound as a constant stream in human life, a larger fabric in which multiple sound and visual media exist and recreate meanings.[25] Composers like Shostakovich, especially those who were deeply connected to cinema practices from the early twentieth century forward, are embedded in this stream today, and represented in certain forms of popular media that continue themes of their works' reception. YouTube, music videos, and other forms that have been generally distanced from any discussion of Shostakovich's music demonstrate how audiences still perceive Shostakovich and his work, and the tropes and ideas with which he is associated. Over a few years, I have observed activity on YouTube, finding a series of homemade videos, uploaded official music videos of international artists, and similar media that address Shostakovich. This "YouTube Shostakovich," an internet ethnography of Shostakovich's reception through a selective medium, focuses on how the composer is portrayed as an icon and is recreated by uploaded videos on YouTube, and how that indexes similar activities outside of that medium.[26] There is more to do with this kind of ethnography; what I provide here is merely a beginning, and a possible way in which Shostakovich as composer and icon is consumed and recreated in these media. Most importantly, and for my purposes here, I am interested in what comes next for Shostakovich and audiovisual media: how we hear Shostakovich across media and venues; and how aspects of his scoring for cinema—which transgressed genres, styles, and codes—manifests today in the uploaded entries in participatory media such as YouTube.

MUSINGS ON YOUTUBE SHOSTAKOVICH

Internet sites such as YouTube are plentiful, and many of them host music, film, and other media that engage composers of the Western concert tradition. On YouTube, a constantly changing media soundscape, uploads of Shostakovich's music, segments of his film scores and/or their films, and old and new concert video/audio recordings abound. A handful of these multimedia uploads use Shostakovich as subject (and sometimes object), and demonstrate an individual's preoccupation with Shostakovich and his concert music as a trope or icon. The majority of these posts engage themes of war, violence, or political commentary. They come in two different types: uploaded homemade videos with Shostakovich's concert music by everyday YouTube users or the sampling of a fragment from a concert piece used as a riff for a popular song, often by well-known musicians. Surely, there are uploads of segments of his film music (often with the films), and of particular concerts of his music. But what I am concerned with here is how individuals—YouTube authors who are responsible for these audiovisual creations—use image and music to illustrate their ideas about politics and war, use Shostakovich to represent a belief, and articulate the intelligibility of his music for their purposes.[27]

Many of Shostakovich's symphonies and string quartets have been used as kind of soundtrack to several homemade films that contest global war and violence. One example is the video creation by YouTube author nikolaos333, who uploaded a series of horrific images from various contemporary wars, predominantly in the Middle East.[28] These collated shots contain images of dead or mangled bodies, explosions, instruments of war, cemeteries, and patriotic symbols from various countries especially implicating the United States, and run parallel to Shostakovich's Eighth Symphony, third movement.[29] (See Video 8.1.) ▶ The images are rhythmically and temporally aligned, sometimes with sync points that appear to mickey-mouse the images, most specifically images of soldiers killing civilians. In his commentary to accompany the video, the author wrote, in Greek, how this specific musical choice captures his feelings about war.[30] Having served as a soldier, he felt that Shostakovich's music was appropriately serious and grief-stricken, and therefore useful for an anti-war video.[31] No doubt Shostakovich has been associated with war for some time, particularly since his Seventh Symphony ("Leningrad"); and several other symphonies have been referred to as the "war symphonies."[32] The leap to associate war with Shostakovich, however intuitive, is unsurprising. The minor mode, low tessitura string opening in the violas, the percussive offbeats in the other strings, and the eventual contrast with high-pitched winds plays on the same codes found in past "dictionaries" that indicate a building of tension and movement.[33] Viewers responded in several languages, commending the uploader or commenting on current politics, riddled with anti-American sentiment. The author also uploaded other segments of Shostakovich's repertory (and that of Stravinsky and Vivaldi), showing some familiarity with the composer. A Shostakovich symphonic movement, one with stark timbral contrasts, percussive emphases, and with a history of being referred to as a "war symphony," clearly resonated with this YouTube author and his individual perspective of current politics, linking the aural codes of this work with modern war.

Another example achieves a similar effect, combining images of war with Shostakovich's music. YouTube author Kagen5690 uploaded a series of World War II images in combination with the composer's Eighth String Quartet, movement two.[34] Less visually dynamic than the video by nikolaos333, this video simply overlays the string quartet movement over random images timed about eight seconds apart. (See Video 8.2.) ▶ There was no mickey-mousing, and no effort made to coordinate with the music as in the previous example. The comments to the video nonetheless reveal political associations, (often incorrect) statements about Soviet history, and praise for the composer. The author also speaks to politics, though vaguely, as provoked by another viewer. The Eighth String Quartet is a well-known work in the West, and one that has been analyzed and discussed at length in regard to Shostakovich's relationship to the state. Similar to the "war symphonies," this quartet has captured popular imagination prior to this video; and with its DSCH and multiple other quotations, the piece has been canonized and strongly associated with grief and loss.[35] Although less charged than other videos, the general tone of the upload and the past history of the quartet suggest a broadly defined association of Shostakovich, grief, and politics.

A last and unusual example of YouTube Shostakovich and associations of war and violence is found in a series of Shostakovich's symphonies uploaded by "Magisch meisje Orkest." Among more than 500 uploaded stills with the music of Haydn, Sibelius, and Tchaikovsky, the Shostakovich symphonies are the only ones to date that show young anime-sketched women holding weapons, or engaging in some sort of battle.[36] Some of the stills associated with Shostakovich's music have changed over time; but of all the uploads of this author, only Shostakovich's music—in this case all fifteen symphonies—has images of girls and guns displayed with each upload. Aside from the disturbing index of young women with weapons and the all attendant fetishistic issues that come with such a series of images collated with the composer's music, the idea that Shostakovich's music is deserving of such imagery continues the same perceptions of violence, albeit general in this case, that have been previously associated with some of his concert music. An upload of Shostakovich's Seventh Symphony ("Leningrad"), one clearly associated with war since its premiere, displays a young woman holding a gun within a war-torn countryside with a zeppelin in the background.[37] (See Figure 8.1.)

The comments to this upload were varied—many focused on the music, and some critiqued or enjoyed the anime image. As with most YouTube comments, heated debates appeared in the comment stream that either angrily protested the inappropriateness of the image with the music, or provided rants about Stalin and the Cold War. In this and other uploads by this author, the fetishistic combination of girl, gun, and Shostakovich is surely individual; but the associations with war, as part of past reception, continues to be conflated with all of his symphonies, including more obvious ones such as the Seventh.

There are even more transformative uses of Shostakovich's music reduced to riffs of a sort that have appeared in popular music over the past six years. Beginning with eclectic performer Peter Fox and the track "Alles Neu" from

Dmitri Shostakovich (1906-1975)

Symphony No.7 in C major, op.60

"Leningrad"

Valery Gergiev

Mariinsky Theatre Orchestra

Konzerthaus, Vienna, 4/12/2010

0:00 / 1:23:00

Shostakovich: Symphony No.7 - Gergiev/MTO(2010Live)

Magisch meisje Orkest

Subscribe 23,653

512,473

＋ Add to   Share   ••• More

2,235 53

Uploaded on Nov 7, 2011
Dmitri Shostakovich (1906-1975)

Figure 8.1: A still from YouTube author Magisch meisje Orkest's upload of Shostakovich's Seventh Symphony.

the album *Stadtaffe* (2008), a string riff from the middle of the finale of Shostakovich's Seventh Symphony became fodder for similar songs thereafter, including Plan B's "Ill Manors" (a single from the eponymous film and its soundtrack, 2012) and Fall Out Boy's "The Phoenix" (from *Save Rock and Roll*, 2013).[38] In Fox's song, he begins with a loop of the half-step undulating motive that appears in the strings in the Symphony's finale, looping it every eight beats, with some variation. This loop becomes the foundation upon which he raps and the American drumline, Cold Steel, lays their rhythms. Fox emulates the galop rhythm from the Shostakovich excerpt and playfully reorients the groove through melodic/rhythmic hemiola in the chorus. The song is critical and playfully mocking of urban life, and accompanies images of Fox moving through urban spaces, ending up in a theater with an orchestra of apes accompanying him on toy piano.[39] (See Video 8.3.) ⊙ Grotesque and witty, the song and its video is an appropriate home for this Shostakovich riff. The offbeat rhythms, the use of a galop rhythm, and usual grotesquerie of Shostakovich's style is emulated here; arguably the repetitive rhythms, minor mode, and string timbre altogether resonated as a familiar *intonatsiya*, becoming fodder for a similarly charged piece of music. Although simply an interesting and potentially resonant riff, the culling of this particular moment of the symphony suggests its enduring popularity, and the associations with tension and possible violence evoked by the code that might still be part of this era's musical dictionary.

British singer/songwriter/filmmaker Plan B borrowed the same riff for his "Ill Manors," a song from his eponymous film soundtrack, also directed by him. Released in 2012, "Ill Manors" consciously uses the same riff to underscore street violence in response to the London riots of 2011.[40] The opening of the video shows Plan B mimicking the actions of a violinist to the rhythms of the Shostakovich loop before he begins commenting on street life, racism, and crime. (See Video 8.4.) ▶ The Shostakovich loop permeates the activist song acting as a foil to the sharp rhythms of his speech and a drummer's backbeat.[41] Creating layers of syncopation, the music is accompanied by images of street violence and disenfranchised youth. The excerpt from Shostakovich's symphony finds a familiar home in this song—with direct statements about class war and street violence, the motive is extracted and remade with similar though generalized meaning. Despite the transnational flow from the urban satire of Fox to the political activism of Plan B, the generalized associations of politics and violence with Shostakovich's symphony continued, if only as simulacra.

With another transnational leap, the motive has recently been taken up by the American band Fall Out Boy in their newest album *Save Rock and Roll* (2013) with their multimedia number, "The Phoenix."[42] The Shostakovich loop is borrowed, but transformed by starting a half-step higher than Fox's and Plan B's songs. (See Video 8.5.) ▶ The eight-beat organization that Fox originally used in "Alles Neu" is present, with additional rhythms added atop the riff often emphasizing a duple feel, and emphasis on beats 7-8-1. With greater emphasis on a duple feel than the previous examples, and a general rock sensibility, this song uses the Shostakovich loop as just one of many lines within it, as opposed to treating the loop as organic material that the singer/rapper ornaments and plays against in counterpoint. Certainly, the accompanying video is violent, but is staged as a comic book fantasy than political commentary.[43] The connection to war and politics is severed in this usage of the Shostakovich loop. Instead when asked about how the song was formed, Patrick Stump, the front man for the band replied:

> I was listening through one of his [Shostakovich's] symphonies and found one little string moment that I loved. . . . We tweaked it a lot, but the bones of the song were done on [that] first inspiration. So thanks to Dmitri Shostakovich.[44]

Stump makes no reference to the exact symphony or to any political under-pinnings in this interview. Shostakovich in this case was simply the "first inspiration." It is possible that Stump found this "little string moment" in the Seventh Symphony after hearing Fox's song, which debuted in 2008, since "Alles Neu" had been imported to the United States and had been incredibly popular across Europe for several years.[45] Regardless, the implied political/violent meanings of the *intonatsiya* of this riff are left behind in this song. Certainly, the riff be heard as aggressive and motoric, and can imply a more general violence (as supported in the video), but the politics of satire or war are absent. The code of the riff (and Symphony from which it was taken) arguably persists, though transformed though a new style and band.

The reduction of a Shostakovich symphony to a riff as foundation for new and often political music, and the illustrative uploading of concert music with video accompaniment show an eclectic recycling of a composer with new media. The recycling is global—from east to west in the case of Fox, Plan B, and Fall Out Boy and across the (computer-owning) world in the case of the homemade videos. This is an example of how a composer, in this case Shostakovich, is used and circulated transnationally in popu-lar culture today, and how he is iconic for many.[46] This kind of circulation implies that the sorts of codes that Shostakovich used in his symphonic music are still understandable today, and that a musical dictionary has endured. The active participation of audiences today through YouTube, and the listening to the past that performers still enact keeps those codes alive. Shostakovich's music, and Shostakovich as iconic figure, continues to be part of our current dictionary, and visual media is integral to the (re)cycling of that dictionary. Shostakovich's music for cinema operated similarly.

Shostakovich was clearly inclined to the imagistic, lived in a time and place that favored theatrical approaches to concert music, and wrote for music and image through opera, theater, ballet, and film. Audiences, wher-ever placed and for a multitude of reasons, associate his music with images. In a post-literate age, as some writers have argued, the manifestation of certain media have been (and still are) competing with the written word, at times replacing that earlier technology. Modes of audiovisual expression (e.g., uploading videos to YouTube) have changed, but the inclination to hear images—to hear Shostakovich—as imagistic, as hero, and/or as icon arguably carries through these newer media, while having been mediated through previous forms and venues such as the concert stage and the cin-ema house. Film was, for Shostakovich, a working medium, a way to explore musical expression, sometimes a way to appease state authorities, a way to earn income, and a way to speak to a general public—just as any other kind of musical expression. As noted by Kozinstev in this chapter's epitaph, Shostakovich's music (or orchestration) as a form of "Babel" speaks to the multivalency of his music and its potential ability to communicate with audiences.[47] As Taruskin has noted, Shostakovich was a "civic artist," one who intended communication with people within, but not subservient to, a state and its contemporaneous politics.[48] Cinema, and the codes that it generated and perpetuated, was one way to speak with those audiences. Film, and the various incarnations of moving media that are now becoming dominant in a post-literate century, are now recycling and expressing his music in similar but new ways, and with another form of iconicity. His participation in the creation of music for Soviet cinema, and the new forms of media (and recent media authors) that have responded to his music, demonstrate an interstitial Shostakovich that has been recreated over time. Such a phenomenon speaks to the plasticity and intelligibility of his music.

Shostakovich's recycling of the current musical dictionary transgressed genres—he and the directors with whom he worked borrowed from musical histories because of the need to satisfy demands in cultural politics, define the aesthetics of realism and socialism, and determine the space that music and sound would occupy in Soviet Russian cinema, that is, understanding sound's relationship to image as mediated by aesthetic concerns and technology. Codes, as variably and broadly defined here, were part of a larger process of filmmaking and film scoring. Being one of the first Russian composers for cinema necessitated Shostakovich's experimentation alongside the many film artists with whom he worked. The experimental nature of this work—the questioning of the nature of the relationship between image and sound—was magnified by the transition from silent cinema to sound-on-film, and momentous changes in Soviet Russian society and cultural politics. It is remarkable how Shostakovich negotiated his new role as film composer in the late 1920s and 1930s in the Soviet Union, and that he maintained a film music career for much of his life. His participation in early Soviet cinema helped to define the Russian film composer, and ushered in a new era of film music.

NOTES

CHAPTER 1

1. Dmitry Shostakovich, "Yeshchyo raz o kinomuzïke" [Once Again About Film Music], *Iskusstvo kino* 1 (1954): 87.
2. Dmitry Shostakovich, "Muzïka v kino" [Music to Cinema], *Literaturnaya gazeta* 1, no. 5 (1939).
3. Richard Taruskin, "Shostakovich and Us," in *Defining Russia Musically* (Princeton: Princeton University Press, 1997), 497.
4. For example, John Riley, *Dmitri Shostakovich: A Life in Film* (London: I. B. Tauris, 2005).
5. In only the past few years has Russian film music garnered any attention from musicologists. See for example, Peter Kupfer, "Music, Ideology, and Entertainment in the Soviet Music Comedies of Grigory Aleksandrov and Isaak Dunyaevsky" (PhD diss., University of Chicago, 2010); Kevin Bartig, *Composing for the Red Screen: Prokofiev and Soviet Film* (Oxford: Oxford University Press, 2013). See also, in music theory, Erik Heine, "The Film Music of Dmitri Shostakovich in *The Gadfly, Hamlet,* and *King Lear*," (PhD diss., University of Texas at Austin, 2005). When I first published work on Shostakovich's film music in 2006, scholars of Shostakovich's music tended to openly dismiss his film scores. See Joan Titus, "Modernism, Socialist Realism, and Identity, in the Early Film Music of Dmitry Shostakovich, 1929–1932" (PhD diss., Ohio State University, 2006) for more information.
6. In the past few years and since my initial publication of my research, some new attention has been paid to Shostakovich's film scores in the United States and in Russia. See Titus, "Modernism, Socialist Realism, and Identity, in the Early Film Music of Dmitry Shostakovich."
7. See Laurel Fay, *Shostakovich: A Life* (Oxford: Oxford University Press, 2000) and Elizabeth Wilson, *Shostakovich: A Life Remembered* (Princeton: Princeton University Press, 1994).
8. On a related note, Marina Frolova-Walker makes a case for Stalinist art as boring. See Marina Frolova-Walker, "Stalin and the Art of Boredom," *Twentieth Century Music* 1, no. 1 (March 2004): 101–124.
9. See Katerina Clark, *The Soviet Novel: History as Ritual*, 3rd ed. (Bloomington: Indiana University Press, 2000).
10. Boris Groys, *The Total Art of Stalinism: Avant-Garde, Aesthetic Dictatorship, and Beyond*, trans. Charles Rougle (Princeton: Princeton University Press, 1992). See also the work of Evgeny Dobrenko, including his *Aesthetics of Alienation: Reassessment of Early Soviet Cultural Theories* (Evanston: Northwestern University Press, 2005).

11. David Bordwell, *Narration in the Fiction Film* (Madison: University of Wisconsin Press, 1985); David Herman, *The Cambridge Companion to Narrative* (Cambridge University Press, 2007); Gerard Genette, *Narrative Discourse Revisited* (Cornell University Press, 1988); and Marie-Laure Ryan, *Narrative Across Media: the Languages of Storytelling* (University of Nebraska Press, 2004).

12. These ideas took root in the writings of other thinkers as well. See the work of Boleslav Yavorsky (1877–1942); and modern work such as David Haas, *Leningrad's Modernists: Studies in Composition and Musical Thought, 1917–1932* (Peter Lang: New York, 1998); Malcolm Brown, "The Soviet Russian Concepts of 'Intonazia' and 'Musical Imagery,'" *The Musical Quarterly* 60, no. 4 (October 1974): 557–567; Elena Orlova, *Intonatsionnaia teoria Asafyeva kak uchenie o spetsifike muzykal'nogo myshleniya* [The Intonational Theory of Asafyev as a Doctrine of the Totality of Musical Thought] (Moscow: Muzïka, 1984); and Jiří Smrž, *Symphonic Stalinism: Claiming Musical Classics for the New Soviet Listener 1932–1953* (Berlin: Lit Verlag, 2011), to name a few.

13. See Boris Asafyev, *Musical Form as Process* and *Intonatsiya*. *Intonatsiya* was published in 1947 but had been conceived and discussed in Asafyev's writings beginning in the 1910s. See Haas, chapter 3 for a summary of some of these writings. See James Tull, "B. V. Asaf'yev's Musical Form as a Process, Translation and Commentary" (Ph.D., diss., The Ohio State University, 1976 for English translation and commentary.

14. Various writers of late have written about audio-visual hearing, or cinematic hearing, which resonates in part with this idea of a musical concept beyond the usual melody. See for example Michael Long, *Beautiful Monsters: Imagining the Classic in Musical Media* (Berkeley: University of California Press, 2008) and John Richardson, *An Eye for Music: Popular Music and the Audiovisual Surreal* (Oxford: Oxford University Press, 2012). Asafyev wrote at length about "sound complexes" and *intonatsiya*.

15. See Haas for a discussion of how Asafyev's writings emerged in the musical work of Leningrad modernists.

16. In using the word/phrases "code," "code complex," or "sound complex" (the last being Asafyev's creation), I am certainly aware that these words cue a long history of analysis in semiotics, structuralism, musical topics and tropes, and the like. Instead of retelling these histories, or finding yet another word, I use the word(s) "code" and "code complex" most frequently throughout this book as a simple reference. There is no intention on my part to ignore past work in semiotics or structuralism, most famously that of Charles Sanders Peirce, Umberto Eco, Ferdinand de Saussure, Yuri Lotman, Mikhail Bakhtin, Jean-Jacques Nattiez, Eero Tarasti, Carolyn Abbate, Julia Kristeva, Christian Metz, Claude Lévi-Strauss, and Roland Barthes, among others not listed here. I have considered this past work for several years, and have decided to use "code" or "code complex" as a form of shorthand.

17. I have previously argued that this openness to an "intonational reserve" jibes with a kind of polystylism of the 1920s in Leningrad. Haas has also discussed this in terms of how Asafyev's theories were a significant part of pedagogical and compositional practice at that time and place. See Titus, "Modernism, Socialist Realism, and Identity, in the Early Film Music of Dmitry Shostakovich, 1929–1932," 27ff.; and Haas.

18. Tull, "B. V. Asaf'yev's Musical Form as a Process," 160.

19. Haas, 61.

20. See for example A. V. Goldobin and B. M. Azacheyev, *Pianist-illyustrator kin-ematografischeskikh kartin* [Accompanying Cinematograph Pictures on the Piano] (Kostroma, 1912). Giuseppe Becce, Ludwig Brav, and Hans Erdmann, *Allgemeines Handbuch der Film-Musik* (Berlin-Lichterfelde: Schlesinger 1927); Erno Rapée, *Erno Rapee's Encyclopaedia of Music for Pictures* (New York: Belwin, 1925); Erno Rapée, *Motion Picture Moods for Pianists and Organists: A Rapid-Reference Collection of Selected Pieces, Adapted to Fifty-Two Moods and Situations* (New York: Schirmer, 1924).

21. See Titus, "Modernism, Socialist Realism, and Identity, in the Early Film Music of Dmitry Shostakovich"; Sergey Bugoslavsky and Vladimir Messman, *Muzïka i kino, na kino-muzïkal'nom fronte printsipy i metody kino-muzïki opyt kino-muzïkal'noy kompozitsiy* [Music and the Cinema, on the Film-Musical Front of the Principles and Methods of Film-Music Experience of Film-Musical Composition] (Moscow: Kinopechat', 1926); D. Blok and S. Bugoslavsky, *Muzïkal'noe soprovozh-deniye v kino* [Musical Accompaniment in the Cinema] (Moscow: Teakinopechat, 1929); and Yuri Tsivian, *Early Cinema in Russia and Its Cultural Reception* (Chicago: University of Chicago Press, 1994).

22. Haas, 60; and Orlova.

23. Ibid.

24. Arved Ashby refers to Mahler as interstitial, an observation that I borrow here. See Arved Ashby, *Absolute Music, Mechanical Reproduction* (Berkeley: University of California Press, 2010), 250.

25. In this study, I omit *Love and Hatred* (*Lyubov i nenavist*, dir. Al'bert Gendel'shtein, 1934) and one of Shostakovich's early cartoon scores, *Tale of a Priest and His Servant Balda* (*Skazka o pope i o rabotnike ego Balde*, dir. Mikhail Tsekhanovsky, 1934), due to a significant lack of resources at the time of research. I hope to publish on these scores at a later date.

26. Cited from I. I. Ioffe, *Muzïka sovetskogo kino* [Music of the Soviet Cinema] (Leningrad: State Musical Scientific-Research Institute, 1938), 45. Here Ioffe cites a stenogram of a presentation dated 9 June 1937.

27. Titus, "About the Music to the *New Babylon*."

28. Ibid.

29. For more on the positive hero, see Clark, *The Soviet Novel: History As Ritual.*

30. Claudia Gorbman, *Unheard Melodies: Narrative Film Music* (Bloomington: Indiana University Press, 1987).

31. *Youth of Maxim* began the trilogy, and was followed by *Return of Maxim* (*Vozvrashcheniye Maksima*, dirs. Grigory Kozintsev and Leonid Trauberg, 1936–37) and *Vyborg Side* (*Vïborgskaya storona*, dirs. Grigory Kozintsev and Leonid Trauberg, 1938).

32. C. Vaughan James, *Soviet Socialist Realism: Origins and Theory* (London: Macmillan Press, 1973), 87.

33. He also wrote string quartet fragments around this time as stand-alone pieces.

34. See Joan Titus, "Dmitry Shostakovich as Film Music Theorist," in *Music and Politics in Twentieth-Century Europe: Essays in Memory of Neil Edmunds*, edited by Pauline Fairclough (London: Ashgate Press, 2012), 249–260.

CHAPTER 2

1. See chapter 1: Introduction, for discussion of codes.

2. See Joan Titus, "Silents, Sound, and Modernism in Dmitry Shostakovich's Score to the *New Babylon* (1928–1929)," in *Sound, Speech, and Music in Soviet*

and Post-Soviet Cinema, ed. Masha Salazkina and Lilya Kaganovsky, 38–59 (Bloomington: Indiana University Press, 2014).

3. Kozintsev and Trauberg also cited the works of Émile Zola and Friedrich Engels as inspirations for the film's story. See Joan Titus, "Modernism, Socialist Realism, and Identity in the Early Film Music of Dmitry Shostakovich, 1929–1932" (PhD diss., Ohio State University, 2006), 159–160. Other authors have claimed different inspirations for the film. Theodore van Houten, for example, claims that the 1900 socialist workers' opera *Louise* by Gustav Charpentier was also an inspiration. See Theodore van Houten, *Dmitri Sjostakovitsj, een leven in angst* (Van Gruting: Westervoort, 2006), 67.

4. Grigory Kozintsev, *The Deep Screen* [*Glubokiy ekran*] (Moscow: Iskusstvo, 1971), 113.

5. See the discussion of this topic in David Bordwell, *Narration in the Fiction Film* (Madison: University of Wisconsin Press, 1985), 250.

6. *Fabula* translates as "story." See Bordwell, *Narration in the Fiction Film*, 235ff.

7. After the film had been shot, but was being reedited (January 1929), Trauberg wrote that he did not understand what "intelligible to the millions" meant. Based on the choice of topic and the intent to show links between the French Commune and the Soviet Union, the directors likely intended that the *New Babylon* be comprehensible, but may not have understood (or wanted to understand) how to be "intelligible to the millions." Leonid Trauberg, "An Experiment Intelligible to the Millions," in *The Film Factory: Russian and Soviet Cinema in Documents 1896–1939*, ed. Richard Taylor and Ian Christie (London: Routledge & Kegan Paul, 1988), 250–251.

8. See the "Party Cinema Conference Resolution," in *Film Factory*, ed. Taylor and Christie, 212.

9. "Sovkino," a shortened word for "Soviet Kino," was the State Organization for Cinema, a consolidation of local film institutions under one government-controlled organization.

10. TSGALI SPB, f.257, op.5, d.31, pages 2–5, "Novyi Vavilon, Zapravleniye," 10 August 1928 and "V pravleniye Sovkino," 25 August 1928.

11. "Letter to Sovkino," 7 December 1928, TSGALI SPB f.257, op.5, d.31, page 12. See also Nina Gornitskaya, ed., *From the History of Lenfil'm Studio: Articles, Reminiscences and Documents of the 1920s* [*Iz istorii Lenfil'ma, Stati, vospominaniya, dokumenty, 1920–e gody]* (Leningrad: Iskusstvo, 1968–), 252–253, for Sovkino's discussion of their decision to have conservatory trained composers write for their films.

12. Laurel Fay, *Shostakovich: A Life* (Oxford: Oxford University Press, 2000), 32.

13. "Protokol," 14 November 1928, TSGALI f. 257, op.5, d.31, page 8.

14. "Agreement" (Dogovor) from Lenfil'm Studio, 31 January 1929, in TSGALI SPB, f.257, op.5, d.31, page 29. Clearly, the studio had been discussing Vladimirov's involvement prior to this date; a *Kino front* (organ of Lenark'a) issue from mid-January 1929 announced that Vladimirov would be working with Sovkino, amidst several advertisements for *New Babylon*. "Announcements," *Kino front*, no.3, 15 January 1929, 5.

15. Dmitry Shostakovich, *Dmitry Shostakovich to Elushka Valenka, April 3, 1924*, letter, Library of Congress, Washington, DC.

16. Kozintsev, *The Deep Screen*, 120. For details on the process of the hiring of Shostakovich, see chapter 3 of Titus, "Modernism, Socialist Realism, and Identity," 178ff.

17. Kozintsev, *The Deep Screen*, 120. If Kozintsev saw a rehearsal of *Nose*, it would have been in the latter half of 1928. According to Fay, publicity for the opera, which included lecture-demonstrations, began in the summer of 1928, and the premiere of the suite of the opera occurred on 25 November 1928. The opera was not premiered until 18 January 1930. See Fay, 54. For his impression of the rehearsal of *Nose*, see also Grigory Kozintsev, "Sackcloth and a Fife" [Deryuga i dudochka], in *D. Shostakovich, Articles and Materials* [*D. Shostakovich, Stat'i i materialï*], ed. G. M. Shneerson (Moscow: Sovetskiy Kompozitor, 1976), 122. See also Wilson, 86–87.

18. Dmitry Shostakovich, "About the Music to *The New Babylon*" [O muzïke k "Novomu Vavilonu"], *Soviet Screen* [*Sovetskiy ekran*] 11 (1929): 5. For a full translation of this article see Dmitry Shostakovich, "About the Music to *The New Babylon*" [O muzïke k "Novomu Vavilonu"], trans. Joan Titus in *The Routledge Film Music Sourcebook*, ed. James Wierzbicki, Nathan Platte, and Colin Roust (New York: Routledge Press, 2011), 61–64. For a partial translation see Manashir Yakubov, ed., "Dmitry Shostakovich's Music to the Silent Film *The New Babylon*" [Muzïka D. D. Shostakovicha k nemomu kinofil'mu "Novyi Vavilon"], in *Dmitry Shostakovich: New Collected Works*, vol. 122, "The New Babylon" [*Dmitry Shostakovich: Novoye Sobraniye Sochineniy, Tom 122*, "Novyi Vavilon"] (Moscow: DSCH, 2004), 542.

19. Shostakovich, "About the Music . . ."

20. Ibid.

21. Kozintsev, *The Deep Screen*, 109.

22. Eisensteinian montage had a strong influence on Kozintsev and Trauberg and is used extensively throughout this film. See Titus, "Modernism, Socialist Realism, and Identity," particularly chapters 1 and 2.

23. In this list, Shostakovich failed to mention the quote of Pyotr Tchaikovsky's "Old French Song" from his *Album for the Young* (*Detskiy al'bom*) for the scene where an old man plays the piano while the French Commune burns to the ground. He likely failed to list the usage of this tune because it did not appear as a recurring theme throughout the score, unlike the quotations of Offenbach and French revolutionary songs. The Tchaikovsky song instead serves as a moment of "anchorage" (see definition below) for the ultimate defeat of the Commune. For further discussion, see Titus, "Silents, Sound, and Modernism . . ."; and "Modernism, Socialist Realism, and Identity," 209.

24. Shostakovich, "About the Music . . .," 5.

25. Ibid. Read carefully, this article shows many parallels to Kozintsev's writings. For example, Kozintsev also complained of the "hodgepodge" approach to musical compilation in the cinema. See Kozintsev, *The Deep Screen*, 119–120, and for a full translation of this article see *The Routledge Film Music Sourcebook*, 61–64. For a partial translation see Yakubov, 542.

26. Shostakovich, "About the Music . . .," 5. The word *khaltura* here is often translated as "trash" or "garbage." See Yakubov, 542 and Marek Pytel, *New Babylon: Trauberg, Kozintsev, Shostakovich* (London: Eccentric Press, 1999), 26 for alternate translations of this word.

27. Kozintsev, *The Deep Screen*, 120. See also Wilson, 87–88 for her translation and interpretation of this passage. Wilson adds in more text and elaboration than I do here. To compare her translation with the original Russian text that she cites, see also Grigory Kozintsev, *Collected Works in Five Volumes* [*Sobraniye sochineniy v pyati tomakh*] (Leningrad: Iskusstvo, 1982), 1:156. The first volume

of the *Collected Works in Five Volumes* of Kozintsev contains the material from *The Deep Screen.*

28. Vladimir Messman used the term "synthesis" instead of "counterpoint." See Vladimir Messman, "Sound Film," in *Film Factory,* 236. See also chapter 2 of Titus, "Modernism, Socialist Realism, and Identity," 119–120 for a more detailed discussion of Messman's response to the Statement. For more detail on this Statement and its relationship to Kozintsev, Trauberg, and Shostakovich, see Titus, "Modernism, Socialist Realism, and Identity," chapters 2 and 3; and Titus, "Silents, Sound, and Modernism . . .," 40–41.
29. Messman, "Sound Film," in *Film Factory,* 237.
30. Kozintsev, "Sackcloth and a Fife," 122.
31. TSGALI SPB, f.257, op.5, d.31.
32. I translate this as "part," but it can also be translated as "reel."
33. Shostakovich, "About the Music . . .," 5.
34. Siegfried Kracauer, *Theory of Film: The Redemption of Physical Reality* (New York: Oxford University Press, 1960).
35. The following analyses of the film and of the music are built from several extant materials and pieces of information from music and film archives across Russia. Since this is a silent film score, I recognize that any analysis, including mine, or even a modern performance of any version of the score with the film, is necessarily fraught. This particular score has a more complex history than some other silent films; it was disorganized from its first premiere, has scattered manuscripts and musical fragments, and continued to be difficult to perform in subsequent showings across the world. Arguably, there is no perfectly synchronized version of music and film for *New Babylon.* What does exist is a series of versions of the film with various compilations of the score. For my purposes here, I carefully examine tunes and sections of the film and score as informed by the extant manuscripts, extant film scenarios, documents from Lenfil'm studios, other materials from the directors or film workers, and every available extant version of the film and version of the published score or recording. As a result, my discussion of the music as it relates to film is closer to how the directors and composer envisioned it, rather than its resulting reality. Several versions of the film and score exist separately and in pieces; and the most reputable current edition of the score, which represents a conscientious and thoughtful piecing together of extant materials, was published by DSCH in 2004. Throughout this chapter, I reference the DSCH edition as a kind of shorthand, and cite other documents as needed. See the Abbreviations of Archives and Libraries Consulted page for a list of archives consulted. A list of the versions of the film and of the music appears at the end of the chapter, as does a discussion of reception history.
36. See also Roland Barthes, "Rhetoric of the Image," in *Image—Music—Text* (New York: Hill and Wang, 1997), 32–51 and Gorbman, 32.
37. Yakubov, 231. Also VMOMK, f.32, inv. no. 26, "Chast' 4."
38. Yakubov, 308ff., measure 77ff.
39. Raymond Monelle, *The Musical Topic: Hunt, Military and Pastoral* (Bloomington: Indiana University Press, 2006).
40. Yakubov, 401.
41. To see a published representation of this musical moment, see Yakubov, 401–428, measures 221–380.
42. See Partitura to "Novyi Vavilon," in VMOMK; and RIII, f.94, op.1, ed.khr.5, 1929; and Yakubov for a published edition of this section.

43. In the DSCH edition, the E-flat major begins in measure 142 and modulates to A-flat major by measures 149–150.
44. Neil Edmunds, *The Soviet Proletarian Music Movement* (Oxford: Peter Lang, 2000), 217.
45. For a nuanced history of "Ça ira" and its changes see Laura Mason, *Singing the French Revolution: Popular Culture and Politics, 1787–1799* (Ithaca: Cornell University Press, 1996). For histories of the French Revolution see Albert Soboul, *A Short History of the French Revolution* (Berkeley: University of California Press, 1977) and Colin Jones, *The Great Nation: France from Louis XV to Napoleon 1715–1799* (New York: Columbia University Press, 2002).
46. Edmunds, 217.
47. Shostakovich, "About the Music . . .," 5.
48. When I refer to a "full orchestra" in this context, I am referring specifically to the entirety of the ensemble as Shostakovich orchestrated it. His orchestral parts indicate that the theater orchestras for which he wrote were likely no larger than forty to fifty instruments, but these would be adjusted depending on the cinema house and context.
49. In his treatise on instrumentation, for example, Hector Berlioz described the bassoon as having a "tendency towards the grotesque." Hector Berlioz, *Treatise on Instrumentation*, enlarged and revised by Richard Strauss (New York: Kalmus Editions), 190.
50. There are appearances of the "Marseillaise" in fragment throughout this part, building up to this full statement.
51. Yakubov, 343.
52. See David Bordwell, *The Cinema of Eisenstein* (Cambridge: Harvard University Press, 1993), 44.
53. See Yakubov, 343–349. See the first part, measures 271–277.
54. Robynn Stilwell, "The Fantastical Gap Between Diegetic and Non-Diegetic," in *Beyond the Soundtrack: Representing Music in Cinema*, ed. Daniel Goldmark, Lawrence Kramer, and Richard Leppert (Berkeley: University of California Press, 2007), 184–202.
55. Kozintsev, *The Deep Screen*, 115–116.
56. Ibid., 120.
57. According to van Houten, Trauberg claimed that he thought up the layering of the two ideas. "I thought of mixing the cancan with the *Marseillaise* and Shostakovich just wrote it down like that . . . all he needed was a list with the length of the scenes . . . ." Interview with Trauberg 10 July 1984 in Van Houten, *Leonid Trauberg and His Films*, 150–151.
58. I use "anchor" to reference Roland Barthes' *ancrage*. For more on the idea of *ancrage*, or anchorage, see Roland Barthes, "The Rhetoric of the Image," in *Image—Music—Text* (New York: Hill and Wang, 1977), 32–51.
59. See for example Shostakovich's theater works, such as *Hamlet* and *Bedbug*.
60. Kozintsev, *The Deep Screen*, 114.
61. See chapter 3 of Titus, "Modernism, Socialist Realism, and Identity," 192–196 for greater detail and discussion of this section.
62. Yakubov, 12 and 28, measure 34ff and measure 151ff.
63. For a mentioning of this connection, see John Riley, "Myth, Parisity, and Found Music in *New Babylon*," *DSCH Journal* 4 (Winter 1995): 27. It is difficult to say that this was taken from *Bedbug*, since *New Babylon* and *Bedbug* were written at the same time. See also Hélène Bernatchez, *Schostakowitsch und die Fabrik des*

Exzentrischen Schauspielers (Munich: Martin Meidenbauer Verlagbuchhandlung, 2006) for another discussion of this galop and its relationship to *Bedbug*.

64. To compare the galop used in *New Babylon* to the one in *Bedbug*, see "Galop," in Dmitry Shostakovich, *Music to Plays—For Piano*, edited and compiled by Lev Solin (Moscow: Sovetskiy Kompozitor, 1977), 9–13.

65. Shostakovich also reused theater music in his following film, *Alone*, borrowing from his theater piece, *Hamlet* (see chapter 2). Reusing material between different pieces of music was Shostakovich's habit throughout his life. In this period, however, borrowing appears to be a practical issue; however, it is possible that Shostakovich associated specific styles or genres, like the galop, with specific meanings.

66. Shostakovich, "About the Music . . .," 5.

67. See Yakubov, 83, 222, 388, and 455 for these waltzes. For a more shortened discussion of each of these waltzes and their origins, see Titus, "Silents, Sound, and Modernism . . ."

68. See Yakubov, 222–223, part 4, measures 19–34, which corresponds to the cue "The actress sings," which accompanies the actress singing (silently) on screen, supporting the signification of the bourgeoisie and "waltz." Compare this with the first appearance of this waltz fragment found on page 108, measures 197ff. in part 2.

69. See Act II, Entr'acte of Jacques Offenbach, *La Belle Hélène*, Chatelet Theatre Musicale de Paris/Marc Minkowski (EMI Records/Virgin Classics, 7243-5-45477-2-0, 2001) approximately 40 seconds into track 1. This waltz comes back at the end of the Act as the main tune of the Finale. This particular recording is based on the critical edition of the opera by Robert Didion, which contains sections, specifically in Act II, that do not appear in other editions of the opera. One edition of the score from Kalmus, for example, did not have this tune in the beginning of the Entr'acte, but did have it at the end (pp.328ff. in Kalmus edition, "Je crains . . ."). See Act II of the second volume of Jacques Offenbach, *Die Schöne Helena (Opera in Three Acts)*, orchestral edition, Edwin Kalmus, 3 vols., (New York, 1980). Bernatchez also noted this quotation from Offenbach in *New Babylon*, but did not cite the Entr'acte. See Bernatchez, *Schostakowitsch und die Fabrik des Exzentrischen Schauspielers* for her discussion of this and other Offenbach quotations in *New Babylon*.

70. Jean-Claude Yon, Liner notes to Offenbach, *La Belle Hélène*, Chatelet Theatre Musicale de Paris/Marc Minkowski.

71. The voicing (instrumentation) and form is different between the two works, but the key is the same (D minor/G major). Compare Yakubov, 387–390 (measures 109–140) and "waltz" (track 9) on *Dmitri Shostakovich, Theatre Music*, which corresponds to the piano reduction of the waltz made by the composer; and "Waltz," in Shostakovich, *Music to Plays—For Piano*, 16. Riley did not mention this borrowing, but it is clear that Shostakovich borrowed measures 110–140 of part 6 from the waltz of *Bedbug*. Bernatchez also mentions that this waltz is like a galop from *Bedbug*, but she fails to specify any further details. See Bernatchez, 145–146.

72. The statement of the waltz in *Bedbug* has an ABA form (if the part of the phrase is broken into segments), where the statement of the waltz in *New Babylon* is AB, without a return to the first part of the phrase. The voicing, due the piano arrangement, is also different in the *Bedbug*. Compare Yakubov, 387–390 (measures 109–140) and "waltz" (track 9) on *Dmitri Shostakovich, Theatre Music*,

which corresponds to the piano reduction of the waltz made by the composer. See "Waltz," in Shostakovich, *Music to Plays—For Piano*, 16.

73. Eric Roseberry, liner notes to Dmitri Shostakovich, *Theatre Music*, Rustem Hayroudinoff (Chandos, 9907, 2001).

74. Titus, "Modernism, Socialist Realism, and Identity"; Jean-Claude Yon, liner notes to Offenbach, *La Belle Hélène*; and Eric Roseberry, liner notes to Dmitri Shostakovich, *Theatre Music*.

75. Shostakovich, "About the Music . . .," 5.

76. Esti Sheinberg, *Irony, Satire, Parody, and the Grotesque in the Music of Shostakovich: a Theory of Musical Incongruities* (Aldershot: Ashgate, 2000), 63 and 210.

77. Ibid., 233–238.

78. For a printed realization, see measures 500–516 for the secondary dominant and dominant buildup (with D and G pedal tones) in Yakubov, 450–455.

79. The end of each phrase clearly cadences on the tonic. See Yakubov, 450–455, measures 522–523, 536, and 543.

80. Ibid. For a printed version of the first phrase, second phrase, final independent measure, see measures 516, 523–536, and 543.

81. The exercise in expressing the internal state of characters is further developed in the film *Alone* (1929–31), collectively made by Shostakovich, Kozintsev, and Trauberg.

82. Kliment Korchmaryov, "Muzïka k fil'me 'Novyi Vavilon'" [The Music to the *New Babylon*], *Izvestiya* 77 (4 April 1929). When mentioning the "piano," it is unclear in his article if Korchmaryov is referring to the piano version of *New Babylon*, which may be interpreted as "complicated"; or the role of the piano in the orchestral score, which is generally restricted to the Tchaikovsky quotation from "Old French Song" in the *Album for the Young* (*Detskiy al'bom*). It is also possible that the piano may have had a significant role, or had been the sole instrument in the performance of the score in the screening that Korchmaryov attended.

83. Shostakovich, "About the Music . . .," 5. This particular section has been mistranslated in the past. Instead of "exercise by Hanon," the word "galop" has appeared in Pytel's English translation. See Pytel, 26. It has also appeared incorrectly in German translation as well. See Bernatchez, 123 and 252.

84. For a printed realization, see Yakubov, 225, measures 44–54.

85. Charles Louis Hanon, *The Virtuoso Pianist, in Sixty Exercises*, trans. Theodore Baker (New York: G. Schirmer, 1928).

86. The designation "Act I, No.3" refers to the edition of *La Belle Hélène* as it appears in Offenbach, *La Belle Hélène*, Chatelet Theatre Musicale de Paris/Marc Minkowski. This melody from the "Song of Oreste" reappears twice, for the "March and Couplets for the Kings" and in the Finale of Act I. In her book, Bernatchez also notes that this melody resembles the "Song of Oreste" and briefly states that this melody assists the "film situation" in understanding how the bourgeoisie are presented in the film. See Bernatchez, 123–124.

87. In Yakubov's edition of the score, this music corresponds with directions from Shostakovich's manuscript, which are "People dance at a rehearsal" and "Officer smiles." See Yakubov, 225.

88. The similarity between the borrowing in *New Babylon* and these possible sources is subtle. The strongest candidates for the borrowed allusion in *New Babylon* are numbers two and three of the Hanon exercises, both of which share similar melodic contour and intervallic leaps. Of the two exercises, the second most closely resembles the *New Babylon* excerpt, particularly in the three-note

groupings, and the leap of a third, followed by a fourth (making up a major sixth). Compare Yakubov, 225 with Hanon, 3–4. The primary indicator that this may also be an allusion to the "Song of Oreste" is the seventh leap in the clarinet in measure 48. See also Bernatchez, 123–124.

89. This juxtaposition is indicated by notes in the manuscript and viewings of the film: rehearsals 1–9 as follows: "Preparations were made to retrieve the operetta"–"Getting ready"—"The actress sings"—"Soldiers drag cannons" (bits of *Marseillaise*)—"People dance at rehearsal" (the above cited "galop")—"Officer smiles." See also Yakubov.

90. Titus, "Silents, Sound, and Modernism . . ." and Titus, "Modernism, Socialist Realism, and Identity," 211–212.

91. Shostakovich's acknowledgement of this idea of contrasts and its resemblance to cinematic form could open a path to new methods of analyzing non-film instrumental music that listeners may perceive as narrative. I have argued elsewhere that Shostakovich's concert music can be read as cinematic if read within the context of his experience as a film composer. See for example Titus, "Modernism, Socialist Realism, and Identity," Introduction, chapter 2, and Conclusions.

92. Yuri Tsivian, *Early Cinema in Russia and Its Cultural Reception* (Chicago: University of Chicago Press, 1994).

93. Ibid.

94. TSGALI SPB, f. 257, op.5, d.31, pages 2–5, "Novyi Vavilon, Zapravleniye" 10 August 1928 and "V pravleniye Sovkino" 25 August 1928 as well as the remaining pages of this section.

95. Derek B. Scott, *Sounds of the Metropolis: The Nineteenth-Century Popular Music Revolution in London, New York, Paris, and Vienna* (Oxford: Oxford University Press, 2008), 73–74. See also Robert Brécy, *La Chanson de la Commune: Chanson et poèmes inspirés par la Commune de 1871* (Paris: Éditions Ouvrières, 1991) and Marc Robine, *Anthologie de la chanson française: Des trouvères aux grands auteurs de XIXe siècle* (Paris: Éditions Albin Michel, 1994), 128–132.

96. Ibid.

97. Scott, 73.

98. Ibid., 205 and Brécy, 239.

99. *Ancrage*, or anchorage is a term borrowed from Roland Barthes. See Roland Barthes, "Rhetoric of the Image," in *Image—Music—Text* (New York: Hill and Wang, 1997), 32–51.

100. Sergey Eisenstein's *Bronenosets Potyomkin* (*Battleship Potemkin*) is one example.

101. Pavel Muratov, "Kinematograf [The Cinematograph]," *Sovremennye zapiski* 26 (1925): 294, quoted in Yuri Tsivian, *Early Cinema in Russia and Its Cultural Reception* (Chicago: University of Chicago Press, 1994), 99. Blok and Bugoslavsky, in their chapter of genres and composers commonly quoted in the cinema, list among the past composers the operas of Pytor Tchaikovsky, Giuseppe Verdi, and the chamber music of Frederic Chopin. See D. Blok, and S. Bugoslavsky, *Muzïkal'noe soprovozhdeniye v kino* [Musical Accompaniment in the Cinema] (Moscow: Teakinopechat, 1929), 101–124. For a detailed discussion of these early manuals, see Titus, "Modernism, Socialist Realism, and Identity," chapter 2.

102. Fay, 50; Egorova, 10; and Wilson, 86. Fay cites documents from the studio that reveal that they blamed Shostakovich for the film's failure. See "To the administration of Sovkino" (V pravleniye Sovkino), 8 April 1929 in TSGALI SPB, f. 257, op. 5, d. 31, page 79, St. Petersburg, Russia for Lenfil'm's summary of events

surrounding the premieres of the film. Trauberg also complained that the audiences misunderstood the images; and that the mismatch between image and music, not simply the music itself, resulted in a misunderstanding of the film's "montages." See David Robinson, "When Filmmaking Was All About Circus and Scandal," *Times* (London), 20 January 1983, 8.

103. Several issues of *Kino Front*, the organ of *Lenark'a*, were dedicated to the "scenario crisis" of the film, and various debates over its intelligibility. *Kino Front*, Nos.3–13, January–March 1929.

104. Kozintsev, *Glubokiy ekran*, 101–102. Kozintsev related that the musical score added "fuel to the fire."

105. Yuli (Yulian) Vaynkop, "Muzïka k 'Novomu Vavilonu,'" [Music to *New Babylon*] *Rabochiy i teatr* (1 April 1929): 9. Altered translation from Yakubov, "Muzïka D. D. Shostakovicha k nemomu kinofil'mu 'Novyi Vavilon,'" 545.

106. "To the administration of Sovkino" (V pravleniye Sovkino), 8 April 1929 in TSGALI SPB, f. 257, op. 5, d. 31, page 79.

107. TSGALI SPB, f. 257, op. 5, d. 31.

108. Ibid. After having met Vladimirov in 1924, Shostakovich eventually worked as a *pianist-illustrator* at one of the theaters where Vladimirov worked, the *Picadilly*. See Galina Kopïtova, "Taper" in *Shostakovich v Leningradskoy konservatorii 1919–1930*, vol. 3, (St. Petersburg: Kompozitor, 2013), 236–237.

109. See Dmitri and Ludmilla Sollertinsky, *Pages from the Life of Dmitri Shostakovich* (London: Robert Hale, 1980), 55–56.

110. Vaynkop, 9. Altered translation from Yakubov, "Muzïka D. D. Shostakovicha k nemomu kinofil'mu 'Novyi Vavilon,'" 545.

111. Leo Arnshtam, "Bessmertiye" [Immortality], in Schneerson, 115–116. Leo Arnshtam (1905–1979) was among many things a musician, a sound designer, and later a film director. He worked with Shostakovich on several film projects over the course of his life. Often referred to as "Lev" in Russian and English sources ("Lev" is the common Russian form of "Leo"), his birth name was "Leo." Later in life, he commented on this point of confusion in his *Muzïka geroicheskogo* [Music of the Heroic] (Moscow: Iskusstvo, 1977).

112. Sollertinsky, 55–56.

113. Fay, 50 and Wilson, 86. "Letters to F.F. Krish" in I. A. Bobykina, *Dmitry Shostakovich v pis'makh i dokumentakh* [Dmitri Shostakovich through His Letters and Documents] (Moscow: Glinka State Central Museum of Musical Culture, 2000), 196–201.

114. "To the administration of Sovkino" (V pravleniye Sovkino), 8 April 1929 in TSGALI, f. 257, op. 5, d. 31, page 79.

115. Ibid.

116. Ibid. and "Letters to F.F. Krish," in *Dmitry Shostakovich v pis'makh i dokumentakh*, 196–201.

117. "Protokol Muz. Soveshchaniya pri Khud. Byuro k/f." 20 February 1929, TSGALI, f.257, op.16 ed. khr. 67, page 17. This translation from Fay, 50 and 298. The purpose of this screening was to evaluate Shostakovich's music, and determine its success. Among the people in attendance were Sollertinsky, Vaynkop, Shostakovich, and Vladimirov.

118. M. Gartsman, "Ne plokho, no i ne sovsem yeshchyo khorosho" [Not Bad, But Not Yet Entirely Good], *Sovetskiy ekran* 15 (9 April 1929). Also translated in part in Yakubov, "Muzïka D. D. Shostakovicha k nemomu kinofil'mu 'Novyi Vavilon,'" 546.

119. Gosfil'mofond, Sovkino report from "Novyi Vavilon" [New Babylon], Sectsia No.1, f. no.2, op. no.1, ed. khr. no.597, 50–54. Although the report does not directly state that Shostakovich's music was used for the showings of the film, Shostakovich was asked to write versions for piano and small ensemble for smaller venues. See "Letter to Sovkino," 7 December 1928, in TSGALI SPB, f. 257, op. 5, d. 31, page 12, St. Petersburg, Russia and "Pis'mo zam. direktora Leningradskoy kinofabriki 'Sovkino' tov. Bïkova v pravleniye 'Sovkino'" [A Letter from the Deputy Director of the Leningrad Film Studio Sovkino to comrade Bïkov in the Management of Sovkino], in Gornitskaya, ed., *Iz istorii Lenfil'ma*, 254–255.
120. Gartsman, "Ne plokho, no i ne sovsem yeshchyo khorosho."
121. Kliment Korchmaryov, "Muzïka k fil'me 'Novyi Vavilon'" [The Music to the *New Babylon*], *Izvestiya*, 77 (4 April 1929). When mentioning the "piano," it is unclear in his article if Korchmaryov is referring to the piano version of *New Babylon*, which may be interpreted as "complicated"; or the role of the piano in the orchestral score, which is generally restricted to specific parts of the score, most famously including the Tchaikovsky quotation from "Old French Song" in the *Album for the Young* (*Detskiy al'bom*). It is also possible that the piano may have had a significant role in the performance of the orchestral score in the screening that Korchmaryov attended. According to Lenfil'm and Leo Arnshtam, the *partitura* was written in several variants, including some for piano. Lenfil'm studio heads and the musical directors of cinema houses agreed early in the process that a piano score would be made for this film, particularly for the "provinces." See Protokol, 14 November 1928, TSGALI SPB f. 257, op.5, d.31, page 8, and "Letters to Krish," in Bobykina, 199.
122. See Titus, "Silents, Sound, and Modernism . . ." and Titus, "Modernism, Socialist Realism, and Identity," chapter 3, 60–64 for a detailed discussion of the scathing attacks of multiple critics on the film. Pavel Petrov-Bïtov features prominently among many of the attackers on the film.
123. I. I. Ioffe, *Muzïka sovetskogo kino* [Music of the Soviet Cinema] (Leningrad: State Musical Scientific-Research Institute: 1938), 33.
124. Dmitry Shostakovich, *Shostakovich: Music from the Films New Babylon and Golden Hills*, Moscow Philharmonic Orchestra and USSR Ministry of Culture Symphony Orchestra/Gennady Rozhdestvensky (Russian Disc, 11064, 1994). Mark Fitz-Gerald also claimed to have released the first complete recording of the score in 2011: Dmitry Shostakovich, *The New Babylon*, The Basel Sinfonietta/Mark Fitz-Gerald (Naxos, 8.572824-25, 2011).
125. Marek Pytel, *New Babylon: Trauberg, Kozintsev, Shostakovich* [Booklet to DVD] (London: Eccentric Press, 1999), 16.
126. Ibid. Bernatchez, *Schostakowitsch* . . . contains the original mistranslation. I corrected this mistranslation in my contribution to the Routledge collection. See Titus, "About the Music to *The New Babylon*," 61–64.
127. My interpretation here has been based in viewing all of the aforementioned films in comparison with Strobel's version. This was done alongside examination of all of the known manuscripts of this film, and conversations with various enthusiasts that have re-edited the film.

CHAPTER 3

1. Joan Titus, "Modernism, Socialist Realism, and Identity, in the Early Film Music of Dmitry Shostakovich, 1929–1932" (PhD diss., Ohio State University, 2006).

2. It was common for films of the twenties to use the name of the actor as the name of the character.

3. Aleksandr Dovzhenko (1894–1956) was a Ukrainian avant-garde film director. He developed what has been referred to as a poetic approach to montage techniques, where he used long, impressionistic shots of the Russian countryside and its people, such as in his film *Earth* (1930). His interests in folklore and the everyday life of the "folk" permeated his later works, and became a symbol of his style. Of the main film directors of the time, Dovzhenko was described as the most "lyrical" of them.

4. A *bai* is commonly defined as a Central Asian landowner.

5. This reel (reel 6) is lost, so the details of the events of the reel are unknown. Early drafts of the scenario, however, show that this part of the storyline was a later addition. See TSGALI SPB, f.257, op.16, d.192.

6. A common phrase used in reviews of the film when describing the plane that comes from Moscow to retrieve Kuz'mina.

7. There were multiple versions of this ending, some of which were far more elaborate than this ending. Kozintsev appears to have been unhappy with their final choice: he claimed that the last scene of the film was "unsuccessful," deeming it "lifeless" and too "schematic." See Grigory Kozintsev, *Glubokiy ekran* [The Deep Screen] (Moscow: Iskusstvo, 1971), 156; and TSGALI SPB, f.257, op.16, d.192.

8. This quote was related by Anatoly Lunacharsky in "Conversation with Lenin," in *Lenin i kino* [Lenin and Cinema], ed. G. M. Boltyanskiy (Moscow/Leningrad: 1925), 16–19. It can also be found in Richard Taylor and Ian Christie, eds., *The Film Factory: Russian and Soviet Cinema in Documents 1896–1939* (London: Routledge & Kegan Paul, 1988), 56–57.

9. TSGALI SPB f.257, op.16, d.192.

10. See Ian Christie, "Making Sense of Early Soviet Sound," in *Inside the Film Factory: New Approaches to Russian and Soviet Cinema*, ed. Richard Taylor and Ian Christie (London: Routledge, 1991), 184–185 for further discussion of this idea.

11. Kozintsev credited Trauberg with having found this article about a woman who nearly froze to death in Siberia. Grigory Kozintsev, "Odna" [Alone], *Iskusstvo kino* 1 (1967): 45. Originally published in *Glubokiy ekran*, 1966.

12. TSGALI SPB, f.257, op.16, d.192. The scenario underwent tremendous change, and the heads of the studio consistently worked with the directors in negotiating changes in the scenario.

13. TSGALI SPB, f.257, op.16, d.192, entire folder and Kozintsev, *Glubokiy ekran*.

14. TSGALI SPB, f.257, op.16, d.192, entire folder. There was a significant push, as indicated in the protocol memos between the directors and various department heads, to have a proper "nationalist" film that would jibe with the Cultural Revolution.

15. Though the studio had specific directives, some of the figures that worked with the directors, such as Moisey Rafes, head of the Artistic Department (Khudoshestvennyi otdel'), had modernist inclinations while pushing a clearly Soviet agenda. TSGALI SPB, f.257, op.16, d.192, pp.100–115.

16. Titus, "Modernism, Socialist Realism . . .," 238–242.

17. In some memos, studio heads such as Rafes and Grinfel'd discussed the possibility of typage as part of character development. In similar memos, they also insisted on creating a character type similar to the heroic figure of Joan of Arc. TSGALI SPB, f.257, op.16, d.192.

18. Kozintsev, "Odna," 47. Fast-paced montage and superficial character typage were also typical of Kozintsev's and Trauberg's earlier eccentric films as well, including *The Adventures of Oktyabrina* (1925) and *The Devil's Wheel* (1926).

19. E. Misalandi, Booklet from the VHS cassette of *Odna* [Alone] (1931; Belye Stolbye, "Krupnï Plan"/Gosfil'mofond/Musey Kino, 2002). See also Joan Titus, "Socialist Realism, Modernism, and Dmitry Shostakovich's *Odna* (*Alone*, 1931)," in *Shostakovich Studies 2*, ed. Pauline Fairclough (Cambridge: Cambridge University Press, 2010), 100–120.

20. Kozintsev, *Glubokiy ekran*, 151.

21. TSGALI SPB, f.257, op.16, d.192, p.38.

22. TSGALI SPB, f.257, op.16, d.192; Kozintsev, *Glubokiy ekran*; and Yakubov, essay "Muzïka D. D. Shostakovicha k kinofil'mu 'Odna.' Istoriya sozdaniya, otsenka kritiki" [Dmitry Shostakovich's Music to the Film *Alone*: How it was Composed, Critics' Appraisal], in *Dmitry Shostakovich: Novoye Sobraniye Sochineniy, Tom 123, "Muzïka k kinofil'mu 'Odna',"* [*Dmitry Shostakovich: New Collected Works*, vol. 123, "Music the Film *Alone* Op.26"] (Moscow: DSCH, 2004), 317–321 (Russian) and 330–334 (English).

23. *Sharmanka* translates as "hurdy-gurdy" or "barrel-organ player."

24. TSAGLI SPB, f.257, op.16, d.192.

25. As I later relate when discussing *Youth of Maxim, Alone* was designed to be the musical film, while *Youth of Maxim* was the speaking film. See chapter 6.

26. Kozintsev, *Glubokiy ekran*, 156. In 1934, Kozintsev wrote, in an article about *Youth of Maxim*, that they worked in the "Oirat *aimak*"; that is, the Buryat Autonomous Soviet Socialist Republic, or what is now the modern-day Republic of Buryatia. This Republic included the Altai and Baikal regions. G. Kozintsev and L. Trauberg, "Yunost' maksima" [Youth of Maxim], *Izvestiya*, n.291, 14 December 1934.

27. TSGALI SPB, f.257, op.16, d.192.

28. TSGALI SPB, Ibid. In 2004, Ol'ga Digonskaya found several misplaced manuscripts of Shostakovich. Since then, she has been working to incorporate them into Shostakovich's repertory. See for example Ol'ga Digonskaya, "Kinomuzyka Shostakovicha: neisvestniye avtografi, simfonichestskiy fragment 1945," *Muzykal'naya akademiya* 2 (2006): 92–107.

29. Cited from I. I. Ioffe, *Muzïka sovetskogo kino* [Music of the Soviet Cinema] (Leningrad: State Musical Scientific-Research Institute: 1938), 45. Here Ioffe cites a stenogram of a presentation dated 9 June 1937.

30. Trauberg claimed that this song was his own in an interview from 1984. He states, "I wrote the song and instructed Shostakovich on how to compose it, and he wrote it right away, a very good song." See Theodore Van Houten, *Leonid Trauberg and His Films: Always the Unexpected* ('s-Hertogenbosch: Art & Research, 1989), 144.

31. See also Titus, "Socialist Realism, Modernism, and Dmitry Shostakovich's *Odna* (*Alone*, 1931); and Titus, "Modernism, Socialist Realism . . .," chapter 4.

32. Kozintsev, *Glubokiy ekran*, 151–152.

33. Ibid.

34. Ioffe, *Muzïka sovetskogo kino,* 34; Pavina Rïbakova, "Muzïka Shostakovicha k zvukovym fil'mam 'Odna' i 'Zlatïe gorï'" [Shostakovich's Music to the Sound Films *Alone* and *Golden Mountains*], *Rabochiy i teatr* 24 (August 1933): 39; Yakubov, "Muzïka D. D. Shostakovicha k kinofil'mu 'Odna'," 320 and 332; and Titus, "Modernism, Socialist Realism . . .," 253–256 for further discussion.

35. He used the galop trope in his previous film score to *New Babylon*, and in theater works such as *Bedbug*, among other works.
36. This march bears a strong resemblance to the first theme of the "chase" music of Shostakovich's theater piece *Hamlet* (1932). It is likely that he reused this march of *Alone* for the first theme/section of this number in *Hamlet*. On a related note, Digonskaya writes that some musical segments used in *Alone* appear in Shostakovich's ballet, *Bolt* (1931). She asserts that Shostakovich probably used the music from the film for the ballet after the film score was written. See Ol'ga Digonskaya, "Odna" in *Shostakovich v Leningradskoy conservatorii 1919–1930*, vol. 3, (St. Petersburg: Kompozitor, 2013), 279.
37. See Michel Chion, "Audio-Vision and Sound," in *Sound*, ed. Patricia Kruth and Henry Stobart (Cambridge: Cambridge University Press, 2000), 205 for further discussion.
38. TSGALI SPB, f.257, op.16, d.192, pp.129–130.
39. Ibid.
40. Kozintsev, *Glubokiy ekran*, 156.
41. Shostakovich had experience with foreign films, including American ones, when learning to accompany the silent cinema. See Galina Kopïtova, "D.D. Shostakovich i A. L. Volynsky, Shkola russkogo baleta, kinoteatr 'Svetlaya lenta'," in *Dmitry Shostakovich: Issledovaniya i materialy, vypusk 2*, (Moscow: DSCH, 2007), 5–32.
42. I found this fragment in the Lenfil'm archive, TSAGLI SPB, f.257, op.16, ed. khr. no.2025, 69 ob. As far as I know, it was not found among the newer manuscripts that Olg'a Digonskaya discovered in 2004.
43. Ibid.
44. Richard Taruskin, "Golden Cockerel, The," in *The New Grove Dictionary of Opera*, ed. Stanley Sadie, *Grove Music Online, Oxford Music Online*, http://www.oxfordmusiconline.com/ (accessed March 4, 2012). My thanks go to Ol'ga Digonskaya for immediately recognizing the reference to Rimsky-Korsakov when first viewing this manuscript several years ago.
45. Ibid.
46. Ibid.
47. See Kozintsev, *Glubokiy ekran*, 152.
48. For a full score version, see Yakubov, measures 6–11. Digonskaya also discusses "Chizhik-Pizhik" in Shostakovich's output, with different emphasis on the tune's history. See Digonskaya, "Odna," 274–275.
49. Gilbert Rappaport, "The Poetics of Word and Music in *Five Satires (Pictures of the Past)* by Dmitrii Shostakovich (op. 109): Representations through the Prism of Russian Cultural History," unpublished paper. It was recently published as "*Five Satires (Pictures of the Past)* by Dmitrii Shostakovich (op. 109): The Musical Unity of a Vocal Cycle," in *Contemplating Shostakovich: Life, Music and Film*, ed. Alexander Ivashkin and Andrew Kirkman (Lodon: Ashgate, 2013), 47–78.
50. Gerard McBurney, "Fried Chicken in the Bird-Cherry Trees," in *Shostakovich and His World*, ed. Laurel Fay (Princeton: Princeton University Press, 2004), 243.
51. For Dmitry Pokrass' version of this march, see Dmitry Pokrass, "Marsh Budyonnogo" (March of Budyonï, 1920) from Mikhail Druskin, *Russkaya revolyutsionnaya pesnya* [Russian Revolutionary Song] (Leningrad: Gosudarstvennoye muzykal'noye izdatel'stvo, 1959), 46; and Amy Nelson, *Music for the Revolution: Musicians and Power in Early Soviet Russia* (University Park, Penn.: The Pennsylvania State University Press, 2004), 85 for another version of the "March of Budyonï," written by Aleksandr Davidenko. Davidenko's version has a similar

descending musical line and a different text. The text in Davidenko's version is the same as the film's intertitles, while the music in Pokrass's version is virtually the same as Shostakovich's music. For a comparison of the folk tune with Shostakovich's underscoring, see Titus, "Socialist Realism, Modernism, and Dmitry Shostakovich's *Odna* (*Alone*, 1931), 115–116. See also Digonskaya, "Odna," 279.

52. Kliment Korchmaryov, 'Muzïka k fil'me "Odna,"' [Music of the Film *Alone*] *Sovetskoye iskusstvo*, 58 (15 June 1931).

53. See also Druskin, Russkaya revolyutsionnaya pesnya, 46–47; and Nelson, Music for the Revolution.

54. In Russian, the name of the song is "Dolyushka russkaya." This title is in the feminine gender, which implies that it is the Russian woman's lot.

55. This song only appears in the phonogram. See Yakubov, "Muzïka D. D. Shostakovicha k kinofil'mu 'Odna,'" 366 and Ioffe, *Muzïka sovetskogo kino*, 34. Yakubov takes his version of the song from Ioffe's book, which was the first publication of the song. Ioffe took his transcription from the phonogram (soundtrack) of the film.

56. Sudarevo is also a region in Russia (Urochishche Sudarevo) in the Pskov Oblast'.

57. For examples, see Neil Edmunds, *The Soviet Proletarian Music Movement* (Oxford: Peter Lang, 2000) and Amy Nelson, *Music for the Revolution: Musicians and Power in Early Soviet Russia* (University Park: Pennsylvania State University Press, 2004).

58. TSGALI SPB, f.257, op.16, d.192, p.38.

59. Ibid.

60. There are other plucked lutes from this region used for accompanying narrative songs that could also be in place of the Kazakh *dombra*, such as the *komuz* (long-necked lute played by Kyrgyz performers) and the *doshpuluur* (plucked lute). See Theodore Levin, *Where Rivers and Mountains Sing: Sound, Music, and Nomadism in Tuva and Beyond* (Bloomington: Indiana University Press, 2006), 99–100 and 147–148.

61. See for example, VMOMK, f.32, ed. khr.2290.

62. The directors had several problems with the recording technology that hindered the final version of the film. For more detail, see Titus, "Socialist Realism, Modernism, and Dmitry Shostakovich's *Odna* (*Alone*, 1931)," 119–120 and Titus, "Modernism, Socialist Realism . . .," 281–283.

63. The indication for a *sharmanka* was present even from the earliest scenarios. TSGALI SPB, f.257, op.16, d.192.

64. Ibid.

65. Kozintsev, *Glubokiy ekran*, 156–157. TSGALI SPB, f.257, op.16, d.192.

66. This motif is sometimes mistakenly attributed to the *bai*. See I. I. Ioffe, *Muzïka sovetskogo kino* [Music of the Soviet Cinema] (Leningrad: State Musical Scientific-Research Institute: 1938), 35–36.

67. When this motif appears at the meeting of the *bai, kulaks*, and village advisor, the trombone glissandi are omitted and the instrumentation slightly scaled down. See Yakubov, *Novoye Sobraniye Sochineniy, Tom 123, "Odna,"* Number 33 (midway through the number), 184–185.

68. Kozintsev, *Glubokiy ekran*, 155.

69. Ibid.

70. Mikhail Cheryomukhin, *Muzïka zvukovogo fil'ma* [Music of Sound Film] (Moscow: Goskinoizdat, 1939), 127.

71. See Manashir Yakubov, ed., *Dmitry Shostakovich: Sobraniye Sochineniy, Tom 18, "Nos"* [Dmitry Shostakovich: Collected Works, vol. 18, "Nose"] (Moscow: Muzyka, 1981), 73, measures 1–5.
72. See Manashir Yakubov, ed., *Dmitry Shostakovich: Novoye Sobraniye Sochineniy, Tom 52a, "Ledi Makbet Mtsenskogo uezda"* [Dmitry Shostakovich: New Collected Works, vol. 52a, "Lady Macbeth of Mtsensk District t"] (Moscow: DSCH, 2007), 192, measures 570–575; and Richard Taruskin, "When Serious Music Mattered," in *Shostakovich: A Casebook*, ed. Malcolm Brown (Indiana University Press, 2004), 376.
73. See Yuri Keldysh, Mark Aranovsky, L. Korabel'nikova, and Yu. Khokhlov, eds., *Muzïkal'nyi entsiklopedicheskiy slovar'* [The Musical Encyclopedic Dictionary] (Moscow: Sovetskaya entsiklopediya, 1990). It has also been used in reference to film music in the Soviet era. See Cheryomukhin, *Muzïka zvukovogo fil'ma*, 143. Cheryomukhin mentions both "leit-timbres" and "leit-colors" in this text. Asafyev also considered timbre a marker of twentieth-century music. See chapter 1: Introduction.
74. Ioffe, *Muzïka sovetskogo kino*, 35–36.
75. Kozintsev related that the association of the woodwinds and flute with the *bai* was created by Shostakovich. See *Glubokiy ekran*, 154.
76. Ioffe, *Muzïka sovetskogo kino*, 35–36; and Taruskin, "When Serious Music Mattered," 376.
77. Cheryomukhin, *Muzïka zvukovogo fil'ma*, 128.
78. Ibid., 127.
79. For a full score of Example 3.5 see Yakubov, page 74, measures 1–5.
80. For a full score of Example 3.6 see Yakubov, page 101, measures 10–14.
81. Kozintsev, *Glubokiy ekran*, 154.
82. Korchmaryov, "Muzïka k fil'me 'Odna.'" For an analysis of this film as it embodies the debate between modernism and socialist realism, see Titus, "Socialist Realism, Modernism, and Dmitry Shostakovich's *Odna (Alone,* 1931)."
83. Kozintsev, *Glubokiy ekran*, 154.
84. The attempt to record speech inevitably failed because the delivery of promised recording equipment was never fully realized. There were many indications in the early scenarios to synchronize speech; in fact there was a lengthy debate between Kuz'mina and the shaman initially planned. After many attempts to record quality sync speech the directors stopped. Only one instance of sync speech exists in the final film. See TSGALI SPB, f.257, op.16, d.192; Titus, "Socialist Realism, Modernism, and Dmitry Shostakovich's *Odna (Alone,* 1931)"; and Titus, "Modernism, Socialist Realism . . ." for further detail.
85. Ioffe, *Muzïka sovetskogo kino*, 11.
86. Ibid., 35–36. When Ioffe described music as speech, he addressed the scene where the *bai* interrupts Kuz'mina as she teaches the children. The first two staves of the musical example that he provides between pages 35 and 36, however, is the beginning music from the "snoring scene," not from the scene of *bai* and Kuz'mina. The remaining lines are from a later incarnation of the music of the "snoring scene" from the end of the fifth reel, probably where the *kulaks* and *bai* are making a deal over the sheep. See Yakubov, *Novoye Sobraniye Sochineniy, Tom 123, "Odna,"* Number 33, 185–187.
87. Typage is the term used to describe an actor who is chosen for the way they appear as opposed to the way they act. Eisenstein used typage in his films, notably *Battleship Potemkin*. See Titus, "Modernism, Socialist Realism . . .," chapter 2.

88. The "fantastical gap" is a phrase coined by Robynn Stilwell and James Buhler to describe the sometimes indescribable space between the diegetic and non-diegetic, calling attention to the potential inflexibility of these concepts. See Robynn Stilwell, "The Fantastical Gap Between Diegetic and Non-Diegetic," in *Beyond the Soundtrack: Representing Music in Cinema*, ed. Daniel Goldmark, Lawrence Kramer, and Richard Leppert (Berkeley: University of California Press, 2007), 184–202.

89. VMOMK, f.32. My heartfelt thanks go to Ol'ga Digonskaya for showing these manuscripts to me soon after discovering them.

90. Ibid.

91. Cornet was the instrument of choice, as opposed to trumpet, as indicated in the multiple orchestral parts to the score housed in the Lenfil'm's archive. TSGALI SPB, op.16, ed. khr. no. 2025.

92. In my estimation, between the film documents and scenarios, and the sketches in both Glinka Museum and Lenfil'm archives, it appears that Shostakovich was composing for these hypothetical instruments are early as summer/fall 1929. TSGALI op.16, ed. khr. no. 2025; VMOMK f.32, inv.109; and VMOMK f.32, ed. khr. 2290.

93. Kozintsev, *Glubokiy ekran*. op. 16, d.192.

94. Ibid.

95. Kozintsev relates a fascinating opinion of the shaman whom he invited to Leningrad to record. He related, "I met Kondratiy Tanashev. He was a professional shaman and knew his business. He worked on real fuel, never free-wheeling: an epileptic, he knew the signs, how to take advantage of an oncoming fit. Besides that, he was an inveterate drunkard. He used to heal sick children before my very eyes in the dark, smoky, yurt. He would strike his tambourines with a stick, wail, intone some sort of incantation in a husky voice and then leap up, twirl round and round, stamping his boots... We took Tanashev to Leningrad to film him in the studio. He obliging repeated (several times) the whole gamut of his incantations. Nothing of their power came over on the screen." See Grigory Kozintsev, *King Lear: The Space of Tragedy: The Diary of a Film Director*, trans. Mary Mackintosh (Berkeley: University of California Press, 1977), 225–226 for further discussion.

96. See Kozintsev, *Glubokiy ekran*, 154.

97. The last word of the phrase actually translates as "living sounds that grow into generalizations [*obobshenii*]," but here I used Yakubov's translation, which does evoke the idea of "real" sounds as symbols. See Kozintsev, *Glubokiy ekran*, 154 for the original Russian.

98. My translation. See Kozintsev, *Glubokiy ekran*, 154 for the original Russian and Yakubov, "Muzïka D. D. Shostakovicha k kinofil'mu 'Odna,'" 331 for another translation.

99. This montage scene was apparent in the early scenarios as well, with the intercutting of the bard with Kuz'mina as opposed to the shaman. TSGALI SPB, f.257, op.16, d.192.

100. Egorova mentions that there is "polyphonic sound montage" in *Alone*, perhaps referencing scenes like this one, though she does not specify what she means by this phrase. See Tatiana Egorova, *Soviet Film Music: A Historical Survey*, trans. Tatiana A. Ganf and Natalia A. Egunova (Amsterdam: Harwood Academic Publishers, 1997), 17. Polyphonic layering of sound was also common to other films such as Vsevolod Pudovkin's *Deserter* and Dziga Vertov's *Enthusiasm*. She

also compares the early film experiments of sound layering with "constructivist" symphonies by composers such as Aleksandr Mosolov and Vladimir Deshevov. Egorova, *Soviet Film Music*, 14.

101. Greg Castillo has discussed this issue of taking elements of peripheral culture of the Soviet Union and melding into the socialist realist aesthetic in architecture under Stalinism. See Greg Castillo, "Peoples at an Exhibition: Soviet Architecture and the National Question," in *Socialist Realism Without Shores*, ed. Thomas Lahusen and Evgeny Dobrenko (Durham: Duke University Press, 1997).

102. Levin, *Where Rivers and Mountains Sing*.

103. For an overview of overtone singing, see Carole Pegg, "Inner Asia," in *Grove Music Online, Oxford Music Online*, http://www.oxfordmusiconline.com/ (accessed October 28, 2011).

104. Levin, *Where Rivers and Mountains Sing*.

105. Korchmaryov, "Muzïka k fil'me 'Odna,'" For further discussion see Titus, "Socialist Realism, Modernism, and Dmitry Shostakovich's *Odna* (*Alone*, 1931)," 114–115.

106. "The Exhaustive Shostakovich," accessed October 28, 2011, https://exhaustiveshostakovich.wordpress.com/; and John Riley, *Dmitri Shostakovich: A Life in Film* (London: I. B. Tauris, 2005).

CHAPTER 4

1. This approach shared some similarities to scores of the late 1960s.

2. See "Introduction," in *The Film Factory: Russian and Soviet Cinema in Documents 1896–1939*, ed. Richard Taylor and Ian Christie (London: Routledge & Kegan Paul, 1988), 315–317 and discussion of *Alone* in chapter 4.

3. Organ of the ARRK (Association of Workers in Revolutionary Cinematography).

4. Taylor and Christie, *The Film Factory*, 318.

5. Ibid., 315 and "*Proletarskoe Kino* Editorial: "Mï prodolzhaem bor'bu" [We Are Continuing the Struggle]," in *The Film Factory*, 321–322. Originally found in *Proletarskoe kino* 5 (February 1932): 1–2.

6. *The Film Factory*, 315.

7. The theme of industrialization was also related to these new themes for cinema. Also, as a result of various economic and ideological reasons, film production significantly dropped each subsequent year from 1930 forward. In 1931, Soviet filmmaking dropped from 147 films (1930) to 103 (1931), then to 90 in 1932 and later 35 in 1933. This was the result of several factors, including censorship of film scenarios, economics, and to some degree the advent of sound technology. See Denise Youngblood, *Movies for the Masses, Popular Cinema and Soviet Society in the* 1920s (Cambridge: Cambridge University Press, 1992), 32–33.

8. According to Shumyatsky, Stalin watched *Alone* and *Golden Mountains*, which prompted him to give more financing to sound development. See Ian Christie, "Making Sense of Early Soviet Sound," in *Inside the Film Factory: New Approaches to Russian and Soviet Cinema*, ed. Richard Taylor and Ian Christie, (London: Routledge, 1991), 186.

9. Tatiana Egorova, *Soviet Film Music: A Historical Survey*, trans. Tatiana A. Ganf and Natalia A. Egunova (Amsterdam: Harwood Academic Publishers, 1997), 21.

10. Gosfil'mofond, "Zlatïe gorï" [The Golden Mountains], ed.khr.847, document 72.

11. Yutkevich claimed that he spoke with Maxim Gorky about the idea in 1929. RGALI, f.3070, op.1, ed.khr.501, "Stenogram of discussion of Yutkevich's paper during the discussion at Lenark'a about the film 'Golden Mountains.'

(S. I. Yutkevich vystupleniye na diskussi v Lenark'e o fil'me S. I. Yutkevich 'Zlatïe gorï,' stenogram diskussi)," 21 November 1931, page 2.

12. Egorova's time frame is therefore strange, since by early 1931, most of *Alone* was shot and the soundtrack was being recorded. See Egorova, 21ff. A collection of documents from Gosfil'mofond also shows that Arnshtam was not involved in the creation of the scenario early in the process. It is unclear from these documents exactly when he would have joined the group. Gosfil'mofond, "Zlatïe gorï," ed. khr.847.

13. I take this date from Arnshtam's essay "Zlatïe gorï" [Golden Mountains], in *Muzïka geroicheskogo* [Music of the Heroic] (Moscow: Iskusstvo, 1977), 66. See also L. Arnshtam, "Zlatïe gorï" [The Golden Mountains], *Sovetskiy ekran* 23 (1971): 18–19, which is the first (and most edited) incarnation of this essay. In the editor's note in volume 41 of the collected works of Shostakovich, Yakubov states that it was 6 September 1931, but he gives no evidence of this being the correct date. I am inclined to believe Arnshtam's date, since most of the press about the film was written in late November of 1931. See Ian Christie, where he discusses the *Khudozhestvennï* Theater in "Making Sense of Early Soviet Sound," 187; and Manashir Yakubov, ed., "Ot redaktsii" [Editor's Note], in *Dmitry Shostakovich, Sobraniye Sochineniy v soroka dvukh tomakh, tom 41, "Muzïka k kinofil'ma, partitura"* [The Collected Works in Forty-Two Volumes, vol. 41, "Music to the Film Scores, Orchestral Score] (Moscow: Muzïka, 1987), 7.

14. TSGALI, f.257, op.16, d.554, Zlatïe gorï," *montazhnï list k novoy redaktsii*; and Gosfil'mofond "Zlatïe gorï," ed.khr.847 and "Zlatïe gorï" (nemoi), *montazhnï list*.

15. Since the earlier version of the film is unavailable, it is difficult to say with certainty how and what was taken out of the film for the 1936 version. A copy of the *montazhnï list* (editing sheet) from 1936 is available in the Gosfil'mofond archive. Gosfil'mofond, "Zlatïe gorï," ed.khr.847. Yakubov claims that a revised version of the film was released on 14 August 1936. See Yakubov, "Ot redaktsii," 7.

16. See Arnshtam, "Zlatïe gorï," in *Muzïka geroicheskogo*, 64.

17. John Riley, "If Only I Had . . . the Rest of the Film," *DSCH Journal* 5 (Summer 1996): 38.

18. *Zlatïe gorï* [Golden Mountains], directed by Sergey Yutkevich and Fridrikh Ermler (1931; Belye Stolby: Gosfil'mofond, 1936). I viewed a copy from Gosfil'mofond provided by the Shostakovich Archive in Moscow. My thanks go to Irina Shostakovich and Ol'ga Dombrovskaya for their help in this matter.

19. Dmitry Shostakovich, "Kino kak shkola kompozitora" [Cinema as the Composer's School], *30 let sovetskoi kinematografii* [30 Years of Soviet Cinematography], ed. D. I. Eremin (Moscow: Goskinoizdat, 1950): 355.

20. Sof'ya Khentova, *Shostakovich, Zhizn' i tvorchestvo* [Shostakovich, Life and Works] (Leningrad: Sovetskiy kompozitor: 1985), 1:533.

21. VMOMK, f.32, inv.104, no.6419, Muzïka k kinofil'mu "Zlatïe gorï" Fragmenti; VMOMK, f.32, inv.42, no.4869, Syuita iz muzïki k fil'my "Zlatïe gorï"; VMOMK, f.32, inv.103, post.6419, Muzïka k kino-fil'my "Zlatïe gorï," "fragmenti" "traktir"; and RGALI, f.2048, Opis' No.3, 33.

22. This suite, which consists of six parts including the fugue, but not *Golden Mountains* tune, was premiered in 1931 and was first published by Muzgiz in 1935, long after the film's first release. See Riley, "If I Only . . .," 37 and Yakubov, "Ot redaktsii," 8. The suite is an abridged version of the film score, highlighting most of the main melodies and musical ideas that correspond to major events in the film. Only the first, second, and a fragment of the fifth movements

correspond with the phonogram of the film. The fugue, the "Intermezzo," and most of the "Finale"—also known as movements (a.k.a, "numbers," as they appear in the manuscripts) three, four, and five—do not appear in the 1936 version of the film. It is also possible that this suite could have served, at least in part, as the score for the silent version of the film, since they both are almost thirty minutes long and include the majority of the music needed for the film.

23. Yakubov, *Sobraniye Sochineniy v soroka dvukh tomakh, tom 41.*
24. See VMOMK, f.32, inv.103, post.6419; VMOMK, f.32, inv.104, n.6419; VMOMK, f.32, inv.42, no.4869; and RGALI f.2048, Opis' No.3, 33. My thanks go to Irina Shostakovich, Ol'ga Dombrovskaya, and Ol'ga Digonskaya for their help in allowing me to see these manuscripts.
25. Sergey Yutkevich, "Vspominaya Shostakovicha" [Remembering Shostakovich], *Muzïkal'naya Zhizn'* 2 (1995): 23.
26. Yutkevich, "Vspominaya Shostakovicha," 23.
27. Arnshtam, "Zlatïe gorï," in *Muzïka geroicheskogo,* 64.
28. Many reviews spoke of *Golden Mountains* as a "speaking" film. *Alone* was often typified as a film where the music "spoke," while *Golden Mountains* was a true "speaking" film with music. Yutkevich expressed a similar view. RGALI, f.3070, op.1, ed.khr.501, "Stenogram."
29. Arnshtam, "Zlatïe gorï," in *Muzïka geroicheskogo,* 63.
30. These numbers are apparent in the manuscripts of *Golden Mountains.* See for example VMOMK, f.32, inv.42, no.4869.
31. Yutkevich described this process during a meeting after the film's premiere. RGALI, f.3070, op.1, ed.khr.501, "Stenogram."
32. Leo Arnshtam, "Zvukovoye oformleniye 'Vstrechnogo'" [Sound Design in *Counterplan*], *Vstrechnyi, kak sozdavalsya fil'm* [*Counterplan*—How the Film was Created] (Moscow: Kinofotoizdat, 1935), 98.
33. See, for example, chapter 2 on *New Babylon* for a discussion of how Grigory Kozintsev envisioned films as symphonies.
34. Arnshtam, "Zvukovoye oformleniye 'Vstrechnogo,'" 98. He considered *Golden Mountains* more "symphonic" than *Counterplan,* yet saw "symphonic" moments in that score as well.
35. Egorova, *Soviet Film Music,* 21.
36. RGALI, f.3070, op.1, ed.khr.501, "Stenogram."
37. Ibid., and Egorova, 10.
38. Khentova, *Shostakovich, Zhizn' i tvorchestvo,* 1:273.
39. Ibid. Arnshtam also considers the film to be leitmotivic. See Arnshtam, "Zlatïe gorï," in *Muzïka geroicheskogo,* 63.
40. See Egorova, *Soviet Film Music;* I. I. Ioffe, *Muzïka sovetskogo kino* [Music of the Soviet Cinema] (Leningrad: State Musical Scientific-Research Institute: 1938); M. Cheryomukhin, *Muzïka zvukovogo fil'ma* [Music of Sound Film] (Moscow: Goskinoizdat, 1939).
41. Arnshtam called this waltz "Spring Flowers," but the waltz is called "Les Violettes." See Emile Waldteufel, *Die schönsten Walzer,* vol. 1 (Frankfurt: Henry Litolff's Verlag). Compare Example 4.2 with this edition (page 4, measures 1–8 of Number 1), which is nearly identical with the exception of key. For the version as it appears in the published suite, see Manashir Yakubov, ed., *Dmitry Shostakovich, Sobraniye Sochineniy v soroka dvukh tomakh, tom 41 "Muzïka k kinofil'mam, partitura"* [The Collected Works in Forty-Two Volumes, vol. 41, Music to the films, orchestral score] (Moscow: Muzïka, 1987), 122, measures 10–20.

42. See chapter 2 on *New Bablyon*.
43. P. P. Petrov-Bytov was the commentator at this point in the meeting. RGALI, f.3070, op.1, ed.khr.501, "Stenogram of discussion (S. I. Yutkevich vystupleniye na diskussi v Lenark'e o fil'me S. I. Yutkevich 'Zlatïe gorï,' stenogram diskussi," 21 November 1931, pages 20–21.
44. The suite reproduces the exact music from this part of the scene.
45. See Number 2 of the suite in Yakubov, *Sobraniye Sochineniy v soroka dvukh tomakh, "Muzïka k kinofil'ma, partitura"* for the full reproduction of the music to this moment in the scene.
46. Robynn Stilwell, "The Fantastical Gap Between Diegetic and Non-Diegetic," in *Beyond the Soundtrack: Representing Music in Cinema*, ed. Daniel Goldmark, Lawrence Kramer, and Richard Leppert (Berkeley: University of California Press, 2007), 184–202.
47. See chapter 2 on *New Babylon*.
48. Arnshtam, "Zlatïe gorï," in *Muzïka geroicheskogo*, 63.
49. It is important to note that this song, "Golden Mountains" (Zlatïe gorï), has been transmitted orally, hence many possible versions do exist, of which the transcribed example is one.
50. This instrumentation is taken from the manuscripts of *Golden Mountains*, specifically the more finished draft of the score found in RGALI f.2048, op. no.3, 33, where Shostakovich indicates the instrumentation for this scene.
51. For the text of this song, see B. Zharov, *Lyubimye russkiye narodnye pesni* [Favorite Russian Folk Songs] (Moscow: Muzïka, 1985), 58.
52. Anahid Kassabian, *Hearing Film: Tracking Identifications in Contemporary Hollywood Film Music* (New York: Routledge, 2001).
53. See chapter 3 on *Alone*.
54. Ioffe, *Muzïka sovetskogo kino*, 38.
55. See Michel Chion, "Audio-Vision and Sound," in *Sound*, ed. Patricia Kruth and Henry Stobart (Cambridge: Cambridge University Press, 2000) and Michel Chion, *Audio-Vision: Sound on Screen*, ed. and trans. Claudia Gorbman (New York: Columbia University Press, 1994). Also cited in David Sonnenschein, *Sound Design: the Expressive Power of Music, Voice, and Sound Effects in Cinema* (Studio City: Michael Wiese Productions, 2001), 153.
56. Arnshtam also spoke of "music anticipating action" in his article on the *Counterplan*, which describes what Chion calls acousmatism. See Arnshtam, "Zvukovoye oformleniye 'Vstrechnogo,'" 96–97. This can also be described as a sound bridge.
57. See chapter 2 on *Counterplan*.
58. Ioffe, *Muzïka sovetskogo kino*, 38.
59. Riley claims that this was also used for his operetta, *The Great Lightening*. Riley, "If I Only . . .," 36.
60. Yutkevich, "Vspominaya Shostakovicha," 23. American newspapers such as the *New York Post* and *New York Herald Tribune* mentioned Eisenstein's introduction of *Golden Mountains*, published on 14 April 1932. Gosfil'mofond "Zlatïe gorï," ed.khr.847.
61. Arnshtam, "Zlatïe gorï," in *Muzïka geroicheskogo*, 66.
62. The term "continuity editing" is borrowed from discussions of Hollywood cinema. See David Bordwell, Janet Staiger, and Kristin Thompson, *The Classical Hollywood Cinema, Film Style and Mode of Production to 1960* (New York: Columbia

University Press, 1985), 194–213. I use the phrase "musical continuity editing" here as a musical version of continuity editing.

63. A sound bridge occurs when sound or music that belongs to the next scene is heard in advance before the image appears. See Frank E. Beaver, *Dictionary of Film Terms* (New York: Twayne Publishers, 1994), 317.

64. A *chastushka* is a vocal-instrumental genre often in the poetic form of a single stanza couplet that has four lines of text, often in a specific syllabic structure (8+7+8+7). They vary in context, but can sometimes have playful connotations. See Izaly Zemtsovsky, "Russian Federation, Traditional Music, Russian, Chastushka" *Grove Music Online, Oxford Music Online*, http://www.oxfordmusiconline.com/ (accessed 6 October 2006).

65. After the son-engineer speaks and gives the watch to Peter, an orchestral version of the waltz appears, which corresponds exactly to the whole of Number 2 in the suite.

66. At times Shostakovich wrote in small fragments that were intended for other sections. In one instance in a manuscript at the Glinka Museum Archive, he wrote notes in the margin indicating a rearrangement or rewriting of a fragment. VMOMK, f.32, inv.104, n.6419.

67. RGALI, f.2048, op. No.3, 33.

68. Only the "BA'" part of the original "ABA'" appears as the workers disperse (beginning with the orchestral flourish of the B section).

69. The music of the boss and the finale music can be found in the suite in the first number (Introduction) and the last number (Finale).

70. This is after the fifth appearance of the waltz in that same scene.

71. Asafyev considered timbre a significant *intonatsia* of twentieth-century music. See chapter 1: Introduction.

72. VMOMK, f.32, inv.104, n.6419.

73. The attacks on the film's plot organization and aspects of style made an impression on Yutkevich, who later apologized for the film in a 1932 speech to the ARRK. See S. Yutkevich, "Vstupitel'noye slovo k diskussii (Stenogramma vystupleniya na diskussii o fil'me "Zlatïe gorï," v moskovskii ARRK)" [Introductory Words to Discussion (stenogram of a speech on the discussion about the film "The Golden Mountains" in the Moscow ARRK)"], *Proletarskoe kino* 1 (1932): 5–9.

74. B. R., "'Zlatïe gorï' proizvodstvo 'Sovkino'" [The Golden Mountains, a Sovkino Production], *Komsomol'skaya pravda* 314 (19 November 1931): 4; Yakov Grinval'd, "Oktyabr'skii podarok sovetskogo kino" [An October Gift to Soviet Cinema], *Vechernyaya Moskva* 265 (9 November 1931): 2; N. OS., "Zlatïe gorï" [The Golden Mountains], *Izvestiya* 328 (29 November 1931); and K[onstantin] Fel'dman, "Ha pereput'i" [At the Crossroads], *Kino* 62 (16 November 1931): 2.

75. Shostakovich, "Kino kak shkola kompozitora," 355.

76. See chapter 2 on *New Babylon*.

77. See Joan Titus, "Dmitry Shostakovich as Film Theorist," in *Music and Politics in Twentieth-Century Europe: Essays in Memory of Neil Edmunds*, ed. Pauline Fairclough (London: Ashgate Press, 2012), 249–260 for further discussion.

78. See N. OS., "Zlatïe gorï" [The Golden Mountains], *Izvestiya* 328 (29 November 1931); B. R., "'Zlatïe gorï' proizvodstvo 'Sovkino'" [The Golden Mountains, a Sovkino Production], *Komsomol'skaya pravda* 314 (19 November 1931): 4; Yakov Grinval'd, "Oktyabr'skii podarok sovetskogo kino" [An October Gift to Soviet Cinema], *Vechernyaya Moskva* 265 (9 November 1931): 2; and A. Agranovsky,

"Pobeda zvukovogo kino" [A Victory of Sound Film], *Pravda* 325 (26 November 1931).

79. Lev Baks and G. Kudryavtsev, "Pobeda" [Victory], Unknown source in Gosfil'mofond "Zlatïe gorï," ed.khr.847. Emphasis made by the original authors. In this case and in general reference to the film materiality in Soviet film theory, "plasticity" refers to the rhythm of the editing, and the material of the celluloid and its contained images.

80. Cheryomukhin, *Muzïka zvukovogo fil'ma*, 60.

81. Ioffe, *Muzïka sovetskogo kino*, 38.

82. Ibid., 37.

83. From a paper by N. Rabinovich 17 April 1939 from the cabinet of film music of the State Scientific-Artistic Institute of Theater and Music (About the Work in Sound Cinema), quoted in Nina Gornitskaia, ed., *Iz istorii Lenfil'ma, Stati, vospominaniya, dokumentï,1930–e gody. Vypusk 4* (Leningrad: Iskusstvo, 1975), 12.

84. Pavina Rïbakova, "Muzïka Shostakovicha k zvukovym fil'mam 'Odna' i 'Zlatïe gorï'" [Shostakovich's Music to the Sound Films *Alone* and *Golden Mountains*], *Rabochiy i teatr* 24 (August 1933): 40.

85. Rïbakova, "Muzïka Shostakovicha," 40.

86. Ibid., 41.

87. Arnshtam, "Zvukovoye oformleniye 'Vstrechnogo,'" 98.

88. Ibid.

89. Arnshtam, "Zlatïe gorï," in *Muzïka geroicheskogo*, 63.

90. Ioffe, *Muzïka sovetskogo kino*, 37–38.

91. Cheryomukhin, *Muzïka zvukovogo fil'ma*, 60. "Well" can also be translated as "successfully." Notably, the fugue was used more often that Cheryomukhin mentions here. See chapter 7 on *Girlfriends*.

92. See also Number 3 in the published suite.

93. See Number 3 in the published suite. The manuscript then shows a reduction of voices back down to three, then two before abruptly ending. VMOMK, f.32, inv.104, n.6419.

94. Neil Lerner, "Musical Texture as Cinematic Signifier: The Politics of Polyphony in Selected Documentary Film Scores by Virgil Thomson and Aaron Copland," *Film Music 2: History, Theory, Practice*, ed. Claudia Gorbman (Sherman Oaks: The Film Music Society, 2004), 1–25. In his article, Lerner describes the fugue as a "cinematic signifier" of sobriety in the American documentary film *The Plow that Broke the Plains* (1936), carries the connotation of academicism. In another documentary film, *The River* (1937), a fugue is used over a visual montage of the destruction of the Mississippi.

95. Lerner argues that the relative audibility of the fugue adds to its sobriety, making it an effective tool in documentary films. Lerner, "Musical Texture as Cinematic Signifier," 18.

96. S. Bugoslavsky, "Formalizm v kinomuzïke" [Formalism in Film Music], *Kino* (16 February 1936), 3.

97. T. Khrennikov, "Muzïka v kino" [Music in Cinema], *Iskusstvo kino* 1 (January–February 1950): 26.

98. See Yutkevich, "Vstupitel'noye slovo k diskussii (Stenogramma vystupleniya na diskussii o fil'me "Zlatïe gorï," v moskovskii ARRK)."

CHAPTER 5

1. Youngblood claims it was January, but Shumyatsky says February. The script was completed by the late summer, and editing began in September; public release of the film was on the target date 7 November 1932. See Denise Youngblood, "Cinema as Social Criticism: The Early Films of Fridrikh Ermler," in *The Red Screen: Politics, Society, Art in the Soviet Cinema*, ed. Anna Lawton (London: Routledge, 1992), 81 and B. Shumyatsky "Kak voznik i stavilsya 'Vstrechnyi'" [How *Counterplan* Arose and Was Produced], in *Vstrechnyi, kak sozdavalsya fil'm*, 5.

2. This phrase is found in many places including Manashir Yakubov, ed., "Ot redaktsii" [Editor's Note], in *Dmitry Shostakovich, Sobraniye Sochineniy v soroka dvukh tomakh, tom 41, "Muzïka k kinofil'ma, partitura"* [The Collected Works in Forty-Two Volumes, vol. 41, "Music to the Film Scores, Orchestral Score"] (Moscow: Muzïka, 1987), 10.

3. See Sof'ya Khentova, *Shostakovich, Zhizn' i tvorchestvo* [Shostakovich, Life and Works] (Leningrad: Sovetskiy kompozitor: 1985), 1:326–327, citing G. V. Ignatyev, "Slovo o vstrechnom," [A Word about Counterplan] *Smena*, (13 March 1977). For greater detail on the scenario drafting process, see Joan Titus, "Modernism, Socialist Realism, and Identity, in the Early Film Music of Dmitry Shostakovich, 1929–1932" (PhD diss., Ohio State University, 2006), 332–336.

4. One of the scenarists, D. Del' discusses this point. See "Kak pisalsya stsenarii 'Vstrechnogo'" [How the Scenario of *Counterplan* was Written], in *Vstrechnyi, kak sozdavalsya fil'm* [Counterplan—How the Film was Created] (Moscow: Kinofotoizdat, 1935), 20. So does Khentova, *Shostakovich, Zhizn' i tvorchestvo*, 1:325–326. RAPP and RAPM were the Association for Proletarian Writers and Association for Proletarian Musicians.

5. Quoted from Khentova, *Shostakovich, Zhizn' i tvorchestvo*, 1:327–328.

6. Gosfil'mofond, "Vstrechnyi," no. C526.

7. RIII f.94, op.2, ed.khr.2 "Vstrechny, avtograf, partitura." Yutkevich, "Vspominaya Shostakovicha" and V. R. Gardin *Vospominaniya, tom II* [Reminiscences, vol. 2] (Moscow: Goskinoizdat, 1953), 2:96; and Khentova, *Shostakovich, Zhizn' i tvorchestvo*, 1:533.

8. TSGALI, f.257, op.16, d.2028 and RIII f.94, op.2, ed.khr.2. See also Khentova, *Shostakovich, Zhizn' i tvorchestvo*, 1:328 and "Vspominaya Shostakovicha" and Gardin, *Vospominaniya*, 96.

9. Khentova, *Shostakovich, Zhizn' i tvorchestvo*, 1:328.

10. Yutkevich, "Vspominaya Shostakovicha," 23.

11. RIII f.94, op.2, ed.khr.2, for example, Shostakovich has specific notes on how to proceed with instrumentation and texture.

12. Ibid.

13. Arnshtam claims that it was he and Volk that did the sound design entirely, but Yutkevich states that Shostakovich worked with Arnshtam on the design of factory sounds in the film. See Leo Arnshtam, "Zvukovoye oformleniye 'Vstrechnogo'" [Sound Design in *Counterplan*], *Vstrechnyi, kak sozdavalsya fil'm* [*Counterplan*—How the Film was Created] (Moscow: Kinofotoizdat, 1935), 99–100 and Yutkevich, "Vspominaya Shostakovicha," 23–24.

14. Arnshtam, "Zvukovoye oformleniye 'Vstrechnogo,'" 99–100. Hawaiian guitar was a popular instrument of this time in Soviet Russia, and used in this film, hence Arnshtam's reference.

15. See, for example, Dziga Vertov's *Enthusiasm* (1930) and *Man with a Movie Camera* (1929) and Dziga Vertov, *Kino Eye: The Writings of Dziga Vertov*, ed. Annette Michelson and Kevin O'Brien (Berkeley: University of California Press, 1984).

16. Arnshtam, "Zvukovoye oformleniye 'Vstrechnogo,'" 99–100.

17. See I. Volk, "The Sound Techniques of the Counterplan," 103–104.

18. In the scene of Babchenko and his wife eating at home, one can hear a hum in the background, possibly produced by the film equipment. In his description of *Counterplan* Riley implies that this might have been intentional. See *Dmitri Shostakovich: A Life in Film* (London: I. B. Tauris, 2005), 20. Volk, however, wrote that nuance was planned, and that cameras were able to be silenced in favor of other sounds because the equipment was far more sophisticated than in previous films. See Volk, "The Sound Techniques of *The Counterplan*," particularly 103–104 for information on the types of systems used in the film such as Pavel Shorin's SH6 and MV2. See also Titus, "Modernism, Socialist Realism, and Identity . . .," 350–351, for further discussion of Volk's article.

19. Arnshtam, "Zvukovoye oformleniye 'Vstrechnogo,'" 100.

20. See chapter 7 on *Girlfriends* for similar blending of modern instrumentation with notions of realism.

21. See chapter 2 on *Alone*.

22. Arnshtam, "Zvukovoye oformleniye 'Vstrechnogo,'" 99.

23. For more on anempathy, see Michel Chion, *Audio-Vision: Sound on Screen*, ed. and trans. by Claudia Gorbman (New York: Columbia University Press, 1994). Arnshtam also discusses how music can act in parallel or in contrast to the images. He outlines a basic set of formulae that he feels most film music follows, which is somewhat reminiscent of Shostakovich's discussion of *New Babylon*. See Arnshtam, "Zvukovoye oformleniye 'Vstrechnogo,'" 96–97.

24. The sketch of this scene exists in the Glinka archive f.32, inv.260, n.6517 in a folder on various sketches, including those of the "Song of the Counterplan." Yakubov has also published this page in *Sobraniye Sochineniy v soroka dvukh tomakh, tom 41*, 475, titled as it is the sketch "Scherzo," as seen in Example 5.1.

25. See Example 4.3 in chapter 4 on the *Golden Mountains*.

26. The instrumentation is for trumpet, trombone, tuba, winds, and timpani. Shostakovich often notated instrumentation in either a second of third draft of his piano scores, as seen in sketches of his earlier film scores as well. The instrumentation was indicated as such in the orchestral parts as well. TSGALI, f.257, op.16, d.2028, pages 98ff.

27. This is the scene that follows the scene where Babchenko gets drunk at home with his phonograph and his cat.

28. See chapter 3.

29. Frid, *Muzïka v sovetskom kino*, 88.

30. Ibid.

31. Ibid.

32. Note that these are some of the same terms that are used later in the thirties to distinguish between "good" music and "bad" music, as with *Lady MacBeth of Mtsensk District*. Shostakovich himself noted this in his article on *Lady MacBeth* from 1935, where he says that people were recognizing that he finally composed "humane" music. He states, "I can recall: the musicians who had heard *Lady MacBeth*, spoke out in the following way: look, finally, they said, Shostakovich has shown depth and humanity. When I asked where do you see the humanity, most of them answered that I had spoken for the first time with serious

language about serious tragic events." See Dmitry Shostakovich, "God posle 'Ledi Makbet'" [The Year After Lady Macbeth], *Krasnaya Gazeta* (1935).

33. Gardin, *Vospominaniya*, 2:96 quoted in Khentova, *Shostakovich, Zhizn' i tvorchestvo*, 1:328. Gardin also states that having the actor act and the composer compose after the fact was a mistake on the part of the directors—a sentence that Khentova notably left out of her book.

34. Gardin, *Vospominaniya*, 2:96.

35. Esti Sheinberg, *Irony, Satire, Parody, and the Grotesque in the Music of Shostakovich: A Theory of Musical Incongruities* (Aldershot: Ashgate, 2000).

36. In her book, *Shostakovich, Life and Works*, 1:328, Khentova states, "So, having watched a scene where on the quay there were bicycles, [Shostakovich] asked S. I. Yutkevich on what second they arise in the frame (shot), and the *partitura* included a witty find—sounds similar to sounds on a bicycle."

37. Yutkevich, "Vspominaya Shostakovicha," 23.

38. From a note by Max Steiner, 1940. See "Introduction," in *Music and Cinema*, ed. James Buhler, Caryl Flinn, and David Neumeyer (Hanover: University Press of New England for Wesleyan University Press, 2000), 15.

39. The beginning of a shift in texture from xylophone to winds and strings, from Fragment Number 1. See Yakubov, *"Muzïka k kinofil'mam, partitura,"* 199, measures 108–120.

40. This corresponds to the beginning of Fragment Number 2 in the Collected Works. Note the constant shifts in texture in the first 30 measures. The siren enters around rehearsal 3, if reading this published version of the score. See Yakubov, 206, measure 1–30.

41. See chapter 4 on *Golden Mountains*.

42. This excerpt correlates to Fragment Number 3 of the Collected Works, rehearsal 4 in Yakubov, 208.

43. E. Frid, *Muzïka v sovetskom kino* [Music in Soviet Cinema] (Leningrad: Muzïka, 1967), 89.

44. Ibid.

45. See chapter 2 on *New Babylon*.

46. This term is borrowed from Russian nomenclature of the time, often indicating music seen as exotic to Russia, that is, central European, and having the characteristic of moodiness and depression. See the *Encyclopedia of Contemporary Russian Culture*, ed. Tatiana Smorodinskaya, Karen Evans-Romaine, and Helena Goscilo (New York: Routledge, 2007), 243–244.

47. Ibid.

48. Amy Nelson, *Music for the Revolution: Musicians and Power in Early Soviet Russia* (University Park: Pennsylvania State University Press, 2004) and Neil Edmunds, *The Soviet Proletarian Music Movement* (Oxford: Peter Lang, 2000).

49. Frid, *Muzïka v sovetskom kino*, 89. In the copy of the film that I viewed, I did not see the label of the bottle. It instead looked like a generic vodka bottle.

50. See chapters 2 and 3.

51. Frid, *Muzïka v sovetskom kino*, 89. When referring to "intellectual" cinema, she specifically cites Eisenstein's *October* and his comparison of Kerensky with a bust of Napoleon. Additionally, in the version of *Counterplan* that I have seen, I did not see a close-up of the bottle as Frid explains; the shorter version that I viewed that lacked that specific shot. There is an indication in the documents at Gosfil'mofond that 1) the film was significantly re-edited just prior to release; and 2) that much consideration in re-editing and releasing the film again in 1936

and 1937, with the editing of specific shots. Gosfil'mofond, "Vstrechnyi," ed.khr. No. 400, and Titus, "Modernism, Socialist Realism, and Identity. . .," 333–336. According to N. Kolin, the film consisted of 2 hours and 20 minutes. Kolin, "Materiali k istorii fil'ma o 'Vstrechnom' " "Materials to the History of the Film about *Counterplan*], in *Counterplan—How the Film was Created*, 148. The version I have viewed, however, is 1 hour and 47 minutes, suggesting that this may be a re-edited version of the original. I was able to view this film thanks to Irina Shostakovich and Ol'ga Dombrovskaya at Shostakovich Apartment Archive in Moscow.

52. Edmunds, *Soviet Proletarian Music Movement*, 18.

53. This song can be found in recent recordings, such as Red Army Choir, *The Best of the Red Army Choir*, compact disc, Silva America, 25 June 2002.

54. See Mikhail Druskin, *Russkaya revolyutsionnaya pesnya* [Russian Revolutionary Song] (Leningrad: Gosudarstvennoye muzykal'noye izdatel'stvo, 1959), 51–52. His example bears a close resemblance to the version heard in the film.

55. For a published version of this song, see Fragment Number 10, the "Song of the Counterplan" from the music to the film *Michurin* (dir. Aleksandr Dovzhenko, 1948). This fragment shows the song sung by full chorus with orchestral accompaniment, much in the manner as it appears in the opening credits of *Counterplan*. Manashir Yakubov, ed., *Dmitry Shostakovich, Sobraniye Sochineniy v soroka dvukh tomakh, tom 41, "Muzïka k kinofil'mam, partitura,"* [The Collected Works in Forty-Two Volumes, vol. 41, Music to the Films, Orchestral Score] (Moscow: Muzïka, 1987), 477.

56. Dmitry Shostakovich, "Moi blizhaishiye rabota" [My Future Works], *Rabochiy i teatr* 11 (1937): 24.

57. See Joan Titus, "Dmitry Shostakovich as Film Music Theorist," in *Music and Politics in Twentieth-Century Europe: Essays in Memory of Neil Edmunds*, ed. Pauline Fairclough (London: Ashgate Press, 2012), 249–260.

58. Tatiana Egorova, *Soviet Film Music: A Historical Survey*, trans. Tatiana A. Ganf and Natalia A. Egunova (Amsterdam: Harwood Academic Publishers, 1997), 31; Khentova, *Shostakovich, Zhizn' i tvorchestvo*, 1:330.

59. I. V. Sokolov, *Istoriya sovetskogo kinoiskusstva zvukovogo perioda, chast' II (1934–1944)* [The History of Soviet Film Art of the Sound Period, Part II (1930–1941)] (Moscow: Goskinoizdat, 1946), 165. Excerpted from M. Cheryomukhin, *Muzïka zvukovogo fil'ma* [Music of Sound Film] (Moscow: Goskinoizdat, 1939), 176.

60. According to Khentova, Ermler seems to have been the one to suggest that the song play over the credits. See Khentova, *Shostakovich, Zhizn' i tvorchestvo*, 1:330. Having an overture to film in this manner was a common trend in Hollywood filmmaking of the thirties, as it was in the Soviet Union.

61. Khentova, *Shostakovich, Zhizn' i tvorchestvo*, 1:329. I. I. Ioffe, *Muzïka sovetskogo kino* [Music of the Soviet Cinema] (Leningrad: State Musical Scientific-Research Institute: 1938), 41.

62. Richard Taylor argues that Soviet cinema, especially of the thirties, was influenced by Hollywood film. I have noticed that the use of the overture, in addition to other parallels between the two cinemas, appears in the film of both countries. See Richard Taylor, "Red Stars, Positive Heroes, and Personality Cults," in *Stalinism and Soviet Cinema*, ed. Richard Taylor and D. W. Spring (London: Routledge, 1993), 69–89.

63. Caryl Flinn argues that music has been assigned a feminine position historical in Hollywood film, and that music can possibly be a voice for female characters.

See Caryl Flinn, "The Problem of Femininity in Theories of Film Music," *Screen* 27, no. 6 (1986): 56–73.

64. See chapter 7.
65. This shift occurs just before rehearsal 6 in the fragment Number 3 of the *Collected Works*.
66. *Music and Cinema*, ed. Buhler, Flinn, and Neumeyer, 15.
67. In the orchestral parts housed in Lenfil'm *fond*, Shostakovich wrote for a folk orchestra for this scene and the opening introduction of the Song. In it he indicated parts for folk instruments of all ranges, including *domra* and *balalaika*. TSGALI, f.257, op.16, d.2028, pages 98ff.
68. Ibid.
69. Several recent writers have claimed this, including Riley, *Dmitri Shostakovich: A Life in Film*, 21 and Egorova, *Soviet Film Music*, 31.
70. See Egorova, *Soviet Film Music*, 33–34.
71. Khentova, *Shostakovich, Zhizn' i tvorchestvo*, 1:337–338.
72. She only stated that in N. Teffi's words, a Vertinsky song, "Tri pazha" (Three Pages) was very close to Shostakovich's song. Also according to Khentova, Chernyavsky tried to claim Shostakovich's song because he believed it resembled some of his songs. See Khentova, *Shostakovich, Zhizn' i tvorchestvo*, 1:336–337. Riley, *Dmitri Shostakovich: A Life in Film*, 19 also cited Khentova for information about plagiarism.
73. Yutkevich, "Vspominaya Shostakovicha," 23.
74. Khentova, *Shostakovich, Zhizn' i tvorchestvo*, 1:329 and 336.
75. Egorova, *Soviet Film Music*, 31.
76. VMOMK, f.32, inv.260, n.6517; RIII, f.94, op.1, ed.khr.2. I also worked with a copy of the fragments from Russian Institute for Art History in St. Petersburg (RIII) and in the Shostakovich Family Archive (SA) in Moscow. Given the limited material available, the foundation of my discussion of the film's music rests on the published fragments, observations from some sketches and scores, and the phonogram (soundtrack) of the previously discussed version of the film.
77. Khentova, *Shostakovich, Zhizn' i tvorchestvo*, 1:332–336. Two of the fragments she cited are also in Yakubov, *Sobraniye Sochineniy v soroka dvukh tomakh, tom 41* (part of Number 3 and the second sketch of the three provided on page 476).
78. Shostakovich, "Moi blizhaishiye rabota," 24.
79. Two of the fragments she cites are also in Yakubov, *Sobraniye Sochineniy v soroka dvukh tomakh, tom 41* (part of Number 3 and the second sketch of the three provided on page 476).
80. VMOMK, f.32, inv.260, n.6517.
81. Yakubov reproduces this sketch in Yakubov, *Sobraniye Sochineniy v soroka dvukh tomakh, tom 41*, 476.
82. See Khentova, *Shostakovich, Zhizn' i tvorchestvo*, 1:332–336 for her description and presentation of the musical examples of the song. The *Komsomol'skaya pravda* newspaper clipping in Figure 5.2 can be compared to Yakubov, *Sobraniye Sochineniy v soroka dvukh tomakh, tom 41*, 477. The excerpt in the Yakubov edition is from the film *Michurin*.
83. See Mikhail Druskin, *Russkaya revolyutsionnaya pesnya* [Russian Revolutionary Song] (Leningrad: Gosudarstvennoye muzïkal'noye izdatel'stvo, 1959) for examples of revolutionary song.
84. "Vstrechnyi" [Counterplan], *Sovetskoe iskusstvo* 52 (15 November 1932).

85. L. Blyakhin, "Vstrechnyi" [Counterplan], *Isvestiya* 318 (15 December 1932): 4. Another writer, A. Evgenev, similarly complained. He cited the *Fragment of an Empire* as "eclectic" and having "freudism" while citing *Golden Mountains* as being "formalist," "schematic," and "aesthetic." See A. Evgenev, "Vstrechnyi" [Counterplan], *Rabochiy i teatr*, 1 December 1932 (34): 17.

86. A. Fevral'sky, "Zametki o 'Vstrechnom'" [Notes on *Counterplan*], *Kino*, 24 December 1932 (59): 3. Throughout various reviews, terms like "emotional," "lyricism," and "organicism" were used to describe the film overall, which in these contexts alluded to the film's successful creation of realism.

87. L. Ginzburg, "Fil'm o lyudyakh, stroyashchikh sotsializm" [Film about People, the Building of Socialism], *Pravda* 327 (22 November 1932): 4.

88. K., "Vstrechnyi" [Counterplan], *Rabochaya Moskva* 265 (12 November 1932). I. Bachelis, "Vstechnyi" [Counterplan], *Komsomol'skaya pravda* 260 (11 November 1932): 4, and "Vstrechnyi," *Sovetskoe iskusstvo*.

89. Shostakovich, "Kino kak shkola kompozitora," 355.

90. "'Vstrechnyi,' krupnaya tvorcheskaya pobeda sovetskoi kinematografii, beseda s predsedatelem pravleniya Soyuzkino t. B.Z. Shuyatskim" [*Counterplan*, A major creative victory of Soviet cinematography, Interview with the head of Soyuzkino t. B. Z. Shumyatsky], unidentified newspaper, 255 (3 November 1932). Gosfil'mofond, "Vstrechnyi," folder no. C526.

91. In a later article, Bogdanov-Berezovsky also states that Shostakovich's music is effective for film, but one should not underestimate the role of the directors and specifically Arnshtam in both *Golden Mountains* and *Counterplan*. See Bogdanov-Berezovsky, "Slushaya zvukovoi fil'm" [Listening to a Soundtrack Film], *Rabochiy i teatr* 24 (August 1933): 14–15.

92. A. Sadovsky, "Vstrechnyi" [Counterplan], *Kino* 51 (6 November 1932): 3.

93. Blyakhin, "Vstrechnyi."

94. "Oktyabr'skii podarok kino, fil'm "Vstrechnyi" [An October Gift to Cinema, the film *The Counterplan*], *Vechernyaya Moskva* (9 November 1932).

95. "Vstrechnyi," *Sovetskoye iskusstvo*. L. Ginzberg, a reviewer for *Pravda*, barely mentioned Shostakovich, but states that speech "appeared to be an organic part of the film," again showing the prevalence of the use of the word "organic" to emphasize realism. See L. Ginzberg, "Fil'm o lyudyakh, stroyash-chikh sotsializm."

96. Ioffe, *Muzïka sovetskogo kino*, 39–40.

97. Ibid.

98. S. Borodovsky, "Strana vstaet so slavoyu" [The Country Rises With Glory], *Vecherniy Leningrad* 234 (11 October 1979): 3. Bachelis, "Vstrechnyi."

99. Egorova, *Soviet Film Music*, 34; Frid, *Muzïka v sovetskom kino*, 87; and *Kompozitory sovetskogo kino* [Composers of Soviet Cinema] (Moscow: Soyuzinformkino, 1983), 13.

100. Arnshtam, "Zvukovoye oformleniye 'Vstrechnogo,'" 99.

101. Borodovsky, "Strana vstaet so slavoyu" and Moldavsky, "Vstrechnyi."

102. Shostakovich, "Kino kak shkola kompozitora," 355.

103. See Egorova, *Soviet Film Music*, 34; Khentova, *Shostakovich, Zhizn' i tvorchestvo*, 1:341; and Fay, *Shostakovich: A Life*, 72.

104. Gerard McBurney, "Fried Chicken in the Bird-Cherry Trees," and Leonid Maximenkov, "Stalin and Shostakovich: Letters to a 'Friend,'" in *Shostakovich and His World*, ed. Laurel Fay (Princeton: Princeton University Press, 2004), 45 and 243.

105. Harold J. Rome and Dmitry Shostakovich, "The United Nations" (New York: Am-Rus Music Corporation, 1942).
106. T.M.P, " 'Thousands Cheer,' Lavish Metro Musical with an All-Star Cast, Makes Its Appearance at War Bond Rally at Astor," *New York Times*, September 14, 1943.
107. This Song was reused in many places in the time between these films and afterward, including in the film *Michurin* (dir. Aleksandr Dovzhenko, 1948). Isaak Dunayevsky also arranged it for chorus. For a list of these instances, though with errors, see John Riley, "From the Factory to the Flat: Thirty Years of the Song of the Counterplan," in *Soviet Music and Society under Lenin and Stalin: the Baton and Sickle*, ed. Neil Edmunds (New York: Routledge, 2004), 67–80.
108. David Bordwell, Janet Staiger, and Kristin Thompson, *The Classical Hollywood Cinema, Film Style and Mode of Production to 1960* (New York: Columbia University Press, 1985), 23–24.
109. Ibid.
110. Maya Turovskaya, "The 1930s and 1940s: Cinema in Context," in *Stalinism and Soviet Cinema*, ed. Richard Taylor and D. W. Spring (London: Routledge, 1993), 44. This report was made by Boris Shumyatsky. In that the same report from which this quote came, Shumyatsky states, "By the entertainment value of a film we mean the considerable emotional effect it exerts and the simple artistry that rapidly and easily communicates its ideological content and its plot to the mass audience." Turovskaya, "The 1930s and 1940s: Cinema in Context," 44–45.
111. For longer discussion of the film and current aesthetics, see Titus, "Modernism, Socialist Realism, and Identity," 341–346.
112. S. Bugoslavsky, "Formalizm v kinomuzïke" [Formalism in Film Music], *Kino* (16 February 1936): 3.
113. T. Khrennikov, "Muzïka v kino" [Music in Cinema], *Iskusstvo kino* 1 (January–February 1950): 26–27.
114. Gosfil'mofond, "Vstrechnyi," folder no. C526.

CHAPTER 6

1. Shostakovich and Kozintsev worked together for over forty years, ending their collaborative relationship with *Hamlet* (1964) and *King Lear* (1971).
2. Denise Youngblood, *Russian War Films* (Lawrence: University of Kansas Press, 2007) and Lilya Kaganovsky, *How the Soviet Man was Unmade: Cultural Fantasy and Male Subjectivity under Stalin* (Pittsburgh: University of Pittsburgh Press, 2008).
3. Aleksandr Karaganov, *Trilogiya o Maksime* [*Trilogy of Maxim*] (Moscow: Iskusstvo, 1981), 19ff.; Grigory Kozintsev, *Sobranniye sochineniy v pyaty tomakh, T.1* [*Collected Works in Five Volumes*, vol.1], ed. V. G. Kozintseva and Ya. L. Butovsky (Leningrad: Iskusstvo, 1982), 379.
4. *Kadr*, 3 December 1932. See also Karaganov, *Trilogy*, 22.
5. Karaganov, *Trilogy*, 19. They relate that the scenario was made in November 1929, and the application was accepted by Lenfil'm in January 1930. At that time it was titled *The Bolshevik*. See the article about their release in *Kadr*, 3 December 1932.
6. Pre-screenings of the film began in December 1934. For the purposes of this book, I save a discussion of the other two films of the *Trilogy* for a later time. I continue a discussion of Shostakovich's film scores in my next volumes, picking up with the *Trilogy* and other film scores that post-date *Girlfriends* (1935–36).
7. See Kozintsev, *Collected Works*, 1:398.

8. Trauberg "L. Z. Trauberg o D. D. Shostakoviche" [L.Z. Trauberg on D. D. Shostakovich] in Karaganov, *Trilogy*, 53. In retrospect, Shostakovich regarded the score to *Alone* as fragmented, not continuous. Here, Trauberg makes it clear that "continuity," in the symphonic sense, was initially intended. See chapter 3 on *Alone*.

9. See chapter 3.

10. TSGALI, f.257, op.16, d.372; Gosfil'mofond ed. khr. No.2841; and Kozintsev, *Collected Works*, 1:391ff.

11. Kozintsev, *Collected Works*, 1:391ff.

12. Notably, the *bayan* player throughout the film gets his own credit revealed at the beginning of the film. Shostakovich's is left out, however, of certain recent releases of the film. See *Legendy russkogo kino—Boris Chirkov*, DVD "Starlain," 2012, for example.

13. Kozintsev and Trauberg worked carefully with the studio to ensure that their scenario was acceptable. This was especially important after they received threats from Lenfil'm studio stating that they would dock their pay after what the studio considered the lukewarm success of *Alone*. See chapter 3.

14. "Shar" is sometimes translated as "balloon." Neya Zorkaya claims that this song was taken from "Krutitsya, vertitsya sharf goluboy" (Whirling, twirling blue scarf), a nineteenth-century romance by Nikolay Titov. The two songs have different music altogether, but the titles do appear to be similar. See Neya Zorkaya, "Trilogiya o Maksima i bol'sheviki ot Maksima do Lenina" [*Trilogy of Maxim* and the Bolsheviks from Maxim to Lenin"], *Slovo*, "Iskusstvo," http://www.portal-slovo.ru.

15. See *Chapayev* and chapter 7 on *Girlfriends*.

16. Kozintsev, *Collected Works*, 1:367. Here, *chantant* can mean cabaret.

17. Ibid.

18. In the scenarios, the directors indicated that the music become louder at the very end, overtaking the image. TSGALI, f.257, op.16, d.372.

19. The *yurodivyi*, or the holy fool, is a known type with a long history in sacred and secular Russian culture. For an overview see Priscilla Hunt and Svitlana Kobets, *Holy Foolishness in Russia: New Perspectives* (Bloomington, IN: Slavica Publishers, 2011).

20. Kozintsev, *Collected Works*, 1:398. See also for general notes about Kozintsev, Ol'ga Dombrovskaya "O muzïke Shostakovicha v fil'makh Kozintseva. Zametki k publikatsii odnogo pis'ma [About Shostakovich's Music to Kozintsev's Films. Notes about the Publication of a Letter], *Kinozapiski* 74, 2005, http://www.kino-zapiski.ru/ru/article/sendvalues/449/.

21. Kozintsev, *Collected Works*, 1:369, 398.

22. The lyrics in Figure 6.4 are taken from the film, and also have been confirmed in the final scenarios. TSGALI, f.257, op.16, d.372.

23. See, for example, the songs of the *bardi*, such as Bulat Okudzhava or Vladimir Vysotsky.

24. Even a cursory scan of the internet (in Russian) shows enthusiastic reception of this song, and how contributors associate it only with the film or with the character of Maxim.

25. Amy Nelson, *Music for the Revolution: Musicians and Power in Early Soviet Russia* (University Park: Pennsylvania State University Press, 2004), 34, 111.

26. Nelson, 34. See also George Weissman, ed., *Balkan Wars, 1912–1913: The War Correspondence of Leon Trotsky* (New York: Anchor Foundation, 1980), 43; Neil Edmunds, *The Soviet Proletarian Music Movement* (Oxford: Peter Lang,

2000), 140; and Boris Schwarz, *Music and Musical Life in Soviet Russia*, enl. ed. (Bloomington: Indiana University Press, 1983), 84.

27. This is after Maxim begins to sing a village song by himself and is silenced by the prison guard, showing that any singing was strictly forbidden in the prison.

28. Nelson, 34.

29. Ibid., 28 and 122.

30. See chapters 3 (*Alone*) and 4 (*Golden Mountains*).

31. The scenarios in the Lenfil'm fond also designate this musical section as "Oi-ra." TSGALI, f.257, op.16, d.372. See also Kozintsev, *Collected Works*, 1:398.

32. Kozintsev, *Collected Works*, 1:369 and 398.

33. Ibid., 1:390.

34. TSGALI f.257, op.16, d.2057 contains the piano score and orchestral parts, each of which are modified with handwritten notes. See also Manashir Yakubov, ed., *Dmitry Shostakovich, Sobraniye Sochineniy v soroka dvukh tomakh, tom 41, "Muzïka k kinofil'ma, partitura"* [The Collected Works in Forty-Two Volumes, vol. 41, Music to Film, Orchestral Score] (Moscow: Muzïka, 1987).

35. In this case, "a+b" indicates a two-part phrase, while "c+c" is a repeat of the same phrase twice. "d" is a set of sequences, as one finds in the quoted song.

36. Kozintsev, *Collected Works*, 1:390.

37. TSGALI, f.257, op.16, d.372.

38. See for example B. Rosentsveig, "Yunost' maksima" [Youth of Maxim], *Rabochaya Moskva*, no.293, 18 December 1934.

39. V. Pudovkin, "Yunost' maksima" [Youth of Maxim], *Izvestiya*, no.294, 12 December 1934.

40. N.A., "500,000 trudyashchikhsya Leningrada smotreli 'Yunost' Maksima'" [500,000 Leningrad Workers Watched "Youth of Maxim"], *Krasnaya gazeta*, 1935.

41. *Chapayev* (1934) was directed by Georgy and Sergey Vasil'yev, with a score composed by Gavriil Popov. Although an interesting score with plenty of music, the focus of this chapter is on Shostakovich's score. I will address Popov's film music in another work.

42. Kaganovsky, *How the Soviet Man was Unmade*.

43. Grigory Kozintsev and Leonid Trauberg, "Nasha rabota nad fil'mom 'Yunost maksima'" [Our Work on the Film "Youth of Maxim"], *Vechernyaya Moskva*, no.298, 28 December 1934.

44. Multiple authors, "Yunost' maksima, tsennïy vklad v Sovetskoye kino" ["Youth of Maxim," A Valuable Contribution to the Soviet Cinema], *Komsomol'skaya pravda*, n.284, 15 December 1934.

45. Multiple authors, "Fil'm bol'shoy vospitatel'nyi sily" [The Film is a Great Educational Force], *Komsomol'skaya pravda*, n.81, 6 February 1935.

46. Boris Chirkov, "Snova maksim" [Maxim Again], *Sovetskaya Rossiya*, 23 January 1975.

47. L. Rovinskiy, "Etot fil'm zavoyuet zritelya—Yunost' maksima" [This Film Conquers the Viewer—Youth of Maxim], *Izvestiya*, 15 December 1934. Articles such as this suggested that "Whirling, twirling . . ." paved the way for the film's intelligibility.

48. The phrase "intelligible to the millions" was the catchphrase of the time. See for example Leonid Trauberg, "An Experiment Intelligible to the Millions," in *The Film Factory: Russian and Soviet Cinema in Documents 1896–1939*, ed. Richard Taylor and Ian Christie (London: Routledge & Kegan Paul, 1988), 250.

49. Rosentsveig, "Yunost' maksima."

50. M. Cheryomukhin, *Muzïka zvukovogo fil'ma* [Music of Sound Film] (Moscow: Goskinoizdat, 1939), 179 and 183.
51. I. I. Ioffe, *Muzïka sovetskogo kino* [Music of the Soviet Cinema] (Leningrad: State Musical Scientific-Research Institute: 1938), 41–42.
52. Trauberg in Karaganov, *Trilogy*, 53ff.
53. In the credits for *Youth of Maxim*, Shostakovich is ignored. In the following films, he is credited.

CHAPTER 7

1. A similar observation can be made of *Love and Hatred* (*Lyubov i nenavist*, dir. Al'bert Gendel'shtein, 1934), where a group of women are central to the story but their gender was less the focus than the Soviet narrative.
2. David Gillespie has a section on women and film in his book, and views the inclusion of women in films as a teleological growth from passive characters of literature to active central characters in Stalinist film, and beyond. This subtle shift in focus from general Soviet women to feminized ones in the 1930s in films such as *Girlfriends*, however, is less the focus of his interesting and general overview. See David Gillespie, *Russian Cinema* (New York: Longman, 2003), 85–88.
3. On the score to *Girlfriends* (and *Love and Hatred*), Egorova is silent, only mentioning them as "symphonic" in passing. See Tatiana Egorova, *Soviet Film Music: A Historical Survey*, trans. Tatiana A. Ganf and Natalia A. Egunova (Amsterdam: Harwood Academic Publishers, 1997), 23.
4. Raisa Vasil'eva was a writer who eventually worked on screenplays until her death in 1938. See also Jamie Miller, *Soviet Cinema: Politics and Perusasion Under Stalin* (London: I.B. Tauris, 2010). Vasil'eva's near-autobiography, *Pervye komsomolki* [The First Komsomols], was rumored to be the basis of *Girlfriends*. In my project on Soviet women, cinema, and music I address Vasil'eva's role in greater detail.
5. Katerina Clark, *The Soviet Novel: History as Ritual* (Bloomington: Indiana University Press, 2000); Lilya Kaganovsky, *How the Soviet Man Was Unmade: Cultural Fantasy and Male Subjectivity under Stalin* (Pittsburgh: University of Pittsburgh Press, 2008); Gillespie, *Russian Cinema*; and Denise Youngblood, *Russian War Films* (Lawrence: University of Kansas Press, 2007).
6. See previous chapters for discussion of those traits in the Soviet press.
7. Youngblood, *Russian War Films*; B. Reznikov, "Girlfriends," *Pravda* no.4, 4 January 1936.
8. Even foreign reviewers commented on how the film resembled *Chapayev*. See the review of the film at the Cameo Theater (Chicago) in Peter Ellis, "Screen: Three Women," *The New Masses*, 17 March 1936, 28. *Three Women* was the American title for *Girlfriends*.
9. See chapter 6 for press on *Youth of Maxim*.
10. See chapters 2 and 3.
11. I am currently working on a separate book project that examines women, music, and Soviet cinema that will provide a closer analysis of this topic in these and other films.
12. Zheimo was a celebrated comedian and child actor prior to her work on *Girlfriends*. She also worked with FEKs, and directors Kozintsev and Trauberg in films such as *Shinel'* (*Overcoat*, 1926), *SVD* (*Soyuz Velikogo Dela*, 1927), and *New Babylon*. Orlova was a known actress in Aleksandrov's films including *Tsirk*

(*Circus*, 1936) and *Volga-Volga* (1938). Both were regarded as spirited blonde women who thwarted the system; some have argued that Zheimo played roles that sometimes demonstrated the power of children to overthrow "wreckers." See Rimgailia Salys, *The Musical Comedy Films of Grigorii Aleksandrov* (Bristol: Intellect Ltd, 2009); and Maria Enzensberger, " 'We Were Born to Turn a Fairy Tale into Reality': Grigori Aleksandrov's *The Radiant Path*," in *Stalinism and Soviet Cinema*, ed. Richard Taylor and Derek Spring (New York: Routledge, 1993), 95.

13. Clark, *Soviet Novel*.
14. Laura Mulvey, "Visual Pleasure and Narrative Cinema," in *Visual and Other Pleasures*, 2nd ed. (New York: Palgrave, 2009), 14–30.
15. Youngblood, *Russian War Films*, 52.
16. Boris Chirkov, Boris Poslavsky, and Boris Babochkin were the actors. Chirkov also played Maxim in *Trilogy of Maxim*.
17. Mulvey.
18. Tania Modleski, *The Women Who Knew Too Much: Hitchcock and Feminist Theory*, 2nd ed. (New York: Routledge, 2005), 69–88.
19. Youngblood asserts that after Stalin, audiences appeared less interested in certain films such as *Shchors* (dir. Aleksandr Dovzhenko, 1939). Similarly, it is unclear whether or not audiences after Stalinism, outside of film enthusiasts, willingly enjoyed *Girlfriends*. See Youngblood, *Russian War Films*, 235.
20. "Devushki revolutsii" [Girlfriends of the Revolution], *Vechernaya krasnaya gazeta*, 4 January 1936.
21. G. Kish, "Podrugi" [Girlfriends], *Pravda*, 16 December 1935.
22. Amo Bek-Nazarov and F. Karen "Rozhdeniye mastera" [Birth of a Master], *Kino*, 28 December 1935.
23. Boris Vetrov, "Podrugi: actyor i obraz" [Girlfriends: Actor and Image], *Kino*, 6 January 1936.
24. Mulvey, "Visual Pleasure . . . ," 25.
25. David Hoffman, *Stalinist Values: The Cultural Norms of Soviet Modernity, 1917–1941* (Ithaca: Cornell University Press, 2003), 111–112. See also Wendy Goldman, *Women, the State and Revolution: Soviet Family Policy and Social Life, 1917–1936* (Cambridge: Cambridge University Press, 1993).
26. B. Bayanov, E. Smirnov, and A. Mar'yamov, "Podrugi revolutsii" [Girlfriends of the Revolution], *Pravda*, January 1936.
27. Yanina Zheimo, "Moi detskiye roli" [My Childhood Roles], *Kino*, 28 December 1935.
28. David Hoffman has discussed how femininity was modeled in visual culture. See Hoffman, *Stalinist Values*, 115–116. See also Emma Widdis, "Dressing the Part: Clothing Otherness in Soviet Cinema before 1953," in *Insiders and Outsiders in Russian Cinema*, ed. Stephen M. Norris and Zara M. Torlone (Bloomington: Indiana University Press, 2008), 48–67.
29. I. F. Popov, "V tvorcheskoi masterskoi S. Yutkevicha" [In the Studio of S. Yutkevich].
30. Clark, *Soviet Novel*.
31. After *Counterplan*, sound films focused most on speech, rather than music to create narrative. As a result, music could be used more selectively. Similar approaches also were favored in early Hollywood cinema.
32. Although almost completely ignored in comparison to films of its time, *Girlfriends* is sometimes mentioned in this way. See Tatiana Egorova, *Soviet Film Music*, 23.

33. Arnshtam referred to them as "preludes" and the term has remained. See Leo Arnshtam, *Muzïka geroicheskogo* [Music of the Heroic] (Moscow: Iskusstvo, 1977), 21.

34. Mikhail Cheryomukhin, "Prodrugi: Muzïka krasochna i dinamichna" [Girlfriends: The Music is Colorful and Dynamic], *Kino*, 6 January 1936.

35. "Underground" Bolshevik is the phrase that some critics used to complimentarily describe Silych's role in the film. See "Podrugi" [Girlfriends], *Vechernyaya moskva*, 16 December 1935.

36. "Girls of the Revolution."

37. "Tyazholey" can also mean severe or hard; and "nevoley" refers to bondage, or oppression. There are multiple translations of this title, including the popular "Tormented by a Lack of Freedom," or "Tormented by Grievous Bondage." See, for example, David Fanning, *Shostakovich: String Quartet No.8* (Aldershot: Ashgate, 2004), Appendix A.

38. Mikhail Druskin, *Russkaya revolyutsionnaya pesnya* [Russian Revolutionary Song] (Leningrad: Gosudarstvennoye muzïkal'noye izdatel'stvo, 1959), 58 and 92. By most accounts, the lyrics in Figure 7.2 align with the third and fourth stanzas of the song in the film. The first two stanzas were partially sung by the children when they first start (beginning with "Zamuchen . . ."), and are stopped so Andrey and Silych can encourage the crowd to listen.

39. See for example Margarita Mazo's nuanced treatment of Russian song in Malcolm Brown, Margarita Mazo, N. A. Lvov, and Ivan Pratch, *A Collection of Russian Folk Songs* (Ann Arbor: UMI Research Press, 1987).

40. In his lullaby in the second half, he emulates some characteristics of folksong. See chapter 2 on *Alone*.

41. Until about 2005, only three fragments from *Girlfriends* were extant, and were housed in RIII, with copies in the Shostakovich Archive in Moscow. Since then, Shostakovich archivist and musicologist Ol'ga Digonskaya has found five more fragments, still leaving fifteen or so remaining sections of music from the film that are lost. Since some of those "sections" are known folk songs, it is possible that there were never composed at all, but created orally on the spot. For detailed information on the found manuscripts see Ol'ga Digonskaya, "Kinomuzïka Shostakovicha: neizvestniye avtografy," *Muzïkalnaya akademiya* 2 (2006), 92–107. Also see the CD liner notes by Digonskaya from "The Girlfriends (Complete)/Salute to Spain/Rule, Britannia!/Symphonic Movement (1945)," Mark Fitz-Gerald, Polish National Radio Symphony Orchestra, 2009, Naxos 8.572138. According to Arnshtam, Shostakovich wrote twelve Preludes; it is unclear to which sections of music he was referring. See Arnshtam, *Muzyka geroicheskogo*, 21.

42. See for example Fanning, *String Quartet No.8* and Sarah Reichardt, *Composing the Modern Subject: Four String Quartets by Dmitri Shostakovich* (Aldershot: Ashgate, 2008).

43. My thanks go to Richard Taruskin for encouraging me to look more deeply at this connection.

44. See chapters 4 on *Counterplan* and 5 on *Golden Mountains*.

45. Since no manuscript of this number currently exists, it has been assumed that Shostakovich authored the arrangement.

46. In the only recording available, Mark Fitz-Gerald calls the ensemble a "banda" likely in reference to opera tradition, where a brass/percussion ensemble plays music (indicated for on-stage but now played off-stage) that opera characters

often hear. See "The Girlfriends (Complete)/Salute to Spain/Rule, Britannia!/ Symphonic Movement (1945)." For more on *banda*, see Philip Gosset, *Divas and Scholars: Performing Italian Opera* (Chicago: University of Chicago Press, 2006), 607.

47. Gosset, *Divas and Scholars*, 607.
48. See chapter 3 on *Alone*.
49. Shorinofone and Tagefone were sound-on-film recording apparatus named after their inventors Pavel Tager and Aleksandr Shorin. The Variophone was a kind of sound technology developed by Evgeny Sholpo and Georgy Rimsky-Korsakov, who worked at Lenfil'm Studios creating this system. See Peter Rollberg, *Historical Dictionary of Russian and Soviet Cinema* (Lanham: Scarecrow Press, 2009), xxvi and following; and Andrey Smirnov's research with the Theremin Center at the Moscow State Conservatory, http://asmir.theremin.ru/genera-tion_z_e.htm.
50. Smirnov, Theremin Center.
51. As Druskin had noted, Shostakovich was familiar with the myriad and emergent trends surrounding him in the 1920s. See chapter 1: Introduction. Shostakovich also attended the conservatory along with Georgy Rimsky-Korsakov and participated in a quarter-tone music group run by Rimsky-Korsakov. See Laurel Fay, *Shostakovich: A Life* (Oxford: Oxford University Press, 2000), 19–20.
52. To date, no manuscripts or edited score exists for these musical sections of the film. Mark Fitz-Gerald did, however, transcribe them for his recording. The transcriptions that follow are my own, and/or were transcribed by trumpeter Christian Anderson.
53. See Robynn Stilwell, "The Fantastical Gap Between Diegetic and Non-Diegetic," in *Beyond the Soundtrack: Representing Music in Cinema*, ed. Daniel Goldmark, Lawrence Kramer, and Richard Leppert (Berkeley: University of California Press, 2007), 184–202.
54. In Mark Fitz-Gerald's transcription and recording, he writes for three trumpets. Through closer scrutiny of the film and an overtone spectral analysis, it is clear that at least four trumpets, if not six, were used in recording this section of the film. It is likely that the first trumpet part, if not all, was doubled creating a formidable sound even in consideration of the quality of sound recording at the time. I thank professional trumpeter Christian Anderson for assistance on this and his insights on trumpet writing and overtone spectral analysis.
55. Raymond Monelle, *The Musical Topic: Hunt, Military and Pastoral* (Bloomington: Indiana University Press, 2006), 160–181.
56. See for example, the first movement of Mahler's Fourth Symphony, second trumpet, and the opening and throughout the first movement of the Fifth Symphony. Monelle also provides several examples from the military, and mottos such as these, some of them from cinema. See Monelle, 113–181.
57. The second movement of this quartet is excerpted, beginning approximately one minute into the work. The excerpt goes on for about 2 minutes, 45 seconds and ends on a harmonic, approximately halfway through the movement.
58. Gosfil'mofond, "Montazhny zapis'" ["Editing record," 1968 restoration], ed.khr.1783.
59. This is one of the three sections of music found in manuscript, and held in RIII (Petersburg) and Shostakovich Archive in Moscow. The others are in RGALI and VMOMK. See Digonskaya, "Kinomuzïka Shostakovicha."

60. Digonskaya, "Kinomuzïka Shostakovicha." Three of these fragments were found prior to 2005. The other five were found by Digonskaya at the Glinka Museum Archive (VMOMK).

61. See for example film music manuals such as Erno Rapée, *Motion Picture Moods for Pianists and Organists: A Rapid-Reference Collection of Selected Pieces, Adapted to Fifty-Two Moods and Situations* (New York: Schirmer, 1924); or Russian accompaniment manuals such as D. Blok and S. Bugoslavsky, *Muzïkal'noe soprovozhdeniye v kino* [Musical Accompaniment in the Cinema] (Moscow: Teakinopechat, 1929).

62. I. I. Ioffe, *Muzïka sovetskogo kino* [Music of the Soviet Cinema] (Leningrad: State Musical Scientific-Research Institute: 1938), 42.

63. Bordwell, et al.; and Claudia Gorbman, *Unheard Melodies: Narrative Film Music* (Bloomington: Indiana University Press, 1987).

64. This name, "The Keys to Happiness," is the same of a fin-de-siècle novel by Anastasia Verbitskaya about the Russian "new woman." The idea that this *traktir* is predominantly for men, and is initially hostile to the young girls is an interesting literary intertextual twist. For an English translation of the novel, see A. Verbitskaya, Beth Holmgren, and Helena Goscilo, *The Keys to Happiness: A Novel* (Bloomington: Indiana University Press, 1999).

65. Shostakovich commonly used the short-short-long rhythmic motive (as well as its inverse) in musical works from this time and beyond.

66. It appears as if a kind of "up-and-downer" was being used. See Gorbman, 77.

67. The trope of a male chorus supporting a revolutionary idea is also used effectively in *Counterplan*. See chapter 5.

68. This was noticed by audiences—an American reviewer described this scene as "over-long and shows a bad Hollywood influence." Ellis, *New Masses*, 28.

69. The well-known Act I, Prelude is often quoted in cinema as are other parts of the opera. The melody and tremolo appears in Lohengrin's arias in Act I, scene iii , "Nun sei bandankt, mein lieber Schwan" and Act III, scene iii , "Mein Lieber Schwan." Another possible choice is the Fountain scene in Modest Musorgsky's *Boris Godunov*, where tremolo strings appear prominently. Thanks to Richard Taruskin for reminding me of the Fountain scene.

70. VMOMK, f.32, No.2303, page 1.

71. The ascending line in the violin at the moment the images fade in to the forest has some resemblance to Mahler's "Urlicht" in *Des Knaben Wunderhorn*, and consequently in the reuse of the song in his Second Symphony. The overall contour and harmonization regardless recalls many romantic works, particularly those by composers of opera, song, or solo violin works.

72. This set of scenes makes great use of the up-and-downer so effectively that it renders the music nearly inaudible during conversations between the lovers. This is likely the result of the poor quality of the extant copy of the film.

73. Ellis, *New Masses*, 28.

74. Hoffman, *Stalinist Values*, 109–117.

75. Ioffe, 42–43.

76. Caryl Flinn argues that music has been assigned a feminine position historical in Hollywood film, and that music can possibly be voice to female characters. See Caryl Flinn, "The Problem of Femininity in Theories of Film Music," *Screen* 27, no. 6 (1986): 56–73.

77. From a note by Max Steiner, 1940. See James Buhler, Caryl Flinn, and David Neumeyer, eds., "Introduction," in *Music and Cinema* (Hanover: University Press of New England for Wesleyan University Press, 2000), 15.

78. See Kathryn Kalinak, *Settling the Score: Music and the Classical Hollywood Film* (Madison: The University of Wisconsin Press, 1992), 168.
79. Flinn, "The Problem with Femininity . . ."
80. Recent general histories about Soviet and Russian film, for instance, rarely mention *Girlfriends*, or discuss it at length. See for example Bridget Beumers, ed., *The Cinema of Russia and the Former Soviet Union* (London: Wallflower Press, 2007). Denise Youngblood, however, is among the first to give significant attention to this film. See Youngblood, *Russian War Films*.
81. Vetrov, "Podrugi: actor i obraz."
82. Kish, "Podrugi."
83. "Devushki revolutsii."
84. Cheryomukhin, "Prodrugi . . . ."
85. Ibid.
86. Dmitry Shostakovich, "About the Music to The New Babylon" [O muzïke k "Novomu Vavilonu"], trans. Joan Titus in *The Routledge Film Music Sourcebook*, ed. James Wierzbicki, Nathan Platte, and Colin Roust (Routledge Press, 2011), 61–64.
87. Ibid.
88. Cheryomukhin, "Prodrugi . . . ."
89. Ibid.
90. Ibid.
91. Ibid.
92. It was premiered in the United States in the first few months of 1936. A Chicago review dates a showing at the Cameo Theater as early as 17 March 1936. See Ellis, "Three Women," 27–28. According to *Vechernyaya Moskva*, it was shown in Paris in October 1936 to positive reviews by Lucien Wahl. See "Podrugi v Parizhe," *Vechernyaya Moskva*, 16 October 1936. Another author stated that it was premiered in Paris later at the *Cinéma du Panthéon* on 19 December 1936. See Roman Gubern and Paul Hammond, *Luis Buñuel, The Red Years, 1929–1939* (Madison: University of Wisconsin Press, 2012), 178.
93. Youngblood, *Russian War Films*, 53 and 235. Shumyatsky relates that Stalin watched it on 25 December 1935, and demanded to watch *Chapayev* after he had finished *Girlfriends*. See Troshin, ed. "'Kartina sil'naya, khoroshaya no ne Chapaev'; Zapiski besed B. Z. Shumyatskogo s I. V. Stalinym posle kinoprosmotrov, 1935–1937," ['The Picture is Good and Strong, but not Chapayev,' Notes of B.Z. Shumyatsky's Conversations with I. V. Stalin after Film Screenings.] *Kinovedcheskie zapiski*, no.62 (2003): 115–187.
94. Ellis; and Wahl.
95. Gosfil'mofond, "Montazhny zapis'," ed.khr.1783. As in other countries, it took time for theaters to turnover to sound, especially in smaller cities.
96. Youngblood, *Russian War Films*, 144; Konstantin Rokossovsky, "Armiya i kino [Army and Cinema]," *Sovetsky ekran*, no.3 (1959): 1; and A. Groshev, "40 let sovetskogo kino [40 Years of Soviet Cinema]," *Sovetsky ekran*, no.16 (1959): 2–3.
97. S. Bugoslavsky, "Formalizm v kinomuzïke" [Formalism in Film Music], *Kino*, 16 February 1936, 3.
98. Ibid.
99. T. Khrennikov, "Muzïka v kino" [Music in Cinema], *Iskusstvo kino* 1 (January–February 1950): 26.
100. Youngblood, *Russian War Films*, 50–53; Goldman, *Women, the State, and Revolution*, 296–343; and Hoffman, *Stalinist Values*, 109–117.

CHAPTER 8

1. I am currently working on two more volumes that address the remaining film scores of Shostakovich, which will trace his film music career through Stalinism and beyond.

2. Grigory Kozintsev and Leonid Trauberg eventually separated in the 1940s, yet Shostakovich continued to work with Kozintsev. The last film on which Shostakovich and Kozintsev collaborated was *Korol' Lir* (*King Lear*, 1971).

3. Shostakovich wrote for two cartoons, *Skazka o pope i o rabotnike ego Balde* (*Tale of a Priest and his Servant Balda*, 1934) and *Skazka o glupom mïshonke* (*Tale of the Silly Baby Mouse*, 1939). The former film has mostly been lost, with a few minutes remaining, while the latter is mostly extant. They stand outside the scope of this book and occupy a different category of film, and deserve their own space outside of this book's discussion of fiction film.

4. Peter J. Schmelz, "What Was 'Shostakovich' and What Came Next?" *Journal of Musicology* 24, no. 3 (Summer 2007): 297–338.

5. For an English translation see James Tull, "B. V. Asaf'yev's Musical Form as a Process, Translation and Commentary" (PhD diss., The Ohio State University, 1976), 146. See also Malcolm Brown, "The Soviet Russian Concepts of 'Intonazia' and 'Musical Imagery,'" *The Musical Quarterly* 60, no. 4 (October 1974): 557–567. Many Russianists have effectively analyzed, discussed, and theorized *intonatsii* and demonstrated its potential applications. See Tull; David Haas, *Leningrad's Modernists: Studies in Composition and Musical Thought, 1917–1932* (Peter Lang: New York, 1998); Brown, "The Soviet Russian Concepts of 'Intonazia' and 'Musical Imagery'"; David Fanning and Pauline Fairclough, eds., *The Cambridge Companion to Shostakovich* (Cambridge: Cambridge University Press, 2008); Elena Orlova, *Intonatsionnaia teoria Asafyeva kak uchenie o spetsifike muzykal'nogo myshleniya* [The Intonational Theory of Asafyev as a Doctrine of the Totality of Musical Thought] (Moscow: Muzïka, 1984).

6. Brown, "The Soviet Russian Concepts of 'Intonazia' and 'Musical Imagery'"; Tull, "B. V. Asaf'yev's Musical Form as a Process"; Haas, chapter 8; Pauline Fairclough, *A Soviet Credo: Shostakovich's Fourth Symphony* (Aldershot: Ashgate, 2006); Michael Rofe, *Dimensions of Energy in Shostakovich's Symphonies* (Aldershot: Ashgate, 2012).

7. Arved Ashby, *Absolute Music, Mechanical Reproduction* (Berkeley: University of California Press, 2010), 250.

8. See Joan Titus, "Modernism, Socialist Realism, and Identity in the Early Film Music of Dmitry Shostakovich, 1929–1932" (PhD diss., The Ohio State University, 2006), 102–105.

9. See chapters 2 and 3.

10. See for example Haas, *Leningrad's Modernists,* 184–186; and Marina Sabinina, *Simfonizm Shostakovicha* [The Symphonism of Shostakovich] (Moscow: Nauka, 1965). In her book, Wilson relates an account of Nadezhda Galli-Shohat, where she describes Shostakovich improvising at the piano while making up a story. See Elizabeth Wilson, *Shostakovich: A Life Remembered* (Princeton: Princeton University Press, 1994), 11.

11. Haas, *Leningrad's Modernists*; Fay, 57–59; Mikhail Druskin "Shostakovich v 20-e gody" [Shostakovich in the 1920s], in *Ocherki, stat'i, zametki* [Sketches, Articles and Notes] (Leningrad: Sovetskiy kompozitor, 1987).

12. Wilson, 27–28; Fay, 29.

13. See chapter 2 on *New Babylon*.

14. Kozintsev, *Collected Works,* 2:423.

15. Ibid. See chapter 5 on *Counterplan*.

16. Joan Titus, "Dmitry Shostakovich as Film Music Theorist," in *Music and Politics in Twentieth-Century Europe: Essays in Memory of Neil Edmunds*, ed. Pauline Fairclough (London: Ashgate Press, 2012), 249–260.

17. For a discussion of Shostakovich's reception in the past several decades, see Schmelz, "What Was 'Shostakovich' and What Came Next?"

18. Solomon Volkov, *Testimony: The Memoirs of Dmitri Shostakovich*, trans. Antonina W. Bouis (New York: Harper & Row, 1979).

19. Laurel E. Fay, "Shostakovich versus Volkov: Whose Testimony?" *Russian Review* 39 (1980): 484–493.

20. Allen Ho and Dmitry Feofanov, *Shostakovich Reconsidered* (London: Toccata Press, 1998); and Ian MacDonald, *The New Shostakovich* (Boston: Northeastern University Press, 1990).

21. See for example Richard Taruskin, "Shostakovich and the Inhuman," in *Defining Russia Musically* (Princeton: Princeton University Press, 1997); Fay, "Shostakovich versus Volkov: Whose Testimony?", etc. These and other scholars, including Malcolm Brown, presented informed and thorough discussions of Shostakovich and his contexts, illuminating Cold War perspectives.

22. Malcolm Hamrick Brown, ed., *A Shostakovich Casebook* (Bloomington: Indiana University Press, 2004). Henry Orlov's chapter, as relayed in an interview by Lyudmila Kovnatskaya, was especially moving in his description of the silencing of Russian émigré writers in the United States.

23. See Brown; Olga Digonskaya; Fairclough; Fay; Alexander Ivashkin, *Contemplating Shostakovich: Life, Music and Film* (London: Ashgate, 2012); Terry Klefstad, "The Reception in American of Dmitri Shostakovich 1928–1946" (PhD diss., University of Texas at Austin, 2003); Schmelz; Taruskin; and Wilson among others.

24. In addition to publication on Shostakovich, there has been (and still are) websites dedicated to his life and work. Most prominently, *DSCH Journal* has an online publication, online followers, and a Facebook site. Fans of Shostakovich have also created their own sites as well (e.g., "The Exhaustive Shostakovich").

25. Jonathan Sterne, ed., *The Sound Studies Reader* (Routledge Press, 2012); Veit Erlman, *Hearing Cultures: Essays on Sound, Listening and Modernity* (London: Bloomsbury Academic, 2004); Trevor Pinch and Karin Bijsterveld, eds., *The Oxford Handbook of Sound Studies* (Oxford: Oxford University Press, 2012).

26. René T. A. Lysloff, "Musical Community on the Internet: An On-Line Ethnography," *Cultural Anthropology* 18, no. 2 (May 2003): 233–263; René Lysloff and Leslie C. Gay Jr. eds., *Music and Technoculture* (Middleton: Wesleyan University Press, 2003).

27. My observation of YouTube phenomena began in 2010. Some of the videos/uploads date farther back, sometimes as far as 2008.

28. Nikolaos333, "Anti-War Video (Shostakovich—Symphony 8—3nd [sic] mvt," https://www.youtube.com/watch?v=MnCq9_Gypjk, accessed January 10, 2011, uploaded September 2, 2008.

29. Another author similarly created a video with Soviet images and this specific movement/work as well. See allabilli, "8th Symphony Dmitri Shostakovich, allegro non troppo, attack," http://www.youtube.com/watch?v=RKshbAYacnA &feature=player_detailpage, accessed February 14, 2014, uploaded September 7, 2008.

30. I am grateful to Olga Tsipis for help in translating this commentary from Greek.

31. There are many anti-war videos on YouTube with various kinds of music; Shostakovich's music is one of several choices made by YouTube authors.

32. The Seventh Symphony was written specifically in response to war, but some of the later symphonies and earlier ones became associated with war by various audiences. One example of this association can be seen in the film *The War Symphonies: Shostakovich against Stalin* (Larry Weinstein, Rhombus Media, 1997).

33. In another upload of this symphony, a commenter replied that the performance was missing tension and fear. See MrRaph87, "D. Shostakovich Symphonie No.8, 3e mvt," http://www.youtube.com/watch?list=PLFCED8F46C1EACFB6& v=sYfliiuj4-c&feature=player_detailpage, accessed February 13, 2014, uploaded June 12, 2009, comment by Jonghun Jung.

34. Kagen5690's channel, https://www.youtube.com/watch?v=IbEe5sfjVUk, accessed February 13 2014, uploaded January 16, 2008.

35. See for example Fanning, *String Quartet No.8* and Sarah Reichardt, *Composing the Modern Subject: Four String Quartets by Dmitri Shostakovich* (Aldershot: Ashgate, 2008).

36. The author calls himself "Magisch meisje Orkest," roughly translated from Dutch as "Magical Girl Orchestra," and has 513 videos uploaded as of February 2014. When I first encountered these on YouTube in 2013, all fifteen of Shostakovich's symphonies were uploaded with images of girls and guns. In the period 2014–2015, a few of the symphonies were re-uploaded (likely because of copyright) with other sorts of images such as a young girl as fighter pilot or urban street kid.

37. Magisch meisje Orkest, "Shostakovich: Symphony No.7—Gergiev/MTO (2010 Live), https://www.youtube.com/watch?v=maOgxgyFljE, accessed February 13, 2014, uploaded November 7, 2011.

38. Peter Fox "Alles Neu (official Video)," http://www.youtube.com/watch?v=DD0A2plMSVA, uploaded July 22, 2008; planbuk, "PLAN B—ill Manors (OFFICIAL VIDEO)," http://www.youtube.com/watch?v=s8GvLKTsTuI, published March 12, 2012; FallOutBoyVEVO, "Fall Out Boy—The Phoenix (Official Video)—Part 2 of 11," http://www.youtube.com/watch?v=5hDZbroaQDc, published March 24, 2013.

39. As seen in the official video uploaded onto YouTube. Fox, "Alles Neu."

40. Dorian Lynskey, "Why Plan B's Ill Manors is the Best British Protest Song in Years," *theguardian.com*, 15 March 2012, http://www.theguardian.com/music/musicblog/2012/mar/15/plan-b-ill-manors.

41. Ibid.

42. FallOutBoyVEVO, "The Phoenix."

43. Neither are there any references to string instruments or string instrument performance in the video, as seen in Fox's and Plan B's songs.

44. Kyle Anderson, "Fall Out Boy's Patrick Stump on Being Back at No. 1, Hanging with Elton John, and Why He Loves Shostakovich," *Entertainment Weekly*, May 14, 2013, http://music-mix.ew.com/2013/05/14/fall-out-boy-patrick-stump.

45. Stump stated that he found, after he had heard Shostakovich's symphony, that Fox has used the same musical idea. He claimed that it was serendipitous that they both used the same "moment" from composer's work. Anderson, "Fall Out Boy's Patrick Stump . . ."

46. There have been similar circulations with Beethoven's symphonic music. Walter Murphy's "Fifth of Beethoven" (1977) and Robin Thicke's "When I Get You Alone" (2013) both use the Fifth Symphony similarly.

47. Grigory Kozintsev, *Sobraniye sochineniy v pyati tomakh*, 2 [Collected Works in Five Volumes, vol. 2] (Leningrad: Iskusstvo, 1982), 2:425.

48. Richard Taruskin, "Shostakovich and Us," in *Defining Russia Musically* (Princeton: Princeton University Press, 1997), 496.

BIBLIOGRAPHY

BOOKS, ESSAYS, AND ARTICLES

Akopian, Levon. *Dmitriy Shostakovich: opyt fenomenologii tvorchestva* [Dmitry Shostakovich: Experience of Phenomenological Art]. St. Petersburg: Dmitri Bulanin, 2004.

Aranovsky, Mark, Yuri Keldysh, L. Korabel'nikova, and Yu. Khokhlov, eds. *Muzïkal'nyi entsiklopedicheskiy slovar'* [The Musical Encyclopedic Dictionary]. Moscow: Sovetskaya entsiklopediya, 1990.

Arnshtam, Leo. *Muzyka geroicheskogo* [Music of the Heroic]. Moscow: Iskusstvo, 1977.

Asafyev, Boris. *Muzykal'naya forma kak protsess, 1930–1947* [Musical Form as Process]. Leningrad: Muzyka, 1971.

Ashby, Arved. *Absolute Music, Mechanical Reproduction*. Berkeley: University of California Press, 2010.

Bachelis, I. "Vstechnyi" [Counterplan], *Komsomol'skaya pravda* 260 (11 November 1932): 4.

Bakhtin, Mikhail. *Rabelais and His World*. Translated by Helene Iswolsky. Bloomington: Indiana University Press, 1984.

Barthes, Roland. *Image—Music—Text*. New York: Hill and Wang, 1977.

Bek, Mikulas, Geoffrey Chew, Petr Macek, eds. *Socialist Realism and Music Colloquia musicologica brunensia 36*. Praha: Koniasch Latin Press, 2004.

Bibikova, Irina, Catherine Cooke, Vladimir Tolstoy, eds. *Street Art of the Revolution: Festivals and Celebrations in Russia, 1918–33*. London: Thames and Hudson, 1990.

Billington, James. *The Icon and the Axe: An Interpretative History of Russian Culture*. New York: Vintage Books, 1970.

Bobïkina, I. A. *Dmitry Shostakovich v pis'makh i dokumentakh* [Dmitry Shostakovich Through His Letters and Documents]. Moscow: Glinka State Central Museum of Musical Culture, 2000.

Bogdanov-Berezovsky, Valerian. *Dorogi iskusstva* [Paths of the Arts]. Leningrad: Muzïka, 1971.

Brown, Malcolm. "The Soviet Russian Concepts of 'Intonazia' and 'Musical Imagery.'" *The Musical Quarterly* 60, no. 4 (October 1974): 557–567.

Castillo, Greg, "Peoples at an Exhibition: Soviet Architecture and the National Question." In *Socialist Realism Without Shores*, edited by Thomas Lahusen and Evgeny Dobrenko. Durham: Duke University Press, 1997.

Clark, Katerina. *The Soviet Novel, History as Ritual*. Bloomington: Indiana University Press, 2000.

Cohen, Annabel. "Associationism and Musical Soundtrack Phenomena." *Contemporary Music Review* 9 (1993): 163–178.

———. "Music Cognition and the Cognitive Psychology of Film Structure." *Canadian Psychology* 43, no. 4 (2002): 215–232.

Cook, Nicolas. *Analysing Musical Multimedia.* Oxford: Oxford University Press, 1998.

Danilevich, Lev, ed. *Dmitry Shostakovich.* Moscow: Sovetskiy kompozitor, 1967.

Dobrenko, E., and K. Gunther. *Sotsrealisticheskii kanon* [The Socialist Realist Canon]. St. Petersburg: Akademicheskii proekt, 2000.

Dobrenko, Evgeny. *Aesthetics of Alienation: Reassessment of Early Soviet Cultural Theories.* Evanston: Northwestern University Press, 2005.

Druskin, Mikhail. *Ocherki, stat'i, zametki* [Sketches, Articles and Notes]. Leningrad: Sovetskiy kompozitor, 1987.

———. *Russkaya revolyutsionnaya pesnya* [Russian Revolutionary Song]. Leningrad: Gosudarstvennoye muzykal'noye izdatel'stvo, 1959.

Edmunds, Neil. *The Soviet Proletarian Music Movement.* Oxford: Peter Lang, 2000.

Emerson, Caryl. "Shostakovich and the Russian Literary Tradition." In *Shostakovich and His World*, edited by Laurel E. Fay. Princeton: Princeton University Press, 2004.

Fairclough, Pauline. *A Soviet Credo: Shostakovich's Fourth Symphony.* Aldershot: Ashgate, 2006.

Fay, Laurel. *Shostakovich: A Life.* Oxford: Oxford University Press, 2000.

Fitzpatrick, Sheila, Alexander Rabinowitch, and Richard Stites, eds. *Russia in the Era of the NEP: Exploration in Soviet Society and Culture.* Bloomington: Indiana University Press, 1991.

Flinn, Caryl. *Strains of Utopia: Gender, Nostalgia, and Hollywood Film Music.* Princeton: Princeton University Press, 1992.

Frolova-Walker, Marina. *Russian Music and Nationalism: From Glinka to Stalin.* New Haven: Yale University Press, 2008.

———. "Stalin and the Art of Boredom." *Twentieth Century Music* 1, no. 1 (March 2004): 101–124.

———. "From Modernism to Socialist Realism in Four Years: The Cases of Myaskovsky and Asafyev." *Muzikologija: Casopis Muzikoloskog Instituta Srpske Akademije Nauka i Umetnosti* 3 (2003): 199–217.

Geldern, James von, and Richard Stites, eds. *Mass Culture in Soviet Russia: Tales, Poems, Songs, Movies, Plays, and Folklore, 1917–1953.* Bloomington: Indiana University Press, 1995.

Gojowy, Detlef. *Neue sowjetische Musik der 20er Jahre.* Regensburg: Laaber-Verlag, 1980.

Groys, Boris. *The Total Art of Stalinism: Avant-Garde, Aesthetic Dictatorship, and Beyond.* Translated by Charles Rougle. Princeton: Princeton University Press, 1992.

Gutkin, Irina. *The Cultural Origins of the Socialist Realist Aesthetic, 1890–1934.* Evanston: Northwestern University Press, 1999.

Haas, David. *Leningrad's Modernists, Studies in Composition and Musical Thought, 1917–1932.* Peter Lang: New York, 1998.

Hooker, Lynn. *Redefining Hungarian Music from Liszt to Bartok.* Oxford: Oxford University Press, 2013.

Huron, David. *Sweet Anticipation: Music and the Psychology of Expectation.* Cambridge: MIT Press, 2006.

James, C. Vaughan. *Soviet Socialist Realism, Origins and Theory.* London: Macmillan Press, 1973.

Kaganovsky, Lilya. *How the Soviet Man Was Unmade: Cultural Fantasy and Male Subjectivity Under Stalin.* Pittsburgh: University of Pittsburgh, 2008.

Katz, Mark. *Capturing Sound: How Technology Has Changed Music.* Berkeley: University of California Press, 2010.

Khentova, Sof'ya. *Shostakovich, Zhizn' i tvorchestvo* [Shostakovich, Life and Works]. Leningrad: Sovetskiy kompozitor: 1985.

Kovnatskaya, Lyudmila, ed. *Shostakovich v Leningradskoy Konservatorii 1919–1930*, vols. 1–3. St. Petersburg: Kompozitor, 2013.

Kramer, Lawrence. *Music as Cultural Practice, 1800–1900.* Berkeley: University of California Press, 1990.

Lobanova, Marina. *Musical Style and Genre: History and Modernity.* Translated by Kate Cook. Amsterdam: Harwood Academic, 2000.

Long, Michael. *Beautiful Monsters: Imagining the Classic in Musical Media.* Berkeley: University of California Press, 2008.

MacDonald, Ian. *The New Shostakovich.* Boston: Northeastern University Press, 1990.

McClary, Susan. *Feminine Endings: Music, Gender, and Sexuality.* Minneapolis: University of Minnesota Press, 1991.

Maes, Frances. *A History of Russian Music: From Kamarinskaya to Babi Yar.* Berkeley: University of California Press, 2002.

Maksimenkov, Leonid. *Sumbur vmesto muzyki: Stalinskaya kul'turnaya revolutsiya 1936–1938* [Chaos Instead of Music: Stalinist Cultural Revolution 1936–1938]. Moskva: Yuridicheskaya Kniga, 1997.

Mayne, Judith. *Kino and the Woman Question: Feminism and Soviet Silent Film.* Columbus: Ohio State University, 1989.

Mazo, Margarita, and Malcolm Brown, eds. *A Collection of Russian Folk Songs by Nikolai Lvov and Ivan Prach.* Ann Arbor: UMI Research Press, 1987.

McQuere, Gordon. "Boris Asaf'yev and Musical Form as Process." In *Russian Theoretical Thought in Music*, edited by Gordon McQuere. Ann Arbor: UMI Research Press, 1983.

Miller, Kiri. *Playing Along: Digital Games, YouTube, and Virtual Performance.* New York: Oxford University Press, 2012.

Morgan, James. "Interview with 'The Nose': Shostakovich's Adaptation of Gogol." In *Intersections and Transpositions: Russian Music, Literature, and Society*, edited by Andrew Wachtel. Evanston: Northwestern University Press, 1998.

Popov, Innokenty. *Nekotorye cherty sotsialisticheskogo realizma v sovetskoy muzïke* [Some Features of Socialist Realism in Soviet Music]. Moscow: Muzïka, 1971.

Robin, Regine. *Socialist Realism: An Impossible Aesthetic.* Stanford: Stanford University Press, 1992.

Rofe, Michael. *Dimensions of Energy in Shostakovich's Symphonies.* Aldershot: Ashgate, 2012.

Sabaneyev, Leonid. "Musical Tendencies in Contemporary Russia." *The Musical Quarterly* 16 (1930): 469–481.

Sabinina, Marina. *Shostakovich—Simfonist: Dramaturgiya, estetika, stil'* [Shostakovich the Symphonist: Dramaturgy, Aesthetics, Style]. Moscow: Muzïka, 1976.

———. *Simfonizm Shostakovicha* [The Symphonism of Shostakovich]. Moscow: Nauka, 1965.

Schwarz, Boris. *Music and Musical Life in Soviet Russia.* Rev. ed. Bloomington: Indiana University Press, 1983.

Shakhnazarova, N. G. *Paradoksy sovetskoi muzïkal'noi kultury 30-e gody* [Paradoxes of Soviet Musical Culture in the 1930s]. Moscow: Indrik, 2001.

Sheinberg, Esti. *Irony, Satire, Parody, and the Grotesque in the Music of Shostakovich: A Theory of Musical Incongruities.* Aldershot: Ashgate, 2000.

Shklovsky, Victor. "Art as Technique." In *Russian Formalist Criticism, Four Essays.* Translated by Lee T. Lemon and Marion J. Reis. Lincoln: University of Nebraska Press, 1965.

Shneerson, G. M., ed. *D. Shostakovich, Stat'i i materialï* [D. Shostakovich, Articles and Materials]. Moscow: Sovetskiy Kompozitor, 1976.

Sinyavsky, Andrey [Abram Terts]. *The Trial Begins and On Socialist Realism.* Translated by Max Hayward and George Dennis. New York: Vintage Books, 1965.

Sitsky, Larry. *Music of the Repressed Russian Avant-Garde, 1900–1929.* Westport: Greenwood Press, 1994.

Slonimsky, Nicolas. "Dmitry Dmitrievitch Shostakovitch." *The Musical Quarterly* 28 (1942): 415–444.

Sollertinsky, Dmitri, and Ludmilla. *Pages from the Life of Dmitri Shostakovich.* London: Robert Hale, Ltd., 1980.

Sterne, Jonathan, ed. *The Sound Studies Reader.* London: Routledge, 2012.

Taruskin, Richard. *Defining Russia Musically.* Princeton: Princeton University Press, 1997.

Titus, Joan. "Montage Shostakovich: Film Popular Culture, and the Finale of the Piano Concerto No.1." Master's thesis, The Ohio State University, 2002.

Tull, James. "B. V. Asaf'yev's Musical Form as a Process Translation and Commentary." PhD diss., The Ohio State University, 1976.

Volkov, Solomon. *Testimony: The Memoirs of Dmitri Shostakovich.* Translated by Antonina W. Bouis. New York: Harper & Row, 1979.

Wilson, Elizabeth. *Shostakovich: A Life Remembered.* Princeton: Princeton University Press, 1994.

Woll, Josephine. *Real Images: Soviet Cinema and the Thaw.* London: I. B. Tauris, 2000.

Yakubov, Manashir. "Muzïka D. D. Shostakovicha k kinofil'mu 'Odna.' Istoriya sozdaniya, otsenka kritiki" [Dmitry Shostakovich's Music to the Film Alone: How it was Composed, Critics' Appraisal]. In *Dmitry Shostakovich: Novoye Sobraniye Sochineniy, Tom 123, "Muzïka k kinofil'mu 'Odna'"* [Dmitry Shostakovich: New Collected Works, vol. 123, "Music the Film *Alone* Op.26"]. Moscow: DSCH, 2004.

———. "Ot redaktsii" [Editor's Note]. In *Dmitry Shostakovich, Sobraniye Sochineniy v soroka dvukh tomakh, tom 41, "Muzïka k kinofil'ma, partitura"* [The Collected Works in Forty-Two Volumes, vol. 41, "Music to the Film Scores, Orchestral Score"]. Moscow: Muzïka, 1987.

Zharov, B. *Lyubimye russkiye narodnye pesni* [Favorite Russian Folk Songs]. Moscow: Muzïka, 1985.

Zhdanov, A., Maxim Gorky, N. Bukharin, K. Radek, and A. Stetsky. *Problems of Soviet Literature, Reports and Speeches at the First Soviet Writers' Congress.* New York: International Publishers, 1934.

FILM AND FILM MUSIC SOURCES

"Oktyabr'skii podarok kino, fil'm "Vstrechnyi" [An October Gift to Cinema, the film Counterplan]. *Vechernyaya Moskva,* 9 November 1932.

Abel, Richard, and Rick Altman, eds. *The Sounds of Early Cinema.* Bloomington: Indiana University Press, 2001.

Adorno, Theodor, and Hanns Eisler. *Composing for the Films.* London: The Athalone Press, 1994.

Agranovksy, A. "Pobeda zvukovogo kino" [A Victory of Sound Film]. *Pravda* 325 (26 November 1931).

Alpers, B. "Mertvoe Iskusstvo" [Death Art]. *Komsomol'skaya pravda* 65 (21 March 1929).
———. "Oshibka 'Feksov'" [The Mistakes of FEKS]. *Sovetskoye iskusstvo* 54 (18 May 1931).
Altman, Rick. "The Silence of the Silents." *The Musical Quarterly* 80, no. 4 (Winter 1996): 648–718.
A-N, E. "Novyi Vavilon v Lenarke" [New Babylon in Lenarka]. *Kino* 26, no. 13 (March 1929): 3.
Arnshtam, Lev. "Zlatïe gorï" [Golden Mountains]. In *Muzïka geroicheskogo* [Music of the Heroic]. Moscow: Iskusstvo, 1977.
Arnshtam, Lev. "Zlatïe gorï" [Golden Mountains]. *Sovetskiy ekran* 23 (1971): 18–19.
Akhushkov, Sh. ed. *Vstrechnyi, kak sozdavalsya fil'm* [Counterplan—How the Film was Created]. Moscow: Kinofotoizdat, 1935.
B.R. "'Zlatïe gorï' proizvodstvo "Sovkino" [Golden Mountains, a Sovkino Production]. *Komsomol'skaya pravda* 314 (19 November 1931): 4.
Babitsky, Paul, and John Rimberg. *The Soviet Film Industry*. New York: Published for the Research Program on the U.S.S.R. by Praeger, 1955.
Bachelis, I. "Vstechnyi" [Counterplan]. *Komsomol'skaya pravda* 260 (11 November 1932): 4.
Balash, Bella [Balázs, Bela]. "Novye fil'my, novye zhizneoshchushcheniye" [New Films, New Life-Feelings]. *Sovetskoe kino* 3–4 (1933): 19.
Baranchikov, P. "Theatr-muzïka-kino, po kinoekranam" [Theater—Music—Cinema, On the Cinema-screen]. *Izvestiya* 77 (4 April 1929).
Becce, Giuseppe, Ludwig Brav, Hans Erdmann. *Allgemeines Handbuch der Film-Musik*. Berlin-Lichterfelde: Schlesinger 1927.
Bleiman, M. "Ob ornamentakh" [About Ornamentation]. *Kino* 59 (24 December 1932).
Blok, D., and S. Bugoslavsky. *Muzïkal'noe soprovozhdeniye v kino* [Musical Accompaniment in the Cinema]. Moscow: Teakinopechat, 1929.
Blyakhin, L. "Vstrechnyi" [Counterplan]. *Izvestiya* 318 (15 December 1932): 4.
Bogdanov-Berezovsky, Valerian. "Slushaya zvukovoi fil'm" [Listening to a Soundtrack Film]. *Rabochiy i teatr* 24 (August 1933): 14–15.
Bordwell, David. *Narration in the Fiction Film*. Madison: University of Wisconsin Press, 1985.
Bordwell, David, and Kristen Thompson. *Film Art: An Introduction*. New York: McGraw Hill, 1997.
Bordwell, David, Janet Staiger, and Kristin Thompson. *The Classical Hollywood Cinema, Film Style and Mode of Production to 1960*. New York: Columbia University Press, 1985.
Borodovsky, S. "Strana vstaet so slavoyu" [The Country Rises with Glory]. *Vecherniy Leningrad* 234 (11 October 1979): 3.
Brown, Royal S. *Overtones and Undertones: Reading Film Music*. Berkeley: University of California Press, 1994.
Bugoslavsky, S. "Formalizm v kinomuzïke" [Formalism in Film Music]. *Kino* (16 February 1936): 3.
Bugoslavsky, Sergey, and Vladimir Messman. *Muzïka i kino, na kino-muzïkal'nom fronte printsipy i metody kino-muzïki opït kino-muzïkal'noy kompozitsiy* [Music and the Cinema, on the Film-Musical Front of the Principles and Methods of Film-Music Experience of Film-Musical Composition]. Moscow: Kinopechat', 1926.
Buhler, James, Caryl Flinn, and David Neumeyer, eds. *Music and Cinema*. Hanover: University Press of New England for Wesleyan University Press, 2000.

Burch, Noël. "On the Structural Use of Sound." In *Theory and Practice of Film Sound*, edited by Elisabeth Weis and John Belton. New York: Columbia University Press, 1985.

Cheryomukhin, M. *Muzïka zvukovogo fil'ma* [Music of Sound Film]. Moscow: Goskinoizdat, 1939.

Chion, Michel. "Audio-Vision and Sound." In *Sound*, edited by Patricia Kruth and Henry Stobart. Cambridge: Cambridge University Press, 2000.

———. *Audio-Vision: Sound on Screen*. Edited and translated by Claudia Gorbman. New York: Columbia University Press, 1994.

———. *The Voice in Cinema*. Translated by Claudia Gorbman. New York: Columbia University Press, 1999.

Christie, Ian, and John Gillet, ed. *Futurism/Formalism/FEKS: Eccentrism and Soviet Cinema 1918–1936*. London: British Film Institute, 1978.

Christie, Ian, and Richard Taylor, eds. *Inside the Film Factory: New Approaches to Russian and Soviet Cinema*. London: Routledge, 1991.

Christie, Ian, and Richard Taylor eds. *The Film Factory: Russian and Soviet Cinema in Documents 1896–1939*. London: Routledge & Kegan Paul, 1988.

Clarida, Robert, and Philip Tagg. *Ten Little Tunes*. New York: The Mass Media Scholars Press, Inv., 2003.

DEBE. "Novyi Vavilon—Kankan v Tumane ili kak Sovkino oposhlilo parizhskuyu communu" [The New Babylon—Cancan in the Fog or How Sovkino Debased the Parisian Commune]. *Komsomol'skaya pravda* 65 (21 March 1929).

Egorova, Tatiana. *Soviet Film Music: A Historical Survey*. Translated by Tatiana A. Ganf and Natalia A. Egunova. Amsterdam: Harwood Academic Publishers, 1997.

Eikhenbaum, Boris. "The Problems of Cinema Stylistics." In *Russian Formalist Film Theory*, edited by Herbert Eagle. Michigan: Michigan Slavic Publications, 1981.

Eikhenbaum, Boris, ed., *Poetika Kino* [The Poetics of Cinema]. Moscow: Kinopechat', 1927.

Eisler, Hanns. *Composing for the Films*. New York: Oxford University Press, 1947.

Ellis, Jack. *A History of Film*. Englewood Cliffs: Prentice Hall, 1990.

Evgenev, A. "Vstrechnyi" ["Counterplan]. *Rabochiy i teatr* 34 (1 December 1932): 17.

Fadeev, A. V. Sutyirin, V. Ermilov, L. Averbakh, V. Kirshon. "Protiv unter-ofitserskikh priemov kritiki" [Against Boorish Critical Techniques]. *Komsomol'skaya pravda*, 23 March 1929.

Fel'dman, K. "Na pereput'i" [At the Crossroads]. *Kino* 62 (16 November 1931): 2.

Feldman, N. "Novyi Vavilon" [New Babylon]. *Vechernyaya Moskva* 68 (25 March 1929).

Fell, John. *A History of Films*. New York: Holt, Rinehart, and Winston, 1979.

Fevral'skii, A. "Zametki o 'Vstrechnom'" [Notes on "Counterplan"]. *Kino* 59 (24 December 1932): 3.

Flinn, Caryl. *Strains of Utopia: Gender, Nostalgia, and Hollywood Film Music*. Princeton: Princeton University Press, 1992.

Frid, E. *Muzïka v sovetskom kino* [Music in Soviet Cinema]. Leningrad: Muzïka, 1967.

Gardin, V. R. *Vospominaniya, tom II* [Reminiscences, Volume II]. Moscow: Goskinoizdat, 1953.

Gartsman, M. "Ne plokho, no i ne sovsem yeshchyo khorosho" [Not Bad, but not yet Entirely Good]. *Sovetskiy ekran* 15 (9 April 1929).

Gillespie, David. *Russian Cinema*. New York: Longman, 2003.

Ginzburg, L. "Fil'm o lyudyakh, stroyashchikh sotsializm" [Film About People, the Building of Socialism]. *Pravda* 327 (22 November 1932): 4.

Glenny, Michael, and Richard Taylor, eds. *S. M. Eisenstein, Selected Works, Volume 1*. London: British Film Institute, 1991.

Glenny, Michael, and Richard Taylor, ed., trans. *S.M. Eisenstein, Selected Works, Volume 2: Towards a Theory of Montage, 1937–40*. London: British Film Institute 1996.

Glukh, M. Kartine—ne dlya massovogo zritelya [The Picture is not for the Mass Viewer]. *Komsomol'skaya pravda* 72 (29 March 1929): 4.

Goldman, Wendy. *Women, the State and Revolution: Soviet Family Policy and Social Life, 1917–1936*. Cambridge: Cambridge University Press, 1993.

Goldobin, A. V, B. M. Azacheyev. *Pianist-illyustrator kinematograficheskikh kartin* [Accompanying Cinematograph Pictures on the Piano]. Kostroma: Izdanie A.V. Goldobina i M.S. Trofimova, 1912.

Gorbman, Claudia. *Unheard Melodies: Narrative Film Music*. Bloomington: Indiana University Press, 1987.

Gornitskaya, Nina, ed. *Iz istorii Lenfil'ma, Stati, vospominaniya, dokumenty,1920-e gody.* [From the History of Lenfil'm Studio: Articles, Reminiscences and Documents of the 1920s]. Leningrad: Iskusstvo, 1968.

———. *Iz istorii Lenfil'ma, Stati, vospominaniya, dokumentï, 1930-e gody* [From the History of Lenfil'm Studios: Articles, Reminiscences, and Documents of the 1930s]. Leningrad: Iskusstvo, 1975.

Grinval'd, Yakov. "Oktyabr'skii podarok sovetskogo kino" [An October Gift to Soviet Cinema]. *Vechernyaya Moskva* 265 (9 November 1931): 2.

Grishanin, V. "He agitka i ne poligramota" [Not Agitka and not a Political Object Lesson]. *Komsomol'skaya pravda* 72 (29 March 1929): 4.

Hoffman, David. *Stalinist Values: The Cultural Norms of Soviet Modernity, 1917–1941*. Ithaca: Cornell University Press, 2003.

Ioffe, I. I. *Muzïka sovetskogo kino* [Music of the Soviet Cinema]. Leningrad: State Musical Scientific-Research Institute: 1938.

K., "Vstrechnyi" [Counterplan]. *Rabochaya Moskva* 265 (12 November 1932).

Kalinak, Kathryn. *Settling the Score: Music and the Classical Hollywood Film*. Madison: University of Wisconsin Press, 1992.

Kassabian, Anahid. *Hearing Film: Tracking Identifications in Contemporary Hollywood Film Music*. New York: Routledge, 2001.

Kenez, Peter. *Cinema and Soviet Society: From the Revolution to the Death of Stalin*. Cambridge: Cambridge University Press, 1992.

Khrennikov, T. "Muzïka v kino" [Music in Cinema]. *Iskusstvo kino* 1 (January–February 1950): 26–28.

Knight, Arthur, Pamela Robertson Wojick and eds. *Soundtrack Available: Essays on Film and Popular Music*. Durham: Duke University Press, 2001.

Kompozitory sovetskogo kino [Composers of Soviet Cinema]. Moscow: Soyuzinformkino, 1983.

Korchmaryov, Kliment. "Muzïka k fil'me "Novyi Vavilon" [The Music to "New Babylon"]. *Izvestiya* 77 (4 April 1929).

———. "Muzïka k fil'me 'Odna'" [Music of the Film "Alone"]. *Sovetskoye iskusstvo* 58 (15 June 1931).

Kosheverova, N. N. "Shostakovich i kino" [Shostakovich and Cinema]. *Muzïkal'naya zhizn'* [Musical Life] 5–6 (1996): 41–42.

Kozintsev, Grigory, and Leonid Trauberg. "Novyi Vavilon" [New Babylon]. *Sovetskiy ekran* 32 (December 1928): 8–9.

———. "Odna" [Alone]. *Iskusstvo kino* 1 (1967): 45–54.

———. *Glubokiy ekran* [The Deep Screen]. Moscow: Iskusstvo, 1971.

———. *King Lear: The Space of Tragedy: The Diary of a Film Director*. Translated by Mary Mackintosh. Berkeley: University of California Press, 1977.

———. *Perepiska G. M. Kozintseva* [The Correspondence of G. M. Kozintsev]. Moscow: Artist, Rezhissyor, Teatr: 1998.

———. *Sobraniye sochineniy v pyati tomakh* [Collected Works in Five Volumes]. Leningrad: Iskusstvo, 1982.

Krakauer, Siegfried. *Theory of Film: The Redemption of Physical Reality.* New York: Oxford University Press, 1965.

Krilov, Tkachevsky, Maiorov, Borodina, Pyil'tsina, Palaktinov, Marchenko, Zakharov. "Zabïli o 'yazïke ponyatnom millionam'" [They Forgot about the "Language Intelligible to the Millions"]. *Komsomol'skaya pravda* 72 (29 March 1929): 4.

Kuz'mina, Yelena. *O tom, chto ya pomnyu* [On What I Remember]. Moscow: Iskusstvo, 1989.

Lerner, Neil. "Musical Texture as Cinematic Signifier: The Politics of Polyphony in Selected Documentary Film Scores by Virgil Thomson and Aaron Copland." In *Film Music 2: History, Theory, Practice,* edited by Claudia Gorbman. Sherman Oaks: The Film Music Society, 2004.

Leyda, Jay *Kino: A History of Russian and Soviet Film.* Princeton: Princeton University Press, 1983.

London, Kurt. *Film Music: A Summary of the Characteristic Features of its History, Aesthetics, Technique and Possible Developments.* London: Faber & Faber Ltd., 1936.

Marks, Martin. *Music and the Silent Film: Contexts and Case Studies, 1895–1924.* New York: Oxford University Press, 1997.

Marshall, Herbert. "The Soviet Cinema, Plans Themes, and Achievements." *British Russian Gazette and Trade Outlook* (September 1933): 311–313.

Martin, Marcel, and Luca and Jean Schnitzer, eds. *Cinema in Revolution.* New York: Da Capo Press, 1973.

Moldavsky, Dm. "Vstrechnyi" [Counterplan]. *Sovetskiy ekran* 23 (1982): 18.

Monosson, L. I. *The Soviet Cinematography.* New York: Amkino Corp., 1930.

Mulvey, Laura. *Visual and Other Pleasures.* 2nd ed. New York: Palgrave, 2009.

Nedobrovo, Vladimir. *FEKS, Grigory Kozintsev, Leonid Trauberg.* Moscow: Kinopechat, 1928.

OS., N. "Zlatïe gorï" [Golden Mountains]. *Izvestiya* 328 (29 November 1931).

Papava, M. "Zhar-ptitsa" [Firebird]. *Kino* 59 (24 December 1932): 3.

Petrova, Inna. *Muzïka sovetskogo kino* [Music of Soviet Cinema]. Moscow: Znaniye, 1964.

P-OV., E. "Rabochiye tormoznogo zavoda o 'Vstrechnyi,' pod obstrelom kritiki" [Workers of the Brake Factory About "Counterplan," Under the Fire of the Critics]. *Rabochaya Moskva* 303 (28 December 1932).

Prendergast, Roy M. *Film Music, A Neglected Art: A Critical Study of Music in Films.* New York: Norton, 1992.

Prezent., Mikh. "Nikakoy poshlosti net" [No Kind of Banality]. *Komsomol'skaya pravda* 72 (29 March 1929): 4.

Pudovkin, Vsevolod. *Film Acting and Film Technique.* Translsted by Igor Montagu. New York: Grove Press, 1960.

Pudovkin, Vsevolod. *Film Technique.* London: George Newnes, Ltd., 1933.

Pytel, Marek. *New Babylon: Trauberg, Kozintsev, Shostakovich.* London: Eccentric Press, 1999.

Rapée, Erno. *Encyclopaedia of Music for Pictures.* New York: Belwin, 1925.

Rapée, Erno. *Motion Picture Moods for Pianists and Organists: A Rapid-Reference Collection of Selected Pieces, Adapted to Fifty-Two Moods and Situations.* New York: Schirmer, 1924.

Richard Taylor, ed. *S.M. Eisenstein, Selected Works, Volume 3: Writings, 1934–1947.* Translated by William Powell. London: British Film Institute, 1996.

Riley, John. *Dmitri Shostakovich: A Life in Film.* London: I. B. Tauris, 2005.

Rïbakova, Pavina. "Muzïka Shostakovicha k zvukovym fil'mam 'Odna' i 'Zlatïe gorï'" [Shostakovich's Music to the Sound Films "Alone" and "Golden Mountains"]. *Rabochiy i teatr* 24 (August 1933): 39.

Ryubanovsky, L. "Zhivye lyudi epokhi" [Living People of the Epoch]. *Komsomol'skaya pravda* 72 (29 March 1929): 4.

Sabaneyev, Leonid. *Music for the Films: A Handbook for Composers and Conductors.* Translated by S. W. Pring. London: Sir I. Pitman & Sons, Ltd., 1935.

Sadovsky, A. "Vstrechnyi" [Counterplan]. *Kino* 51 (6 November 1932): 3.

Semiradsky. "Novyi Vavilon" [New Babylon]. *Sovetskiy ekran* 12 (1929): 4.

Sepman, Isol'da, ed. *Fridrikh Ermler, dokumenty, stat'i, vospominaniya* [Fridrikh Ermler, Documents, Articles, and Reminiscences]. Leningrad: Iskusstvo, 1974.

Shumyatsky, Boris. "Rezhissyor i akter v kino" [The Director and the Actor in Cinema]. *Iskusstvo kino* 2 (February 1936): 8–9.

Slater, Thomas, ed. *Handbook of Soviet and East European Films and Filmmakers.* New York: Greenwood Press, 1992.

Sokolov, I. V. *Istoriya sovetskogo kinoiskusstva zvukovogo perioda, chast' 1* (1930–1941) [The History of Soviet Film Art of the Sound Period, Part 1 (1930–1941)]. Moscow: Goskinoizdat, 1946.

———. *Istoriya sovetskogo kinoiskusstva zvukovogo perioda, chast' II* (1934–1944) [The History of Soviet Film Art of the Sound Period, Part II (1930–1941)]. Moscow: Goskinoizdat, 1946.

Taylor, Richard. "Red Stars, Positive Heroes, and Personality Cults." In *Stalinism and Soviet Cinema*, edited by Richard Taylor and D. W. Spring. London: Routledge, 1993.

Taylor, Richard. *Film Propaganda: Soviet Russia and Nazi Germany.* London: I. B.Tauris, 1998.

Titus, Joan. "Silents, Sound, and Modernism in Dmitry Shostakovich's Score to the *New Babylon* (1928–1929)." In *Sound, Speech, and Music in Soviet and Post-Soviet Cinema*, edited by Masha Salazkina and Lilya Kaganovsky, 38–59. Bloomington: Indiana University Press, 2014.

———. "Dmitry Shostakovich as Film Music Theorist." In *Music and Politics in Twentieth-Century Europe: Essays in Memory of Neil Edmunds*, edited by Pauline Fairclough, 249–260. London: Ashgate Press, 2012.

———. "Essay and Translation of 'About the Music to the *New Babylon*' by Dmitry Shostakovich." In *Film Music: Source Readings, 1910–1951*, edited by James Wierzbicki, Colin Roust, and Nathan Platte, 61–64. London: Routledge Press, 2011.

———. "Socialist Realism, Modernism, and Dmitry Shostakovich's *Odna* (*Alone*, 1931)." In *Shostakovich Studies 2*, edited by Pauline Fairclough, 100–120. Cambridge: Cambridge University Press, 2010.

———. "Modernism, Socialist Realism, and Identity, in the Early Film Music of Dmitry Shostakovich, 1929–1932." PhD diss., Ohio State University, 2006.

Trauberg, Leonid. "Comment est né 'La Nouevelle Babylone,' (1978)." An extract from a letter to Miriam Tsoukandais reprinted in *L'Avant-scene du cinema* 217, (December 1978): 8.

———. *Izbrannye proizvedeniya v 2-kh tomakh* [Selected Works in Two Volumes]. Moscow: Iskusstvo, 1988.

———. *Svyezhest' bytiya* [The Freshness of Life]. Moscow: Kinotsentr, 1988.

Tsivian, Yuri. "Russia, 1913: Cinema in the Cultural Landscape." In *Silent Film*, edited by Richard Abel. New Brunswick: Rutgers University Press, 1996.

———. *Silent Witnesses: Russian Films 1908–1919*. London: BFI, 1989.

———. *Early Cinema in Russia and Its Cultural Reception*. Chicago: University of Chicago Press, 1994.

Turovskaya, Maya. "The 1930s and 1940s: Cinema in Context." In *Stalinism and Soviet Cinema*, edited by Richard Taylor and D. W. Spring. London: Routledge, 1993.

Vaynkop, Yuli. "Muzïka k 'Novomu Vavilonu'" [Music to New Babylon]. *Rabochiy i teatr* (1 April 1929): 9.

Van Houten, Theodore. *'Eisenstein was a Great Eater': In Memory of Leonid Trauberg*. 's-Hertogenbosch: Art & Research, 1991.

———. *Leonid Trauberg and His Films, Always the Unexpected*. 's-Hertongenbosch: Art and Research, 1989.

Workers of KIM: F. Geminder, S. Chernya, L. Dzhaparidze, O. Vintser, Khimera vmesto communï [Chimera instead of the Commune]. *Komsomol'skaya pravda* 72 (29 March 1929): 4.

Youngblood, Denise. "Cinema as Social Criticism: The Early Films of Fridrikh Ermler." In *The Red Screen: Politics, Society, Art in the Soviet Cinema*, edited by Anna Lawton (London: Routledge, 1992).

Youngblood, Denise. *Movies for the Masses: Popular Cinema and Soviet Society in the 1920s*. Cambridge: Cambridge University Press, 1992.

———. *Russian War Films*. Lawrence: University of Kansas Press, 2007.

Yutkevich, S. "Vstupitel'noye slovo k diskussii (Stenogramma vystupleniya na diskussii o fil'me 'Zlatïe gorï,' v moskovskii ARRK)" [Introductory Words to Discussion (stenogram of a speech on the discussion about the film "Golden Mountains" in the Moscow ARRK)]. *Proletarskoe kino* 1 (1932): 5–9.

———. "Na krepkoi pochve" [On Strong Ground]. *Kino* 60 (30 December 1932).

———. "Vspominaya Shostakovicha" [Remembering Shostakovich]. *Muzïkal'naya zhizn'* 2 (1995): 23–26.

Zorkaya, Neya. *The Illustrated History of the Soviet Cinema*. New York: Hippocrene Books, 1989.

WRITINGS BY SHOSTAKOVICH

Grigoryev, L. and Ya. Platek, eds. *Dmitri Shostakovich about Himself and His Times*. Moscow: Progress Publishers, 1981.

Shostakovich, Dmitry. "Avtobiografia" [Autobiography]. *Sovetskaya muzïka* 9 (1966): 24–25.

———. "Bol'shoy Talent, Bol'shoy Master" [A Great Talent, a Great Master]. *Iskusstvo kino* 1 (1956): 46–62.

———. "God posle 'Ledi Makbet'" [The Year After Lady Macbeth]. *Krasnaya Gazeta* (1935).

———. "Declaratsya obyazannostey kompozitora" [Declaration of a Composer's Duties]. *Rabochiy i teatr* 31 (20 November 1931): 6.

———. "Hakanunye prem'erï 'Nosa': Pochemu 'Nos'?" [On the Eve of the Premiere of "Nose": Why "Nose"?]. *Rabochiy i teatr* 3 (15 January 1930).

————. "Kino kak shkola kompozitora" [Cinema as the Composer's School]. In *30 let sovetskoy kinematografiy* [30 Years of Soviet Cinematography], edited by D. I. Eremin. Moscow: Goskinoizdat, 1950.

————. "Moi blizhaishiye rabota" [My Future Works]. *Rabochiy i teatr* 11 (1937): 24.

————. "Muzïka v kino" [Music to Cinema]. *Literaturnaya gazeta* 1, no. 5 (1939).

————. "O muzïke k 'Novomu Vavilonu'" [About the Music to "New Babylon"]. *Sovetskiy ekran* 11 (1929): 5.

————. "Pis'ma v redaktsiyu" [Letter to the Editor]. *Rabochiy i teatr* 16 (14 April 1929).

————. "Yeshchyo raz o kinomuzïke" [Once Again about Film Music]. *Iskusstvo kino* 1 (1954): 85–89.

SCORES

Shostakovich, Dmitry. *Novoye Sobraniye Sochineniy, Tom 122, "Novyi Vavilon"* [Dmitri Shostakovich: New Collected Works, vol. 122, "The New Babylon"]. Edited by Manashir Yakubov. Moscow: DSCH, 2004.

————. *Novoye Sobraniye Sochineniy, Tom 123, "Muzïka k kinofil'mu 'Odna'"* [Dmitry Shostakovich: New Collected Works, vol. 123, "Music the Film Alone, op.26"]. Edited by Manashir Yakubov. Moscow: DSCH, 2004.

————. *Novyi vavilon, syuita iz muzïki k kinofil'mu partitura* [The New Babylon, Suite from the Music to the Film Score]. Edited by Gennady Rozhdestvensky. Moscow: Sovetskiy kompozitor, 1976.

————. *Sobraniye Sochineniy v soroka dvukh tomakh, tom 41, "Muzïka k kinofil'ma, partitura"* [The Collected Works in Forty-Two Volumes, vol. 41, "Music to Film, Orchestral Score"]. Edited by Manashir Yakubov. Moscow: Muzïka, 1987.

INDEX